POVERTY IN RURAL IRELAND

A Political Economy Perspective

Edited by

Chris Curtin
Trutz Haase
Hilary Tovey

Oak Tree Press

Dublin

in association with
Combat Poverty Agency

Oak Tree Press
Merrion Building
Lower Merrion Street
Dublin 2, Ireland

© 1996 Combat Poverty Agency

A catalogue record of this book is
available from the British Library.

ISBN 1-86076-031-7

Combat Poverty Agency Research Report Series No. 22

The views expressed in this report are the authors' own
and not necessarily those of the Combat Poverty Agency.

Printed in Ireland by Colour Books Ltd.

Contents

List of Tables

List of Figures

For Damian Hannan,
who first reminded us that rural
development involves rural
displacement as well.

Acknowledgements

The editors wish to acknowledge the enormous contribution made by a number of people to bring this study to fruition. In particular, we acknowledge the vision and enthusiasm of the Combat Poverty Agency for conceiving the project and making it happen. Particular thanks are expressed to Helen Johnston who patiently managed the project over the years. We would like to express our thanks also to the individual authors, John Jackson, Patrick Commins, Tom Boylan, Eamon O'Shea and Carmel Coyle, as well as Andy Conway and Carol Conway for their contributions. Such a broad range of expertise has brought fresh thinking and ideas to addressing issues of rural poverty. Finally, we recognise the contributions made by the many commentators who read earlier drafts of the work and made critical suggestions for the improvement of the overall book.

Chris Curtin
Trutz Haase
Hilary Tovey

About the Contributors

Tom Boylan is Associate Professor of Economics at University College Galway. One of his main areas of teaching and research is development economics, including industrial and spatial development.

Carmel Coyle is Research Fellow at the Centre for European Economic and Public Affairs at University College Dublin where she has undertaken a number of research projects in the areas of comparative European Government and Public Administration.

Patrick Commins is Acting Head of the Rural Economy Research Centre in Teagasc (the Agriculture and Food Development Authority). His research interests include rural development, structural change in agriculture and agri-rural policies.

Chris Curtin is Professor of Political Science and Sociology at University of Galway. He has published work on community development, agrarian politics and social exclusion.

Trutz Haase is an independent Social and Economic Consultant. He worked formerly as a Research Officer in the Northern Ireland Economic Research Centre and the Combat Poverty Agency, and as a Research Associate in the Educational Research Centre at St. Patrick's College, Drumcondra.

John A. Jackson is Professor of Sociology at Trinity College Dublin. His main work is in the areas of migration and stratification processes.

Dr. Eamon O'Shea is a college lecturer in economics at University College Galway. His main research interests are as follows: ageing, disability, discrimination, poverty and social policy.

Hilary Tovey is a Senior Lecturer in Sociology at Trinity College Dublin. Her research interests include rural and agricultural development, the sociology of food, the sociology of the environment, and the sociology of minority language and culture.

Foreword
Combat Poverty Agency

INTRODUCTION

The way that rural poverty is understood in public debate is largely limited to three aspects: first, in terms of poor areas; secondly, in terms of poor communities; and thirdly, in terms of poor farmers. While these are important aspects, they neglect a whole series of other important questions. In particular, there is a need to become more precise about who within rural communities faces disproportionate risks of poverty. Addressing poverty at the community level without addressing whether there are significant differences in the well-being of people within these communities can lead to an insufficient targeting of the rural poor. It was in this context that the Combat Poverty Agency decided to undertake a study of the character and the underlying causes of poverty in rural Ireland.

FOCUS OF THE STUDY

This study attempts to bring a new perspective into the ongoing debate on the future of those who are disadvantaged and are living in rural areas. In particular, the study aims to identify the rural inhabitants who are at risk of living in poverty and the factors that affect their life chances.

The book has both an analytical and a policy focus. It is an attempt to provide a thorough understanding of the causes and consequences of rural poverty and a useful framework for a more effective formulation of policies aimed at the alleviation of rural poverty. To this end, it draws primarily on what is commonly referred to in the literature as the political economy approach. The advantage of this approach is that it draws attention to:

(1) The way in which the organisation of the economy produces particular forms of investment (and disinvestment) in rural areas

(2) The variety of social groups, their interests in land, property and the environment, and the interaction between social groups and economic processes

(3) The way in which, and the reasons why, the State operates as it does in response to, or as an initiator of, economic reorganisation and rural decline

(4) The effects that the further integration into the European Union may have on people who are experiencing poverty and are living in Ireland's more peripheral areas.

At the same time, the study tries to overcome some of the limitations inherent in the political economy approach. In particular, it seeks to avoid a narrow economistic interpretation of the future outlook of rural areas, and instead tries to understand the particular development opportunities of any one locality as a combination of the economic constraints imposed by the wider economy, public-policy decisions and the way in which the inhabitants of the rural space respond to these forces.

In line with this theoretical orientation, the book's policy framework is wide ranging and addresses the significance of macro-level organisations such as the European Union and the Irish state, regional bodies and agencies, and voluntary and community organisations.

WHO ARE THE RURAL POOR?

The decline in the numbers engaged in agriculture, and the increasing similarity in the composition of the rural and urban labour forces have increasingly raised the question as to whether there is anything distinctly different about poverty in rural areas. Indeed, the limited development opportunities of Ireland's more remote areas may have more to do with their economic and social peripherality than with anything inherently rural. Nevertheless, people living in areas that previously were overwhelmingly agricultural in character continue to perceive themselves as distinct from their urban counterparts. Furthermore, such areas share a number of common characteristics, which makes it convenient to group them together — notably, questions of distance, accessibility of services, the relative importance of land-based activities, and the degree of spatial segregation between differing social groupings. This book concentrates on those who are poor and are living in areas that are characterised by these features.

STRUCTURE OF THE BOOK

The book falls into three main sections: the first section (Chapter 1) provides an overview of poverty in rural Ireland; the second section (Chapters 2 to 8) poses a number of issues in relation to rural poverty and suggests solutions; and the third section (Chapter 9) raises a number of policy implications emanating from the study.

The first, written by the editorial team of Chris Curtin, Hilary Tovey and Trutz Haase, spells out that the book is about the production, the reproduction and the experience of poverty in rural areas. The book puts forward the notion that it is people who are poor in rural areas and that we should be concerned with people rather than rural space per se. This is set in the context of the political economy in terms of the production of poverty — that is, the effect of global restructuring on rural localities, the effect of the organisation of the food industry and the impact of the European Union. This section then looks at how different rural groups respond to these processes and their particular rural experiences.

The second section contains seven chapters in which different authors discuss various aspects of rural poverty and suggest ways of addressing these. The areas covered include the demographic structures of rural areas, particularly the impact of migration. An important issue in discussing poverty in rural Ireland is agricultural production and the role and future of small-scale farming. Natural resource development is becoming increasingly important as an area that has the potential to address poverty in rural Ireland, at least to some extent.

Chapter 4 looks at the potential of forestry, mining, aquaculture and tourism in rural areas and the ability of those who are living in poverty in rural areas to benefit from these developments. Rural industrialisation is discussed as an area where poverty in rural Ireland can potentially be tackled. This is followed by an important chapter on social-service provision, an issue that deservedly has received some attention in rural areas. The Agency has had a particular interest in innovative actions taken by the Forum project in the Poverty 3 programme in the areas of primary health care and rural transport in particular. Important points are raised with regard to the need for policies based on fairness, equity and justice if people living in rural areas, and, in particular, the rural poor are to receive an adequate level of social-service provision. The final two chapters in the second section deal with the role of community development and local government in addressing poverty in rural areas. Both community development and local government have the potential for development in this area, and, if combined, would maximise the positive contribution that these structures could make to addressing poverty in rural areas.

The third section (Chapter 9) raises the policy implications arising from the contributions and discusses some very pertinent issues that must be dealt with if we are to recognise and seriously to address the plight of the rural poor.

KEY POLICY ISSUES

Several key policy issues are raised in this book.

(1) *Rural poverty is an issue that should be placed firmly on the national policy agenda*: The analysis and discussion in this book very clearly highlight the need to identify and understand the causes, experiences and consequences of poverty in rural Ireland, and, while many of the causes and experiences may be similar to those in "urban" Ireland, there are features that are distinctive and need to have particular responses. National development strategies should be directed towards the elimination of poverty as a significant goal.

(2) *Poverty in rural areas can be understood as resulting from global and national policies.* Solutions to addressing rural poverty must be seen in this context. While local solutions obviously have a role to play, they should complement national and European policies, rather than be expected in their own right to address the problems of rural areas.

(3) *The current National Anti-Poverty Strategy can have an important role in recognising and addressing poverty in rural Ireland.* The National Anti-Poverty Strategy, which is being developed and implemented across all government departments through an Inter-departmental Policy Committee, can play a significant role in raising poverty in rural areas as a key issue to be addressed — by "proofing policies" to assess their impact on people who are living in poverty in rural areas; and by taking co-ordinated measures to address this. Such policy responses should be based on the principles of equity and social justice. The editors of the book flag the idea of introducing a "social audit" with respect to addressing poverty in rural areas, and this is worthy of further consideration.

(4) *The focus on addressing rural poverty should be on people rather than space.* Throughout this book the authors emphasise that within rural areas there are people who are particularly marginalised, excluded and often "invisible". Policies in rural areas, especially with regard to rural development, need to recognise the needs of those who are most disadvantaged, and to enable them to participate in the development of their areas.

(5) *While area-based strategies clearly have a role to play, they should complement national policies.* It is evident from this book

that area-based strategies such as the local rural development programme, LEADER, community development projects and projects such as the Poverty 3 Forum project in Connemara have a role to play in addressing rural poverty. However, they need firstly, to complement a strong national commitment to addressing rural poverty — for example, through the National Anti-Poverty Strategy — and secondly, to take into account the needs of the rural poor. There could be an important role for a revised system of local government. The outcome of the Devolution Commission's deliberations could be significant here.

(6) *A number of specific issues raised in the book should be taken on board.* These are:

- The need to ensure that welfare support to low-income farmers and other non land-based rural inhabitants is provided at an adequate level — that is, at least at the minimum adequate rates recommended by the Commission on Social Welfare

- The need to maintain and create non-farm employment opportunities in rural areas

- The need to encourage industrial development in rural areas

- The need to encourage and support organic forms of farming and artisan food producers. This would be in recognition of the need to promote "sustainable development" and environmentally friendly farming methods

- Environmental impact assessments in rural areas should recognise the social impacts of particular forms of development — for example, through a social audit mechanism.

- A commitment should be made to implementing a programme of social services in rural areas based on the principles of equity and fairness rather than purely economic criteria — why should people be disadvantaged because of where they live?

(7) *These key issues and others raised in the book must be seriously considered and acted upon by all those who have some influence on people living in rural areas.* The Agency welcomes this contribution to the debate on poverty in rural Ireland and hopes that it will stimulate active and co-ordinated policies to address the real needs of those who are living in poverty in rural Ireland.

1: Understanding Rural Poverty

*Hilary Tovey, Trutz Haase
and Chris Curtin*

INTRODUCTION

Rural poverty and deprivation are topics that have received a good share of attention in Irish public discussion over many years, and it may well be asked what purpose can be served by bringing out yet another book on the topic. This book is intended to offer a distinctive approach to rural poverty — within the Irish context, distinctive in its treatment of both poverty and rurality; and, in particular, distinctive in the way that it tries to bring the two together.

One of the major aims of the book is to rethink the concepts of poverty and rurality through considering how they may be linked together. Both concepts are widely recognised as ambiguous and open-ended, presenting major problems of definition. In a book of readings on deprivation in rural Britain, Bradley et al. state that: "The concept of 'rurality' just like that of 'deprivation' engenders seemingly endless terminological debate and confusion. Put these two equally chaotic concepts together and one might reasonably expect epistemological turmoil" (1986: 18). Yet, as their own work shows, what one actually gets is often mutually fruitful illuminations, as researchers pursue the goal of a better understanding of poverty itself by asking what is distinctive about *rural* poverty.

In looking at rural poverty, the main aim of this study is not to establish that there is "more poverty" among rural than urban people in Ireland, or that some rural groups are poorer, or others less poor, than urban groups. Although some of the discussions in later chapters may either confirm or challenge such comparisons, it is not intended overall to set up an urban–rural "poverty contest". What is of interest is the question of whether poverty arises and is reproduced in rural Ireland in ways that are distinctive when compared with urban Ireland. Another area of interest is discovering whether poverty is experienced in rural Ireland in distinctively different ways, but it is not intended to make some specific association between being rural and being poor.

It is hoped that this book will contribute to debates around policy and indeed to the evolution of new strategies for intervening in rural poverty. But it is important to state at the outset that it is not intended to be another "handbook for rural development" — and, indeed, its primary focus is not on development issues at all. What it tries to offer is, rather, a discussion document on rural poverty. Its central objective is to increase public knowledge of social change in rural areas, and, in particular, of the way in which resources and opportunities are redistributed between social groups in the course of rural social change.

Clearly, there are developmental implications to be derived from a discussion of, for example, how certain types of change in rural society affect the distribution of rural resources. But this study suggests that attempts at "rural development" are not the only, and may not even be always the best, way of solving problems of rural poverty. There are major questions to be raised about how "development" is understood in this context, some of which are touched on later in this chapter. At this point, however, it is noted only that from the standpoint of the rural poor, intervention to equalise the distribution of existing resources, or to prevent or reduce the marginalisation of specific groups from the available opportunities, may sometimes be more beneficial than trying to increase the overall level of wealth generated within a locality or region.

In the rest of this chapter, then, a case is made for understanding poverty in a particular way, and addressing rural Ireland in a particular way, in order to establish what is meant by the phrase "rural poverty". In both cases, the approach is essentially one that focuses on social dynamics. To talk of "rural poverty" as one particular type of poverty is to suggest that poverty must be recognised, not as any sort of given condition, but as a product of societal developments, and must be investigated in that context. In turn, that requires that "the rural" itself be treated within a societal developmental context.

In the most abstract terms, what is recognised today as "rural Ireland" is a spatial and social manifestation of the uneven process of global capitalist development. Rural Ireland is not developing separately from urban areas. Rather, both rural and urban are subject to broad national and international developmental processes. These have different outcomes in different spaces or localities, and different effects on the different social groups within these localities. "Rural poverty" is thus a dynamic condition, which is produced out of, maintained or changed by dynamic processes in society in general. Discussing the dynamics of poverty as they operate in a rural setting should make its own contribution both to poverty studies in Ireland and to studies of rural Ireland.

THE DYNAMICS OF POVERTY

Until quite recently, research on poverty has been characterised more by terminological debates, and a preoccupation with measurement techniques, than by theoretical and explanatory development. The immense political significance and immediate policy relevance of research findings, understandably, encouraged researchers to concentrate on establishing the empirical dimensions of the problem before all else. This promoted a succession of attempts to define exactly what it means to be "poor" and to how many people in a given society the term "poor" may be applied. As mentioned earlier, this book attempts to shift the focus away from headcounting the rural poor, towards explaining the production of poverty in contemporary rural society. Nevertheless, it is not possible to escape entirely from some discussion of conceptual matters. A brief outline of the main ways of defining and conceptualising poverty in general — which have emerged from the debates of recent decades — may help to explain and elaborate the editors' own perspective on rural poverty in Ireland.

Ferge (1987: 15, 16) suggests that a distinction be made between different definitions of poverty in terms of where they can be located on three different dimensions:

(1)   Absolute versus relative

(2)   Objective versus subjective

(3)   Material versus social definitions of poverty.

As will be argued below, differences in defining poverty along these dimensions partly reflect the empirical complexity of the phenomenon; but they can also be understood as an indication of the extent to which researchers' own values and their political perspectives on processes of development in their societies enter into and shape their research.

Absolute and Relative Conceptions of Poverty

An *absolute* view of poverty assumes that it is possible to determine in some "scientific" or "value-free" way what counts as a minimal acceptable standard of living — "poverty" is then defined as inability to meet this standard. This is often expressed in terms of inability to meet "basic needs", or "minimal subsistence standards" as the basic necessity to sustain physical life. As Townsend (1987) has pointed out, such a definition of poverty can have dangerous political consequences, since it can be used to argue against State intervention to improve the situation of the poor once they have reached the minimal standards decided upon. For example, the use of "minimum subsistence standards" to determine the extent of poverty in Britain in the early twentieth century was derived from nineteenth-century Poor

Law legislation which, in turn, had its origins in pressure from the rich to reduce the cost of maintaining people in workhouses. One way in which that could be done was by establishing a minimum level of diet on which workhouse residents could subsist. Townsend argues that once the concept of minimal subsistence standards was legitimated — through nutritional research, for example — it could be and was used to justify low wage rates, and even lower rates of welfare payment to the unemployed poor.

Few studies of poverty in the developed world now would restrict their definition of poverty to a condition of lacking even the minimum subsistence levels needed to sustain physical life. Most would insist on incorporating some recognition of the way in which what is regarded as a minimum standard of subsistence in a society is influenced by the general standard of living in that society. To that extent, poverty is recognised as something that can vary in meaning between societies — that is, it is a *relative* rather than absolute condition. Where poverty is conceptualised in ways that link it to social inequality, definitions become even more explicitly relative. Such definitions — often accompanied by a terminological switch from "poverty" to "deprivation", "marginalisation" or "social exclusion" — start by determining what is required for an individual or family to enjoy the sorts of living conditions considered usual in that society. People whose resources fall below this level can be regarded as "poor", even if they are not in danger of ceasing to subsist, in the sense that they are marginalised or excluded from exercising "full membership" in their society.

One of the attractive features of this approach is that instead of directing attention onto "the poor" as a discrete group, disarticulated from broader social processes, which an "absolute" approach tends to do (and which, in turn, often implies that the poor are somehow responsible for their own condition of poverty), it focuses attention instead on *inequalities in the distribution of resources* within specific societies. In turn, this can have significant policy implications. While "absolute" poverty is often presented as something that can only be resolved through general economic growth, on the understanding that that is the only thing that could allow more people to meet their needs, "relative poverty" could be overcome through a more equal distribution of existing resources — something that is achievable even in times of economic recession if majority expectations of what is "the usual standard of living" in the society can be reduced.

Objective and Subjective Conceptions of Poverty

The distinction between *objective* and *subjective* conceptions of poverty brings a further dimension into question: should people's perceptions of their own situation, and that of others, be included in measurements of poverty (the "subjectivist" position), or should measurements of poverty be restricted to "external" or "factual" criteria, such as the degree of access to certain standards of nutrition, clothing, housing and transport possessed by an individual or household, as judged by a qualified outsider (the "objectivist" position)? Including people's "subjective" definitions of their own situation does not make poverty impossible to measure "objectively" — in the sense of "scientifically" — although it may mean that different, often more time-consuming, measurement techniques have to be used, which may make large-scale and particularly cross-national types of study more expensive or difficult to undertake.

Subjective measurements of poverty can produce "absolutist" definitions of what it is to be poor. For example, when members of a society are asked how they would rank a series of indicators of deprivation as more or less "basic" (see, for example, Williams and Whelan's (1994) distinction between "primary" and "secondary" deprivation) they are being invited to give their views on what are the absolutely necessary conditions for survival in their society. Equally, there have been examples of "relativist" approaches to the study of poverty which were based entirely on objective measures. For example, Townsend's (1979) study has been widely criticised because the items he included in his "deprivation index" were selected by himself as a researcher, rather than being derived from a study of what ordinary people in the society considered to be essential elements of an acceptable lifestyle. But, in general, the more relativist the conception of poverty, the more likely it is that the perceptions of members of society as to what counts as a "normal" standard of living in their own society will have been included in the measure of poverty used.

Distinguishing between objective and subjective definitions of poverty allows us to recognise that what people feel about their own situation may sometimes differ sharply from how an external observer would describe this. People may feel themselves to be poor who would not be judged poor by a researcher, whether using absolute or relative standards of judgment. More interestingly, people's subjective experience of poverty may emphasise elements of their condition which are not given priority by external observers; or they may not perceive themselves as poor, even when objective standards would categorise them as poor. A number of studies of deprivation in Britain, for example, have found that deprived rural groups are less likely than similarly situated urban groups to describe themselves as poor (Knox, 1986: 102). Flynn (1986) suggests that the reason for this may be that the dominant ideology about rural life in Britain is that it is socially, aesthetically and physically more satisfying than urban life, and that this ideology has been internalised even by the rural poor.

Since this book focuses on the specific features of rural poverty in Ireland, it needs to address the issue of "subjective poverty" and its relationship with rurality. Have Irish rural people tended to hold particular views about how poverty is distributed in Irish society, which would make them more prepared or less prepared to define themselves as poor? Do urban and rural residents agree or differ over who the real "rural poor" are? Is rural residence associated, in Ireland, with distinctive beliefs about the appropriate ways to respond to and deal with poverty? It may not be possible to answer such precise questions as these based on the material covered in later chapters of the book, but it is, nevertheless, important to keep subjective understandings in view and to recognise that they may be implicated not just in the existence, but also in the persistence and the expansion or the decline of poverty in rural Ireland.

Material and Social Conceptions of Poverty

Movement towards the use of more "subjectivist" approaches to studying poverty in recent years has also coincided, among both researchers and policy makers, with increased interest in conceptions of poverty that go beyond the purely material. Economic deprivation remains a central element in defining poverty, but it is increasingly seen as inadequate on its own. People who are poor in material terms are often also poor in social terms (they are unable to meet the obligations or expectations that are associated with normal social relationships in their society), and often also in political terms (they are excluded from participation in decision making within their society). Poverty research, which continues to be preoccupied primarily with measuring poverty in terms of income levels, for example, can be criticised for disregarding the impact on the poor of experiencing *social and political exclusion*.

These are increasingly accepted as very significant features both of how people experience poverty, and of the dynamics of poverty reproduction. Social and political marginalisation or exclusion can leave the excluded less and less in control of their own circumstances, which can, in turn, increase the risk of falling into "material" poverty. Those who make this sort of case also argue that it is necessary to re-think the conventionally recommended solutions to poverty, such as increased social welfare payments or State transfers to the poor. Solving poverty must include not just redressing material deprivation, but also increasing the self-respect of the poor, their opportunities for education and mobility, and their capacity to participate individually or collectively in the core decision-making processes of their society.

Rethinking poverty in terms of *social exclusion* has allowed poverty debates to link up with broader debates about social justice and the "rights of citizenship", which should be available to all members of a society (see, for example, Atkinson and Barnes, 1989: 12). However, there remains considerable debate about whether it is possible to develop objective measures of social and political exclusion, particularly of a sort amenable to measurement in large-scale and cross-national research; and if not, whether it is allowable to infer from material indicators of poverty the presence of socio-political exclusion as well. In a study specifically of rural poverty, such an inference seems likely to be of doubtful validity. At least one study on "marginalised farmers" in Ireland (Leeuwis, 1989) suggests that while economic marginalisation (lack of income from agriculture, exclusion from commercial food production) among small farmers may be related to, even partly caused by, their political and ideological marginalisation, it is much less clear that it has any association with social marginalisation in the sense of exclusion from social relationships and networks at the local level. Indeed, exclusion from local social life may in some cases be more a feature of the lifestyle of large high-income farmers than of small low-income ones.

The terminology of "exclusion" seems to have become widely used nowadays, mainly as a result of a deliberate decision by the EU in the late 1980s to move away from using the term "poverty" (Nolan and Whelan, 1996: 221). The reasons for the shift were political as much as theoretical — a feeling among some member states that "poverty" implied criticism of the régime in which it was found, or an increasing concern about a possible collapse in social integration across the EU as it moved towards full economic integration. But there were also substantive arguments for making the shift in terminology, particularly, as was noted above, the belief that poverty today is a matter not just of financial deprivation, but also, increasingly, of deprivation of rights and

marginalisation from power. "Poverty refers 'only' to financial resources, social exclusion is multidimensional" (*ibid.*: 223).

Poverty as a Dynamic Process

Nolan and Whelan argue that this contrast is more spurious than informative and that "social exclusion" remains a vague concept whose
precise relationship to poverty is not clarified. They also suggest that
a lot of its appeal comes from the claim that "poverty" is a static condition while what we need to examine are dynamic processes, and
that these are better captured by the (more "active") concept of
"exclusion". They disagree with this: "Although empirical poverty research may often have been guilty of adopting a static perspective,
concentrating much of its effort on description of those identified as
poor at a point in time, there is absolutely nothing in the way poverty
is generally conceptualised which has such a static or descriptive
connotation" (op. cit.: 225). Poverty research, they suggest, is increasingly research into the dynamic processes that lead people into a
situation of poverty. There is no need to change to a discourse of social
exclusion to address this issue.

Agreeing that "social exclusion" remains a rather obscure and, in
some respects, politically contentious term, contributors to this book
have, for the most part, used the term "poverty" in preference. But it
is nevertheless important to take note of the issues to which the terminological debates of recent years have drawn attention and which
much previous poverty research has neglected — particularly, that
poverty includes more than simply lack of money; and that it is not
simply a characteristic of an individual or household, but intimately
related to structural processes of reproduction and change at the level
of society as a whole.

The existence and the persistence of poverty, not just in the developing countries of the world, but in the rich and developed states also,
has been documented in many studies since the 1960s. Many poverty
researchers today are prepared to argue that the *existence* of poverty
in the advanced societies can be taken for granted now — what research should be directed towards is *explaining* its existence (see, for
example, Ferge and Miller, 1987). In the Irish case, the existence of
substantial poverty was well documented in the late 1980s (Callan
and Nolan, 1988; Callan et al. 1989), and, in that context, moves towards a focus on the dynamics of poverty in Ireland are now recog-

nised as overdue. But researchers differ over what they understand by "the dynamics of poverty".

The main form which a focus on poverty dynamics has taken among Irish researchers to date (Nolan and Callan, 1994) has been investigating the movements of Irish families or household groups into and out of poverty over a period of time. Williams and Whelan have shown, for example, that households within a broad income band have a propensity to move from above to below the poverty line, or from below to above it, according to changes in their circumstances, particularly in the employment status of the main wage earner in the household. They want to treat poverty as "dynamic" in that sense, because they see this as a way of combating the over-rigid distinctions between "the poor" and "the non-poor" in Irish society, which are produced by "static" views of poverty.

The editors would agree that investigating the dynamics of poverty should include investigating the structured movements — not just of households but also of individuals, and, where relevant, of social or occupational groups — in and out of poverty or through different experiences of poverty over specific periods of time. But in this book's use of the term, a "dynamic" approach to poverty should do more: it should also try to locate such changing experiences as outcomes of broad processes of social and structural change within societies. So, for example, if the sudden loss of employment by a household member can move a household that was previously above the poverty line to below it, the editors would argue that an account of "the dynamics of poverty" in Irish society should include also some explanation of employment and unemployment trends in general, or, more broadly, of how processes of economic development within the society are altering and restructuring access to livelihood resources for different social groups.

In summary, this study of rural poverty in Ireland is primarily about the production of poverty, the experience of it, and the reproduction of it over time, rather than about establishing the extent of rural poverty. It is part of a general attempt by researchers on poverty to shift debate away from measurement and description and towards explanation. In the course of that, however, the study aims also to contribute to developing the way in which poverty itself is defined and conceptualised, researched and made the object of policy debate in Irish society, rural or urban.

The editors believe that it is particularly important to use a definition of poverty which recognises it as relative to general conceptions of a normal or acceptable standard of living in contemporary Ireland, rather than as an absolute condition, and which pays attention to non-material aspects of poverty and to the ways in which those labelled as poor interpret and respond to their situation. The importance of material conditions like access to income and to services and supports in shaping the world of the poor is not thereby discounted. But as has already been noted, rural inhabitants may interpret their material situation in ways that differ from urban people. It is also the case that they may be subjected to rather specific understandings of how to deal with poverty, which are held by leaders of rural society, by the makers of rural policy — themselves probably not "rural" — or by other urban groups in Ireland. To develop that point further, it is necessary to offer some conceptual elaboration of "rural" as well as of "poverty". A more detailed explanation is needed of what we take to be the main dynamics of change in Irish rural society, but before that, there must be some discussion of the meanings attached to "the rural" in Ireland, particularly in relation to the way it has been understood in Irish policy discourses on rural development.

Poverty, Class and Locality in Rural Ireland

As stated earlier, this book focuses as far as possible on the dynamics of poverty — the forces that produce it, and the way in which, in some cases, it becomes reproduced and institutionalised over time, or, in others, social groups are able to escape from poverty. Addressing this through a specific focus on *rural* poverty in Ireland can be justified on two counts.

In the first place, although researchers often disagree on what they understand by "rural", nearly all will agree that, at least until recently, the most significant feature which marked out rural from urban areas, and which gave rural areas experiences in common, has been the dominant position within them of *agricultural production*. Research has repeatedly shown that in developing capitalist societies the path of development and modernisation in agriculture differs markedly from that in most other sectors of production (see, for example, Goodman and Redclift, 1986; Goodman et al., 1987). In turn, this suggests that the generation of poverty is different and distinctive in rural areas.

To make this point is not to assume that agriculture continues to be the dominant production process or user of labour in all of rural Ireland. As later chapters show, Ireland has become an increasingly "urbanised" society in recent decades, both in the sense that more and more people are moving out of the countryside to live in or near towns, and in the sense that industrial and service occupations have replaced farming as the main occupation of a majority of rural dwellers today. Nevertheless, the spatial distribution of the rural population, and many features of their social positions and relationships, still need to be placed in a context of earlier agrarian practices and structures if they are to be fully understood.

On this basis, this study argues that much of the rural poverty in Ireland today is a product of development trends and policies in agriculture, at both national and global levels. Rural poverty is not, of course, confined to farmers. Yet even those landless groups in the countryside who have been heavily dependent on employment in, for example, branch plants of multinational industries, have largely been created out of the particular ways in which inheritance and succession have been organised within Irish farming since the Famine, or out of changes in the use of wage labour on farms as farmers became more technologically developed and more oriented towards profit from the late 1950s onward. Present and past agricultural trends and practices underpin many characteristics of the contemporary non-agrarian but rural social world. The next section develops this point in much greater detail, focusing on how global trends in food production and processing, and international restructuring in industrial production more generally, have shaped the situation of rural areas in Ireland and of the social groups found within them.

The first point, then, is that to the extent that "rural" still implies "agricultural", if only in the limited and qualified way suggested above, analysis of the dynamics of agriculture and food production is a necessary element in understanding poverty in rural areas in Ireland. Secondly, however, ideas of "rurality" in everyday discourse are often linked to notions about *the organisation of space*. Rural areas tend to be defined as exhibiting a distinctive use of space: they are areas in which there is a lower level of population density compared to urban areas, for example, or they are areas in which wealth-generating activities require access to space in a way that urban economic activities do not. The most obvious example of this may again be agriculture, which, in spite of 100 years or so of adopting new technologies that tend to promote increased output from static or declining acreages, still uses extended land areas as a central element in the production of food. But we can also see certain types of tourism, or other forms of resource exploitation, such as forestry, as character-

istically "rural" in the way that they use land or space. This implication of spatial characteristics in the concept of rural has some important consequences when one comes to consider rural poverty.

The idea that rural areas are places with a low population density (which the presence of "Congested Districts" in nineteenth-
century Ireland suggests should be treated as historically specific)
forms part of a tradition of theorising about development problems in
Europe in terms of the concept of "sparsely populated regions".
Within this tradition, population scarcity has also been linked to *spatial peripherality*, in the sense of distance from the developed core of
society. Spatial patterning, and social and political dependence or
powerlessness, are thus interlinked in this characterisation of the rural: the more rural an area is, the more spatially dispersed is its
population, the more spatially distanced it is from the urban centre(s)
of power and administration, and the less it is able to exert autonomous action to make itself more developed.

Traditional "rural development" perspectives and policies have
generally taken for granted that rural poverty , in the sense of economic and social peripherality, is identical with or a result of geographical peripherality, and have sought policy interventions that
would make rural *areas* less marginal or less "spatially excluded". It
is argued here that the equation of rural poverty with certain geographical features of rural localities should be treated as a hypothesis
to be tested in research rather than, as is so often assumed, a matter
of definition.

This is not to suggest that spatial location has no bearing at all on
the existence or otherwise of deprived or excluded social groups.
Quite the contrary, the argument that economic development tends to
be a spatially uneven process both internationally and locally is accepted. Indeed, the presence of *diversity* between local spaces is one
very important source of, or resource for, wealth accumulation in the
course of economic growth; and, in turn, economic development can
quite profoundly alter previous spatial configurations and relationships, as, for example, Commins and Keane (1994) argue in showing
how agricultural production and output has been gradually shifting
from the north-east to the south-west of Ireland in recent years in
response to changing policies and international conditions. This spatial unevenness and spatial restructuring is undoubtedly a significant
factor to be considered when trying to explain why it is that certain
social groups in the countryside experience a movement into poverty,
or, on the contrary, manage to take actions that lift them above the

poverty line. However, from the perspective of this study, it is never areas or localities that are "poor" or "marginalised", "wealthy" or "included", but *people* or social groups.

Distinction Between Localities and Social Groups

There are two simple but nevertheless often overlooked reasons for emphasising the distinction between localities, on the one hand, and social groups, on the other. First, an area that contains many poor people may still be a source of wealth for specific individuals or organisations outside it. The organisation of tourism in a sparsely populated region, for example, or of the extraction of minerals from land which supports only very poor small farmers, allows some individuals or groups to accrue wealth from what is, if one looks only at its inhabitants, easily categorised as an "underdeveloped" or "peripheral" area. This is a reminder of the importance of international and global processes in reshaping the economies and social structures of rural areas (this is developed further in the next section). Second, just as economic development encourages spatial (local or regional) diversity, so it can also encourage inequalities between social groups.

If one thinks of poverty in the broadest sense, in terms of economic, social, political and/or ideological exclusion from participation in society, it seems obvious that very few, if any, localities exist in rural Ireland in which everyone experiences exactly the same degree of exclusion. At the very least, there will be differences in the way that exclusion is experienced by groups of different ages or different genders. Both gender and age, for example, strongly affect patterns of ownership of land or other material resources in rural areas; they also — usually in the reverse pattern — shape access to education and to knowledge, skills and cultural capital. And as rural areas in Ireland have become less dominated by occupations in farming, many have also experienced the emergence of differentiated *social class* structures, by which is meant that access or the lack of access to education or capital, and hence to non-farming occupations, becomes something that is inherited across generations, as the position of parents in relation to such resources in turn constrains or determines the position of their children.

These are very obvious points to make. Yet it seems that they are still necessary, given the way in which the problems of rural people are still predominantly addressed and understood in the Irish literature. For example, the recent report from the National Economic and Social Council (NESC) on development in rural Ireland (NESC, 1994), although it presents its arguments with meticulous care and thoroughness, and does initially (*ibid.*: 5) recognise the fact that not all the inhabitants in a given rural locality experience the same problems, adopts throughout an area-based perspective on rural poverty and rural development. Instead of conceptualising the issue as that of overcoming social exclusion among certain rural groups, it treats it in essence as a problem of the underdevelopment or lack of development of Irish rural localities.

As a result, it is forced into making quite arbitrary decisions about what constitutes an appropriate area for analysis: should this be a "locality" — and how do we establish the boundaries of that? — or should it be a "region" and, if so, how large or small a space is intended by this? Should a "rural area" include local towns which are more and more likely to be the commercial, educational, occupational and leisure centre for the rural population, for example? The Report does make helpful distinctions between "territorial" as against "sectional or functional" types of policy for rural areas, arguing that the type of policy adopted is a separate issue from how it is implemented — for example, through a centralised or decentralised approach, making more or less use of local agents as against agencies of the national or supranational state (NESC, 1994: 18–20). The Council's own preference is ultimately for a territorial type of policy (for example, integrated rural development), which also involves the maximum use of local agents whether individuals, corporate actors or "communities". This allows them to move easily between describing their subject as "rural development policy" and as "local development policy".

Treating "rural" and "local" as interchangeable in this context poses several problems. Since underdeveloped "local areas" are found in cities as well as in the countryside, the specific processes that have created social exclusion and problematic social structures within some rural areas of Ireland easily drop out of sight. At the same time, diversity between and within rural localities also disappears and we are encouraged instead to focus on the problems that they have in common, such as population loss through emigration. Yet it seems clear that although out-migration may be found in both rich and poor agricultural areas, and, more importantly, in both rich and poor rural households, it does not carry the same meanings in terms of choice or of the life-chances associated with it in each case.

If the main concern is with overcoming marginality and exclusion in Irish society, and specifically in Irish rural areas, it seems better to start by looking for those social groups within rural Ireland who are most subject to exclusion, and in the opinion of the editors of this study, this does require a "sectoral" as much as a spatial or "territorial" approach to the issue. It may be the case that solutions to deprivation in rural Ireland require territorial political responses — for example, collective or community action engaging local power-holders as well as the excluded in order to press for changes in state policy; but for the purposes of identifying and analysing the social groups most at risk, and perhaps also for improving their situation, it would appear that sectoral analysis and the identification of policies directed at improving access and increasing equity within different economic sectors are likely to be the most useful.

The language of "rural local development", as developed in the NESC Report, is primarily a language of consensus. It assumes that there is no contradiction between increasing the wealth generated by a "locality" and increasing the standard of living of all groups within that locality; yet studies of mining, fish farming and other forms of rural resource exploitation suggest that this is often not the case and that, in fact, wealth generation through exploitation of rural re-sources can involve a decrease in the standard of living previously enjoyed by some rural groups. It assumes that the State or other supra-local actors have no interest in keeping some rural localities "underdeveloped", or, as we might put it, in "ruralising" some parts of state territory; yet the basis for this assumption is not spelt out, and, in fact, some of the discourse on maintaining rural areas which emerges from state or EU policy statements might suggest otherwise.

Mormont (1990) has suggested that there has been a profound transformation in the meaning of "rural" in European society in re-cent decades, from indicating the presence of a specific form of *society* assumed to have many features distinct from, and perhaps to be in opposition to, urban society, to, simply, "nature" as unsocialised or de-socialised *space*. EU policy statements such as the *Rural World* report (1988) can be seen as supporting this claim, in so far as they speak of "the rural" as having distinct *functions* to perform for society — in particular, the function of maintaining "buffer zones" between built-up areas which can be available to citified humanity as locations for leisure pursuits or just as "lungs" for the intake of relatively un-polluted air. Some rural areas, in other words, may be required by the State to forego development (for example, in allowing no industries to

locate there) or even undergo de-development (for example, in farming practices) and it is not necessarily the case that their inhabitants
will receive appropriate compensation for the resulting reduction in
their living standards, if they are allowed to remain in the area at all.

It is this consensus perspective that allows the authors of the
NESC Report to agree with state and EU policy which insists that
marginal rural areas can best overcome their problems through collective *territorial* action including rural residents, local corporate actors
and local government agents. In contrast, this book argues that such a
policy needs to be subjected to critical evaluation, since it is not evident that everyone benefits equally from it, or even that it does offer
an effective path out of peripherality for rural localities. Other
authors have suggested that "bottom-up" policy approaches which
emphasise the need for local mobilisation around development may
offer to rural groups little more than *ideological* inclusion. They allow
the State to secure legitimacy for its development projects by creating
the appearance that all rural people can participate in the creation of
such projects through their collective or communal action, while in
fact transferring to the local actors only minimal power to identify or
implement appropriate forms of development.

In summary, in investigating rural poverty in Ireland the intention
of this study is not simply to reproduce the many previous accounts
and analyses of territorial peripherality, underdevelopment or exclusion that already exist. The aim is to shift attention onto specific social groups who experience poverty, and whose presence within rural
Ireland is a product of macro-social long-term trends towards spatial
and social restructuring in international industrial and food production processes. In this way, it is hoped to develop the argument that
poverty must be seen as a part, even perhaps a normal but an increasingly unacceptable part, of the dynamics of social change and
development in Ireland and in the world.

THE PRODUCTION AND REPRODUCTION
OF RURAL POVERTY

To understand the factors that contribute to the creation and reproduction of rural poverty, it is necessary to look both at the social processes that take place between individuals or small groups at the local
level, and the social and economic processes that affect whole social
groupings or regions at the national or even global level. Indeed, what
is often perceived by an individual as their own personal fate or mis-

fortune in reality reflects the conjuncture of these two levels, and whether particular individuals finds themselves in poverty is largely determined by the degree to which the individual is able to respond to the economic and social opportunities or crises, over whose occurrence that individual may have little control in the first place.

The purpose of this section is to take a closer look at the national and global developments that affect rural communities, and thereby set the framework within which more localised processes take place. There are four areas in which such an approach may offer explanations beyond what can be extracted from local experience, namely:

(1) The way that the organisation of global food production yields particular forms of investment (and disinvestment) in rural areas

(2) The spatial impact that the global restructuring of production has on the organisation of industry and services in Ireland

(3) The role that the Irish state has in mediating international and localised developments

(4) The effects that European Integration may have on Irish peripherality.

The Political Economy of Food

Though agriculture is no longer the mainstay of every rural community, one still cannot understand the dynamics of rural development without a thorough grasp of the factors that determine the conditions under which agricultural production takes place. Agricultural production is probably the single most regulated commodity of national importance, and who is producing what, where and at what price is strongly influenced by national, European and worldwide agreements. It seems appropriate therefore to start with a brief look at how the production of food is organised at a global level and at the changes that have taken place in this organisation over the past decades.

The rules defining the international post-war food régime[1] gave priority to national regulation, and authorised both import controls and export subsidies necessary to manage national farm programmes.

---

[1] The term "régime" is used here to refer to a coherent and stable set of rules and regulations that has applied across a vast number of countries over a considerable number of years.

Economically and politically more powerful states used the unusual form of subsidised exports and surplus commodities to restructure international trade and production in their own favour. The ability of less powerful states to develop their own national economies, particularly to the extent that they depended primarily on agrarian strategies, was shaped by the opportunities and limits of world food markets. Since the "food crisis" of the early 1970s, the post-war food régime has been in fundamental disarray. Competitive dumping and potential trade wars, particularly between the European Community and the US, have made the practice of national price support systems unbearably costly. Furthermore, trans-national corporations (TNCs) in the agro-food sector have outgrown existing national regulatory frameworks, making it impossible to control them, while, at the same time, TNCs themselves increasingly experienced national regulatory frameworks as an obstacle to further integration of a potentially global agro-food sector.

This shift in the balance between internationally organised food corporations and individual nation states was well documented in the recent negotiations of the GATT. Behind the scenes of the conflict between the US and the EC, which held centre stage at the GATT negotiations, lay the emergence of a new alignment between Japan, which together with other countries had emerged as a major commercial food importer, and a group of successful new agro-food exporters in the Third World. The rise in trade between these countries had irrevocably destabilised the hitherto Atlantic-centred food régime. This development had gradually taken place over the past 20 years or so, but few people would commonly have paid much attention to the particular developments in the global food market. While there exists a popular perception of the fact that the "oil crisis" of the early 1970s led to the subsequent differentiation of the Third World and the emergence of a set of new oil-exporting countries and successful newly industrialising countries (NICs), little attention generally has been paid to the parallel emergence of a whole set of "new agricultural countries", or NACs. To give only a taste of the size of shifts in global food markets, one may consider the following excerpt from Friedmann:

> Within four years of the US soy embargo of 1973, NACs had cut into the previous virtual US export monopoly. By 1977, the US share of world exports of oilseed and meals, of which soy was the largest, was only 54.6 per cent. Ten years later, the US share of world oilmeal exports had fallen to one-sixth. It exported less than

Brazil and only slightly more than Argentina. China, Chile, and India had joined the ranks of major oilmeal exporters. . . . Brazil's successful adaptation of the US model, which shifted the focus from agriculture to agro-industry and from the management of surpluses to commercial exports, involved a complex web of international and social transformations. It gave Brazil a competitive advantage in a technically evolving and increasingly open international food economy — *at high cost to the victims of capitalist transformation of the agro-food economy of Brazil.* . . . Liberalisation has created an unstable situation in which importers (with strong currencies) benefit and the largest exporter wields the greatest power in international rule-making. Paradoxically, liberal trade practices now so desperately pursued by the US to manage short-term deficits, reinforce the long-term shift of advantage to (economically strong) import countries (Friedmann, 1993: 46–7, emphasis added).

If one considers the central importance that soy has in the whole processed food sector, the above excerpt provides a brief glimpse into the depth of changes that have occurred over the past 20 years, principally involving a twofold shift in power relations at a global level. Firstly, there has been a fundamental shift in influence away from the food-raising sector and in favour of the food-input and the food-processing and marketing sectors (Goss, 1980). Secondly, technological advances in food production, together with the protectionist drive of the post-war Atlantic-centred food régime, have led to a situation of general over-production in food stuffs which, in turn, has facilitated a significant shift in influence to food-importing countries.

Recent changes in national farm policies are now catching up with the structural end of the post-war food régime. Changes in agricultural policy, which were unimaginable at the outset of the Uruguay Round of GATT negotiations, now anticipate for the first time an end to national surplus production. The separation of farm income support from production — that is, the end of price supports — seems to be the likely future for North America. In the EU, reforms of the Common Agricultural Policy (CAP), initiated in 1988 and intensified in 1991, point decisively in the same direction. The collapse of the former Eastern Bloc and the subsequent emergence of trading relationships with the European Union have dramatically accelerated this development. It is now widely acknowledged that any eastwards extension of the European Union would have to put a radical end to the remaining price support régimes. Indeed, it seems increasingly to

be mainly a question of *when* farmers will start receiving direct income support instead of being supported indirectly through the prices
of their commodities. To the extent that trade between the European
Union and the former Eastern Bloc states expands further, and certainly if some of these countries are successful in joining the EU,
there is little doubt that a substantial number of farmers who so far
enjoyed the protection of the EU will find it increasingly difficult to
survive solely on their earnings from working the land. Some of those
who decide to discontinue agricultural production may find support in
a combination of rural welfare and tourism projects. In other cases,
farm income supports may be tied to management of rural resources
and to environmental programmes. But there is little doubt that an
ever-larger proportion of people who live in rural areas will not receive their incomes in any way through agricultural production. For
many years already, the idea that contemporary Ireland is primarily
an agrarian country has owed more to myth than to reality. Acknowledging this fact is an important starting point in the search for a realistic path to combat rural poverty.

The Global Restructuring of Production and its Spatial Impact on the Organisation of Production

Though the agriculture sector was looked at first, the underlying
forces that made its global restructuring possible are themselves only
part of the changes that inform the contemporary reorganisation of
production as a whole on a global scale. The principal enabling factor
in this process has been the technological revolution occurring since
the Second World War. This has not only deeply affected production
processes themselves, but has radically changed the existing possibilities in their form of organisation. In particular, the emerging international division of labour has made possible the separation of the
location of production from the spheres of technical and financial
support.

On a global scale, this has resulted in some countries being chosen
as a convenient site for the relocation of part of the industrial activity
from the advanced capitalist societies. Within the advanced capitalist
countries it has evoked a rapid change towards office-based economies, principally devoted to managerial control, business services and
information processing. Individual firms are reacting to the changing
environment in a twofold manner: in the short run they attempt to
identify methods of increasing labour productivity; in the long run

they re-assess their investments, shifting capital from one type of activity to another and from one location to another.

Firms operating in Ireland are no exception to this. But since the "opening up" of the economy in the late 1950s, the behaviour of Irish firms has become much more influenced by developments outside the Irish economy than was previously the case. It is therefore useful to take a brief look at the developments around this fundamental change in Irish economic policy and what this subsequently entailed.

By the late 1950s, Irish economic development had come practically to a standstill. In contrast, many of the Western capitalist economies were experiencing unprecedented and sustained levels of growth at this time, principally as a result of increased labour productivity in the wake of the application of Fordist and Scientific Management methods of production. The idea behind the opening up of the Irish economy was the belief that, by exposing Irish firms to foreign competition, the new labour processes that had developed throughout the Western economies would allow productivity in Irish firms to rise and bring with it similar rates of increase in incomes and profitability.

As it happened, the Irish economy did indeed experience an unprecedented revival during the 1960s. By the early 1970s it was ready to join the European Economic Community, which it subsequently did in 1973. By this time, Ireland also benefited to a considerable extent from the inward investment of foreign multinational companies. Ireland had become one of the favourite locations for internationally mobile production, owing partly to the first downturn of the core European economies in the late 1960s, and partly to the favourable conditions prevailing in Ireland for those multinationals because of the generous tax concessions by the Irish government and massive grants through the IDA.

At least in hindsight, however, the blessings of an economic strategy based on attracting branch plants of multinational corporations have been mixed. Initially there were many new jobs created in these new centres of production. This meant not only an important source for personal incomes and growing GDP, but also an important impetus towards technological renewal. It remains an inescapable fact that productivity in foreign-owned companies has consistently outstripped that of the indigenous sector. But the abolition of trade barriers, which were a prerequisite for joining the European market, also meant the removal of any protection for Ireland's traditional industries and emerging new infant industries. As Ireland had joined the open market as a late starter, its industries tended to be too small to compete successfully in often already-saturated markets. The subsequent job losses were massive, particularly in Ireland's traditional industries. Between 1973 and 1980, over 10,000 jobs were lost in the textile, clothing and footwear sectors alone.

However, the job losses in the indigenous sector were not the only downside of an economic strategy that had left Ireland wide open to fluctuations in the world market. As most of the foreign investment was in the form of branch plants of large multinational corporations, Ireland suffered all the common ill-effects associated with such a strategy. Much of the production in those branch plants was of low value-added content, consisting mainly of low-skill assembly operations; R&D expenditure was minimal as most of those functions remained in the corporation's home countries; forward and backward linkages to indigenous industries remained much below what had been expected; and most of the profits made by those companies failed to be reinvested but were repatriated, creating a considerable loss to the Irish economy.

Possibly the worst effects of this strategy were the inherent ill-effects of the very fact that these companies represented highly mobile investments. As international markets fluctuate, companies decide at the stroke of a pen to open and close factories, with often devastating consequences for the towns and villages in which they had settled. Particularly in more rural locations, branch plants of multinational corporations had often represented the only significant employer in the locality. Having first attracted considerable proportions of the local workforce into the factory, many people would have discontinued their previous, more marginal economic activities. If such a factory were then to close, it could leave the local economy devastated as it was often impossible to re-establish previous economic activities.

It goes beyond the purpose of this introductory chapter to argue in greater detail the pros and cons of such a development strategy. However, it is important here to point out the exceptional degree of vulnerability that the Irish economy has experienced ever since — firstly, as a result of being so small, and secondly, by being one of the most open Western economies.

The Role of the State

The Irish state has been far from neutral in this course of events but has generally provided active assistance in the process of national and regional restructuring. The State had a major role in initiating

the opening up of the economy in the late 1950s and, as Boylan demonstrates in Chapter 5, has continued to play a strategic role through
the publication of key reports such as the Telesis and Culliton Reports (NESC, 1982 and Review Group, 1992). Last but not least, the
State provides the necessary fiscal environment through low taxation
and generous grants from the IDA.

Besides ensuring competitiveness in international markets, the
second reason for the Irish state to be heavily involved in formulating
an overall economic strategy is its concern with the uneven effects that
market-led expansion tends to have on the different regions within its
domain. Throughout the Western capitalist countries, there has been
a growing awareness since the late 1960s that the increasing spatial
concentration of economic problems, particularly in urban areas of
multiple disadvantage, may ultimately turn into a political problem,
threatening the economic and social cohesion of individual nation
states. For this reason, the Irish government, like most other European governments, intervened during the 1970s through a number of
regional policies, principally aimed at manipulating the relative costs
of production at the regional level. As Boylan shows in great detail in
Chapter 5, since the early 1980s, regional development has increasingly been left to the outcome of prevailing market forces, and the
question arises as to why the Irish government, as most other Western governments, has changed so fundamentally its behaviour towards regional economic problems.

Some answers to this question can be sought by looking more
analytically at the general role of the State. O'Connor (1973) argues
that the State plays two major but linked roles in a capitalist system.
First, it promotes capitalist accumulation by providing the general
material conditions of production and reproduction, including the en-
forcement of law and order, the regulation of conflict between capital
and labour, and the representation of the interests of national capital
on the world market. The second role of the State is the legitimisation
of capitalism. As tensions between capital and labour are a constant
threat to the viability of both individual enterprises and the system
as a whole, the capitalist state plays a vital role in ensuring worker
compliance. This is largely done by guaranteeing minimum living
standards for the working class.

However, even within the advanced capitalist world, not all countries or regions are equally equipped to respond to the challenges
posed by the changing economic and political conditions. Economically peripheral regions in particular often face two problems. Firstly,

their traditional industries tend to be unable to adapt to the ever-faster-changing international division of labour, and they often face the complete decline of their staple industries. Secondly, when industries do manage to restructure themselves, the regaining of competitiveness tends to be accompanied by substantial losses in employment.

Ireland's experience is no exception to this. There are fewer examples within the Republic as most of Ireland's leading industries were situated in the north of the country when it was partitioned in 1922, but Northern Ireland's industries provide an excellent example. Shipbuilding and mechanical engineering — two of Northern Ireland's three staple industries — declined sharply in the wake of the simultaneous decline in world demand and a shift in the location of production to the newly industrialising countries (NICs) during the 1970s and 1980s. In contrast, Northern Ireland's textile industry was able to restructure itself. Here, however, productivity gains, which were essential to maintain competitiveness against the new producers in the NICs, led to substantial employment losses throughout the industry.

With the exception of the food processing industry, the Republic of Ireland had few industries that could be called staple industries and, as a whole, the Republic's development had more in common with the experience of other NICs. The restructuring experienced in the food-processing industry, however, was of considerable importance and affected many rural areas. To the extent that Ireland became a small open economy within the wider European economy, many of its traditional industries, like the footwear, textile and confectionery industries, experienced a traumatic decline with partly disastrous consequences for the more rural areas.

The principal problem for peripheral regions within the advanced capitalist countries seems to be their inability to attract any significant share in the new growth sectors of the economy. As national economies rapidly develop towards office-based economies, new employment in the areas of managerial control, business services, and information processing tend to be highly concentrated in the more prosperous countries and regions within it. The continued lack of new employment opportunities and the resulting levels of out-migration from Ireland's more rural areas are a striking reminder of this development.

Following O'Connor's distinction between the two principal roles of the capitalist state, it could be said that it was in its role as a promoter of accumulation that the Irish state generally supported this development, since without a prosperous national economy the legitimacy of the State itself might have been called into question. This, however, leads to a problem: as labour is less mobile than capital, it finds it more difficult to shift from one sector to another and, even more, from one spatial labour market to another. As a consequence, and despite substantial emigration from certain regions, major pockets of long-term unemployment and structural disadvantage have been created. These contain the potential, even if only occasional and temporary, to undermine the State's legitimacy and hence constitute a potential threat to the popular support for the economic system as a whole.

In contrast, it could be said that it was primarily in its role as legitimator of the capitalist system that the Irish state became involved not only in economic policies designed to increase employment generally, but also in spatial policies designed to ensure the absorption of unemployed labour in its most depressed regions. Generally, this has taken the form of reducing the relative costs of fixed capital by subsidising inward investment, while the regional component has been pursued through the provision of special grants or tax incentives for locating in specially designated regions.

As was apparent by the late 1970s, as a strategy of industrial development, the success of the State's intervention has been limited. Externally controlled establishments had developed only minor linkages with the local economy and were likely to be the first to be closed in the event of global recessions. Furthermore, to the extent that manufacturing industry lost out in its overall share of employment, it failed to provide the necessary jobs to absorb an increasingly redundant labour force from the agricultural sector. Even though the Irish government has been somewhat more successful with its strategy than some of its immediate neighbours — notably Northern Ireland and Britain — the resulting problems for the Irish state are enormous.

Rationality Crisis and Legitimation Crisis

In trying to understand how the State reacts to the problem it faces at present, it may be useful to draw on Habermas (1976). Using a similar framework to O'Connor, Habermas distinguishes between two separate elements in this type of crisis. To use his terms, a *rationality crisis* occurs when the state fails to meet the needs of the economic system — that is, it fails to promote capitalist accumulation successfully. A *legitimation crisis* occurs when it fails to maintain mass loyalty to the economic system. Drawing on this distinction, Johnston

(1986) argues that, because of the changes in the global organisation of capital, any particular state's ability to solve this set of crises has fundamentally changed over time: "Under industrial capitalism the state may expect to solve both crises (to the extent that both can be solved, simultaneously) through policies internal to its own territory, under global capitalism it cannot, since whereas *legitimation crises* remain intra-state issues, *rationality crises* increasingly involve inter-state issues" (Johnston, 1986: 277).

This can be illustrated by comparing the world recession of the early 1980s with that of the 1930s — both contain a similar set of crises. In the 1930s a solution to both the *rationality crisis* and the *legitimation crisis* was possible for most states, as they possessed sufficient autonomy of action within the industrial capitalist system. In contrast, during the recession of the 1980s, most states were unable to tackle the *regional legitimation crisis* successfully within the attack on the *rationality crisis*. Under conditions of global capitalism the relative positions of the State and the major capitalist actors have been reversed. In seeking to solve a *national legitimation crisis* it has become imperative for the State to support the maximisation of economic efficiency at the national level. At the regional level, equitable economic conditions are no longer a primary goal and the resulting *regional legitimation crisis* has been subjected increasingly to ideological arguments that seek to obscure it rather than solve it.

The controversy over the real or perceived contradiction between efficiency at the national level and equity at the local level runs like a thread through the chapters of this book. Boylan discusses this difference in paradigms in relation to industrial production, O'Shea in relation to the provision of services, and Curtin in relation to the empowerment of local communities. They all provide ample illustrations of the change in perceptions and national policies following therefrom. Nevertheless, a theoretical understanding of these processes is of importance, as it not only provides an explanation for the major social and economic phenomena that have occurred, but also offers important insights for what one might expect in the future.

It is the contention of the editors of this book that Irish economic and social policy has become inseparable from that of its European partners. The Irish economy is one of the most open amongst the developed capitalist economies and, given its small size, has effectively become a "taker" in the general conditions of competitive markets. It therefore will remain an imperative for the Irish state to maximise economic efficiency at the national level, to maintain its overall legitimation successfully. In such a scenario, one can predict that the State will make only marginal attempts actually to *solve* the underlying regional economic problems. This is not a matter of ill-will or lack of interest, but is the rational response for the State, which has to concentrate on the maximisation of economic efficiency at the national level.

However, if there is no real willingness to address the underlying economic problems of marginalised regions, then, within these regions, the major attack by the State will inevitably be an ideological one — while committing only marginal resources in terms of redistribution towards the most disadvantaged areas and sections of population within them, these are likely to be of high profile, primarily aimed at portraying the State as doing something about the regional crisis. At the same time, there will be little interference with the prevailing mechanisms of market allocations. In particular, the State will strenuously avoid undertaking any significant *structural* adjustments that would be required to achieve more equitable allocations of resources between different sectors of the population and/or geographical regions.

Readers are invited to make up their own minds on this in the light of the evidence provided in the following chapters of this book. Before that, however, the following sections provide a final look at some of the European developments that are likely to influence developments in Ireland.

European Integration and Irish Peripherality

Similar to the question of more equitable development within Ireland, the question arises of whether the struggle for economic competitiveness at the European level will allow the equalisation of peripheral incomes and standards of living, or whether the conditions of intra-core competition in the global capitalist system will intensify and increase regional inequalities. If the latter is the case, this could leave Ireland in an increasingly peripheral situation relative to the European core.

Few will doubt the central importance to competitive advantage of innovation in the social organisation of production, particularly aspects of the large capitalist firm that increase "economies of speed" or "throughput" by reducing unit costs of production. State support of innovation, or, in this case, support by the European "supra-state", is a crucial determinant of which regions successfully compete in the world economy and which regions "fail". In this respect, the latest wave of European integration can be interpreted as the reaction of a number of European government and business élites to the "Euro-pessimism" of the 1980s and the opportunities and challenges presented by the hegemonic decline of the US economy and the economic ascent of Japan. The primary goal of this élite is successful competition in a global market.

European economic and political unification is, at least at its inception, a project first and foremost aimed at achieving competitive advantage in a global market. However, the legitimacy of a new Europe would be seriously challenged if there were significant erosion in the welfare state to which most European citizens have become accustomed. This creates a tension or contradiction between the requirements of competition through "lean production" and the "lean state", on the one hand, and the demands of non-business social forces on the other. The key nexus of intra-European or core-periphery conflict, in this context, will centre around whether the requirements of Euro-core accumulation (which is necessary for European competitive success in the global system) can coexist with the aspirations of European peripheries to achieve upward mobility in the world system (from semi-periphery to core).

Unfortunately for the periphery, the discourse around these aspirations has so far centred on the diversionary subject of the size of core-periphery transfers under the programme of "cohesion". Though these transfers are very visible and seem, at times, to involve huge sums of money, their relative size in relation to European GDP has remained of minute proportions. In contrast, little attention is paid usually to the fact that the possibility for peripheral regions or countries to achieve a vibrant presence in the leading economic sectors has remained highly questionable. As core regions monopolise key technologies, European peripheral states are bound to EU restrictions on trade and industrial policies that prohibit the protection of their indigenous industries. If considerable advances are not made in developing core industries in Europe's more peripheral regions, increased long-term dependency will be the inevitable outcome. This, however, is exactly what Ireland's rural regions have already began to experience.

INVESTIGATING POVERTY IN
RURAL IRELAND

A book devoted primarily to the topic of rural *poverty* is fairly unusual in the Irish context — and perhaps elsewhere as well. In Ireland, discussions of the rural have generally been dominated by a developmental focus, reflecting the enormous importance of the rural,
and particularly the agricultural, economy to Irish national prosperity over most of this century, and also perhaps the extent to which
rural sociology and economics have tended to be segregated into sectoral, policy-oriented state and semi-state institutions.

Poverty and development issues do, of course, overlap, and, undoubtedly, rural policy deliberations have been influenced to some
extent by concern about poverty, particularly poverty among small
farmers. But within the developmental framework, poverty becomes a
policy issue mainly when it affects or is thought to be affecting the
development possibilities of the society as a whole. This has been
particularly true in more recent decades, when small-farm poverty, for
example, has been increasingly addressed as a *failure in production*
at a time when maintaining high levels of farm output has been seen
as a crucial resource for national economic growth. The "policy problem" in relation to poverty, in other words, has been understood as the
insufficiently productive use of potential wealth-generating resources
by some farmers, which not only means that they themselves do not
generate the sort of output that could secure reasonable income levels
for their households, but also that they are not contributing as well as
they could to Irish national wealth (see, for example, NESC 1989).

While the production failure may be explained by various farm-
level factors such as holding size, household demography, the farmer's
access to capital or to knowledge of relevant production and marketing skills, and so on, the solutions proposed tend to be ones that will
enhance the development of Irish society as a whole (for example,
moving such farmers out of farming so that the production resource
that they are tying up — their land — can be worked more efficiently
by someone else) or of particular sectional interests within it (for example, the food industry), rather than necessarily lifting these farmers themselves out of poverty.

An approach that is specifically concerned with poverty in rural
areas needs to question the very developmental models themselves,
which produce such conclusions. From a poverty point of view, analysis must start from a recognition of inequality in the distribution of
resources and life chances as a central feature of Irish society, and

must assess any proposed intervention in the rural in terms of its likely impact on this unequal distribution. Some types of development strategy may reduce disparities in income and/or property ownership even while increasing wealth generation from rural localities as a whole, but others may only do the latter, leaving existing poverty levels untouched.

Turning their attention from developmental towards more distributional issues in Irish society has allowed the contributors to this book to question a broad range of conventional assumptions about rural Ireland and the way in which it fits or does not fit into the wider society. It may be helpful at this point to identify and discuss some of the issues they address, as a means of orienting readers more precisely to the material of the book and to its overall perspective.

In Chapter 2 on "Demography and the Distribution of Deprivation in Rural Ireland", Jackson and Haase present a number of challenges to what are often taken-for-granted assumptions about both poverty and rurality — the validity of measuring rural poverty in terms of spatially aggregated "indicators of disadvantage", the distribution of rural poverty as something that follows a clear east–west pattern across the country, the very distinction between "rural" and "urban". Their most central challenge is to the equation of rural poverty with rural population loss. We have become so familiar with the argument that falling population levels are both an indicator of rural poverty, and give rise to rural poverty — they are part of a cumulative cycle of reduction of services, job losses, emigration, a skewed age range in the remaining population, and further population decline — that we find it difficult even to consider separating the two. Halting and even reversing population decline is thus widely accepted as the primary goal in addressing rural poverty — for example, the recent "Developing the West" initiative has set itself, as a "success outcome", the objective of "stabilising the population of the West".

Jackson and Haase argue that this over-focus on population decline comes from assuming that the ideal situation for a rural, or indeed any, community is to be in a continuous process of self-replacement. This view of community regeneration is one that idealises the absence of change — the "reproduction of the local community" is taken to mean its reproduction in the same form as before. But according to Jackson and Haase, in the context of global developmental trends it is impossible (even if it were desirable, which may be questioned) to prevent population change and turnover from occurring in local rural areas in Ireland. They suggest therefore that we replace this model with one which they call "a dynamic model of population interchange". This would allow for transformations over time in the types of social groups, and in the levels of population density, that characterise rural areas.

Jackson and Haase see the assumption that static self-reproduction, or social immobility, is both best for and "natural" to Irish rural life as strongly influenced by the character of Ireland as "a property-owning democracy". They draw our attention to the rural ideology which connects "belonging" in a locality and the right to participate in local decision-making with ownership, preferably over several generations, of a house in the area. The "static model" is linked also to accounts of "peasant" or "traditional" family farms, which emphasise the inter-generational transmission of household and holding as a single entity as the ultimate goal of the farmer/household head (for example, Arensberg and Kimball, 1968). Of course, what these analyses also show is that static self-reproduction of rural farm families (to the extent that it was ever achieved beyond one or at most two generations) depended on the removal or celibacy of all the children of the household except the designated heir. Population decline was a threat to reproduction of the peasant economy and society, but so also, it should be noted, was population growth, and the achievement of a demographically "balanced" community required the impoverishment or exclusion of large numbers of local people.

Population decline in a rural area need not be an indicator of growing poverty among the remaining residents, if, for example, it is associated with centralisation of land and a consequent improvement of farm output and incomes. The assumption that this is an "impoverishing" type of change for rural areas is a product of what Curtin and Varley (1991) have called "populist" ideology, which itself has often had the effect of concealing and mystifying the presence of poverty in Ireland. More broadly, it can be said that what Jackson and Haase are drawing attention to here is the failure of the Irish state to develop any clear policy on population distribution across the country, a point that is also strongly made by NESC (1995), and which runs through most of the other contributions to this volume in various forms — for example, in critiques of the lack of a proper "regional development" policy in Ireland.

In the absence of discussion of what sort of population distribution and metropolitan-urban-rural balance is desirable in Ireland, policies for population maintenance or population movement in particular areas are made on the basis of unexamined assumptions and traditions. Changing from a "static" to a "dynamic population interchange" model would require, as Jackson and Haase point out, a re-examination of rural policy in a range of areas, to identify where dis-incentives to mobility exist and should be altered. These are not fully spelt out in their discussion. But it would be important, it seems, not to allow a change of models to turn into abandonment of any inter-vention by the State, or "leaving it to the market" to determine popu-lation processes. There is a danger that moving those who need access to urban services out of the open countryside, and leaving this to those who can afford the costs of distance, would merely mean leaving the countryside to be inhabited by the rich.

This would certainly remove the problem of rural poverty but only at the cost of introducing a new form of social exclusion. Redistribut-ing poverty on a spatial level is not a solution to poverty. Moreover, the form taken by interchange of populations in some parts of rural Ireland, where ownership of houses by external tourist groups has become extensive, seems as likely to deepen as to combat feelings of disadvantage and exclusion among the remaining locals, who may be unable to afford to settle their own children locally as land and house prices rise to national or even European market levels, and who ex-perience increasing isolation during the long winter months when many of the new owners are absent.

In their discussion, Jackson and Haase also raise the question of whether it is valid any longer to distinguish between "rural" and "urban" in Ireland, since, in their opinion, the social structures of ru-ral and urban populations are increasingly coming to resemble each other. The over-stress on rural and urban difference is linked, in their view, to a tendency to overlook social stratification in rural areas. This, they say, is something that has been strongly associated with particular areas in our cities and with urban residential segregation, dense patterns of public housing development, and a degraded envi-ronment. In contrast, the rural poor are often scattered sparsely across attractive landscapes, and in private as well as public housing, making them less visible to those whose eyes are attuned to urban poverty characteristics. In practice, Jackson and Haase suggest, there may be little rationale for treating poverty as something that is spe-cifically rural or specifically urban: poverty is found in both settings and is a product of wider restructuring forces which are themselves linked to a process of gradual "urbanisation" of all Irish social life.

This is a strong argument, which runs counter to much of what has been argued in this introductory section of the book. The editors would be somewhat sceptical of the claim that rural poverty has been "invisible" in Ireland, although this may be true of other European countries such as the UK or the Netherlands. The visibility or otherwise of poverty is related to the presence of organisations and interest groups willing to make it an issue — although the main farming organisations in Ireland generally tend to be concerned with securing the interests of richer rather than poorer farmers, they have often emphasised the presence of poverty in the countryside as a way of maintaining levels of state assistance to and supports for agriculture. It could be argued that until quite recently there were few organisations prepared to speak on behalf of the urban, rather than the rural, poor, and that in that sense urban poverty has been the more invisible. There is also a long tradition in Irish thinking, going back to the Great Famine if not earlier, which associates rural areas with frugal, even harsh lifestyles, while cities are seen as places of wealth and luxury (rendering them the more attractive, or the more suspect, depending on the point of view of the thinker).

More importantly, the editors argue throughout this introduction that national and international restructuring processes have a tendency to differentiate spatial areas as much as to homogenise them, so that while some areas in rural Ireland may be becoming "urbanised" it is also the case that some experience increasing "ruralisation" (specialisation in agricultural or other natural resource extraction enterprises, reduction in occupational diversity, loss of national power-holders out of the locality, and, perhaps, reduction in population density).

While it would certainly be foolish to suggest that causes of poverty in urban areas — such as unemployment — have no relevance for rural poverty, it would also be wrong to deny that much of the unemployment in each case derives from different structural conditions and has different effects. In particular, it is experienced differently in rural and urban settings, as Jackson and Haase themselves point out when they say that one reason why rural poverty is sometimes invisible, even to the poor themselves, is the strength within rural communities of the convention forbidding direct acknowledgement of class and material differences between neighbours and face-to-face acquaintances. Nevertheless, in raising the whole question of rural versus urban and the rural–urban distinction, Jackson and Haase are reminding us of an important point which is easily overlooked in studies such as this — that is, that "the urban-rural divide" is a social construct, which varies in meaning from time to time given different sociocultural conditions, and which is on some occasions used to imply, and to mobilise action around, differences that have no real significance in social life.

The two chapters which directly follow this suggest — supporting the editors' position — that to the extent that there is a distinctive "rural" society in Ireland, it rests on a distinctive economic base, one organised around the use and exploitation of nature or natural resources. Commins (Chapter 3) addresses the more obvious form of rural natural resource use in Ireland, agriculture, while in Chapter 4, Tovey discusses other less well-studied forms, which either compete with agriculture — for example, in the case of mining — or have been strongly promoted in recent years as "alternative" or supplementary forms of employment for farm workers, such as forestry or rural tourism.

Commins' analysis strongly supports the editors' argument that understanding poverty among Irish farmers depends on understanding the changes and restructuring that have been taking place in national and international food production systems in recent decades. Going into the issue in considerable detail, he identifies a range of "restructuring trends", which are reshaping Irish agriculture, and argues that their overall outcome has been to "widen the economic inequalities among different categories of farmers". He shows how these restructuring trends, in combination with state and EU policies for agricultural development, continually reproduce groups of farmers who are in or on the margins of poverty, whether they are farmers who have too little land, farmers who produce extensively rather than intensively, or (increasingly, nowadays) farmers engaged in particular sorts of farm system (beef-cattle store production, for example, as against dairying, cattle fattening or tillage). The same developmental trends that give rise to the concentration of production, production resources, and income among a contracting group of "large" farmers, also push more and more "small" farmers out of commercial production altogether, or create and recreate groups of farmers on the fringes of viability.

In Commins' view, given these processes, "It is difficult to envisage the elimination of poverty in agriculture in the medium term" — or perhaps at all. To eliminate poverty among farmers would require radical changes, not just in state goals and developmental policies for agriculture, but also in the restructuring processes, which, as has been suggested earlier, are part of the development of international or global capitalism and would be extremely resistant to attempts at change from a small and semi-peripheral state such as Ireland.

Concept of Poverty as Income Poverty

This is a depressing conclusion, and one which it is important to examine further. Commins assesses "the risk of being poor" among Irish farmers in terms of the risk of falling below certain income levels. To a large extent, this understanding of poverty as primarily "income poverty" is inevitable given the difficulties in getting good data on other dimensions of the problem. Nevertheless, an ESRI comparison of the risk of "income poverty" with measures of "deprivation" among farmers (Nolan and Callan, 1994) has found that they are not identical. Equating poverty with low income is particularly problematic in the case of farmers, where low incomes may be associated with high wealth or large capital assets, and Jackson and Haase point out that the common confusion between income and property is one of the factors that help to conceal the real poverty of many Irish farmers from public recognition.

It is also important to note, as Commins does, that many farm households whose income from farming might place them in the poverty category have income from other sources, which raise them above the relative poverty line. On that definition, farm households that are in "income poverty" are primarily those that rely on state transfers and have no off-farm earnings, and they only amount to a proportion of all the farm households that have been marginalised from commercial agriculture. Or, to put this the other way round, economic marginalisation or exclusion need not necessarily be identical to "income poverty".

A second important point is that the level of material well-being of all household members cannot be equated with the global income coming into the farm household. Commins does not discuss the distribution of income within the household between farm family members, and undoubtedly hard information on this issue is not easily available, but the effect of his approach is to make gender- and perhaps also generation- or age-differences in the risk of poverty invisible.

We may link this to the general neglect, within most discussions of Irish farming, of the fact that agricultural production in Ireland is primarily, or almost totally, organised within family-based enterprises, and that different family members have different interests in regard to the farm labour process and different, and unequal, access to the money earned from the farm and to the capital that it represents. There is some ethnographic evidence (O'Hara, 1994) to suggest, for example, that on some larger, more commercial farms in the east of the country, farmers' wives are more likely to be treated as "housewives" dependent on whatever allowance their husband likes to make them (unless they have their own separate job or business), whereas on more marginal, low-income farms in the west they are more likely to have joint bank accounts with their husbands and to share equally in the financial management of the household. This might suggest a need to qualify Commins' claim that "Poverty in farming households is inextricably linked to small-scale farming", so as to take account of such gender differences. We might also look for a fuller explanation of why it is that there is apparently a higher than usual average of farm operators who are women, on what are identified by agricultural experts as "problem" farms in Ireland.

Would an analysis of poverty in Irish farming in terms of social and political exclusion produce a different picture from one based on farm household income levels? Commins makes a number of points throughout his discussion which suggest that exclusion is a relevant issue, but these are not developed, nor is the relationship between "poverty as exclusion" and "poverty as inadequate income" examined in any depth. It is possible that tendencies towards exclusion and tendencies towards income poverty sometimes run in different directions in the case of farmers, or at least that the experience of income poverty may, in many cases, be considerably mitigated by experiences of social or political *inclusion*, which are not available, to the same extent, to the urban poor or, more particularly, to the non-farm poor in rural areas.

As was mentioned earlier, Leeuwis' (1989) study of small farmers in the Tuam area suggested that low-output, low-income farmers here were in many respects better integrated into their local community than the high-output, high-income farmers whose main social support was their relationship with their local state advisory agent. Of course, larger farmers may have little interest in local inclusion in any case, having a much more spatially extended social field than small farmers.

Commins notes that one of the problems that affect contemporary farmers is their loss to agribusiness of autonomy and control, but this is a problem which does not affect all farmers equally, and indeed it seems likely to affect larger producers, and producers within particular sorts of highly technologically developed farm systems (such as milk production, where the processing industry maintains particularly tight controls over on-farm production processes and techniques) more than the smaller farmer who is more marginalised from commercial farm production. This issue also suggests that the term "exclusion" is less straightforward than at first it might appear — is loss of control to the food industry a form of political exclusion suffered by farmers, or is it a form of social inclusion and incorporation?

More research is needed on these issues within the Irish context before hard conclusions can be drawn about poverty in Irish farming. But a final point is also worth noting — to the extent that the claim by the IFA to represent "all farmers" is accurate, Irish farmers in general enjoy a degree of political inclusion, for example, in being participants in the deliberations of the "social partners", which is not available to other rural inhabitants or to many urban poor such as the long-term unemployed.

An important part of Commins' contribution is his analysis of the various policy responses of the Irish and EU states to the continuous reproduction of inequality and poverty within contemporary farming. He points out that most of the policy responses that have been used to date have had the effect of increasing and cumulating advantage and disadvantage, rather than reducing the gap between them. This is particularly obvious in the case of market price supports under the unreformed CAP, which not only returned higher incomes to larger producers, but also had a knock-on effect on the reproduction of inequality over time as farm profits "became capitalised into land values".

Management of the allocation and distribution of production quotas in dairying provides a similar example of how certain sorts of policy intervention may create additional "property" for some farmers. Milk production quotas in Ireland have become transformed into saleable assets, again benefiting the larger producer. It is interesting to compare the Irish state's management of this with that of the French, for example, where steps were taken to prevent milk production quotas from becoming part of the disposable capital of farmers and where, as a result, "the previous trend towards concentration of production in certain areas has been stopped . . . and the fragile upland milk-producing districts have also been successfully protected" (Naylor, 1993).

Commins also points out that after Irish state policies to intervene in structural trends towards land concentration "came off the policy agenda" in the 1980s, they were replaced by attempts to direct income subsidies towards the poorest farmers, on an areal basis, through the Disadvantaged Areas Scheme, and these in turn lost their poverty focus as the designated areas expanded to cover over 70 per cent of the country. Since even before Ireland entered the EEC, it would appear that there has been a continual resistance among agricultural and agribusiness interests towards any type of state intervention that tries to reallocate resources in such a way as to maintain smaller or less intensive producers within commercial farming.

State Ideologies of Agricultural Development

This has been justified through an ideology of "development" which, following Leeuwis, van der Ploeg and others we might define as recognising "modern farming" only in terms of one very specific model — that is, farming that is very dependent on purchased inputs and easily adapted, in terms of its on-farm production processes and its outputs, to the needs of the larger food-processing system. As Leeuwis (1989) points out, this has meant that a large category of small farmers in Ireland has been systematically subjected to ideological, if not also social, political or economic, exclusion over the period.

In recent years smaller farmers who cannot compete within commercial agricultural production have been encouraged to look for incomes outside farming, through on-farm diversification away from food production, or if within food production, through adopting "environmentally friendly" farming methods which will be rewarded by the State rather than the market (for example, the Rural Environmental Protection Scheme or REPS). The possibility of earning off-farm income and also, if to a lesser extent, of making a living through farm diversification, depends crucially on the condition of the local economy, labour market and levels of consumer demand.

Later chapters suggest, however, as we will see, that the Irish state is withdrawing its commitment to the maintenance of rural non-agricultural economies in recent years, and in the absence of state planning, many agriculturally peripheral rural areas seem likely to face a bleak future. Whether rewards for "landscape management" are likely to give farmers an income that could compensate for lost production possibilities is also questionable, as Commins notes. It would probably need to be combined with assistance in securing markets where food that is produced under environmentally sustainable conditions can realise higher returns than normal, or where farmers engaged in this sort of food production receive higher income supports than others. These suggest that the goals of Irish agricultural policy themselves need to be reconsidered as part of a strategy for tackling poverty in farming — perhaps we should be trying to move away from emphasis on volume of output (if contracted into a smaller and smaller area of the country) towards quality of output and sus-

tainability of production, and the model of the "developed farm" needs
to be changed accordingly.

In raising the question of farming and rural environmental protection, Commins reminds us that agriculture is not just part of a
food-producing industry but is also a way of exploiting certain natural
resources which exist in the countryside. It may be evaluated and
compared, as a form of resource exploitation, with others which are
now becoming available. In Chapter 4, a number of other forms of
natural resource development are examined in relation to rural poverty — primarily, aquaculture, forestry, mining and rural tourism. In
her examination of these, Tovey makes explicit some problems of current state models of rural development which are touched on more
implicitly in Commins' discussion of farming. She suggests, indeed,
that one of the key questions that should be raised about natural resource development in Ireland is whether poverty as such, and solutions to poverty, have any place at all on the current development
agenda, or whether this effectively excludes the poor.

This issue is also highlighted in Chapter 5, by Boylan, who argues
that, particularly in the re-orientation of industrial policy which has
taken place in Ireland since the early 1980s, concern about directing
development to the areas most lacking in it has been replaced by a
concern about meeting national targets in output and economic
growth, regardless of where these are achieved. In Chapter 4, quota-
tions from recent ministerial pronouncements on resource development — for example, through mining — are used to suggest that the
state's main interest in this area is in the contribution it can make to
"the national job and wealth creation effort", on the assumption that
raising national levels of wealth does, eventually, reduce inequalities
between rich and poor, or at the least, raise the standard of living of
the poor above the poverty line. An important element of the discussion in this chapter focuses on whether that assumption is justified —
whether in fact the forms of natural resource development that have
been taking place in rural Ireland recently do lead directly or indirectly to increases in employment or self-employment among those
rural groups who are most in need of access to additional income.

Environmental Claims on the Countryside

A second key question which Chapter 4 identifies arises from recognising the way in which the Irish countryside in recent years has become the object of intense and competing claims by different social

groups, urban as well as rural. While some groups regard the countryside as an arena of resource exploitation, others see it as a landscape and space to be conserved, for leisure and recreation or simply as valuable "nature". In some cases, conservation and exploitation of the countryside are interrelated — for example, when environmental management is linked to efforts to increase tourism, or to restrict access to particularly valued stretches of country to people able to pay for membership of sports or hunting clubs. In other cases, natural resource exploitation is, or is perceived to be, in direct opposition to environmental conservation, as is often the case in disputes over mining or over the location of fish farms.

Tovey suggests that concerns about environmental protection and the claims to guardianship of nature made by environmental groups in Irish society should be examined to see whether they are compatible with, or in conflict with, the claims of the rural poor to a better livelihood. The question is both important and very difficult to answer. An additional problem is that many conservation initiatives are justified on the grounds of their long-term benefits for future members of society, presumably including the descendants of the present-day poor as well as the rich. Thus a decision not to proceed with a development which might create rural jobs immediately may be justified on the grounds that in the long term it would destroy the very resources that are necessary for rural life. Such long-term effects are extremely difficult to calculate and much depends on whether we accept that natural resources are exhaustible or whether we believe that as some are used up today, others will be found to take their place. It is arguable, moreover, that if the needs of the poor are not attended to today, the problem of their descendants' needs may not arise at all. Certainly, in putting environmental considerations above those of poverty considerations in the case of rural resource uses, such as mining, for example, we may be contributing to a situation where the poor and their children will not be able to remain in the countryside whether it is destroyed or whether it is conserved.

Virtually all development decisions nowadays, under EU directives, must treat impact on the environment as one of the internal "costs" to be weighed against the benefits of proceeding with the projected development. However, as the environmental impacts have gained more attention, the issue of the unequal social effects from development seems to attract less. It could be argued that social effects should be similarly "internalised" in the assessment of all rural development projects. This is perhaps anticipated in the developing interest within some EU circles in finding a strategy for "poverty-proofing" all future policy decisions. At the end of the book there is a discussion of some attempts currently being made to meet this inter-est — for example, the development in Britain of "social auditing", which can be linked to, and used to amplify, projects for sustainable development.

Equity, Efficiency and Regional Planning

Chapters 5 and 6 turn to more historically detailed accounts of Irish state development policies, and in particular of the rise and decline of rural or regional planning in Ireland — in one case in respect of rural service provision, in the other in respect of employment creation in the countryside. Both produce rather similar interpretations of this history as one of tensions and conflicts between considerations of "equity" and "efficiency" in state development policy. In his discussion of "Rural Industrialisation and Rural Poverty", Boylan links this eq-uity/efficiency conflict directly to a perceived conflict between the needs of national economic growth at different periods, on the one hand, and the need of rural areas for development, on the other.

In the 1960s, Boylan says, those who opposed regional develop-ment planning on efficiency grounds argued that spatial dispersion of industrial and other sources of employment would act as a constraint on national economic growth. They based this on the observation that the developed economies with which Ireland was trying to catch up were characterised by industrial concentration in a small number of large centres (ignoring the possibility that there is a variety of ways in which societies can "modernise" and that the very different situa-tion of Ireland as a peripheral and "late-developing" economy might make attempts to emulate the developmental experiences of more core countries futile). Nevertheless, there does not appear to be any evidence that the Irish economy experienced a sudden contraction in growth during the decade of dispersed industrialisation (rural indus-trialisation) policy, from the early 1970s to the early 1980s.

This would suggest that the reversion that Boylan identifies from 1982 onwards to a "flexible" location policy for new firms, and what he calls a shift from a "needs" to a "potentials" approach to designation — that is, allowing firms to select the location that suits them best, rather than directing them to the locations of greatest need — did not occur because of any rational acceptance of the validity of the "efficiency" side of the argument. Boylan suggests that it primarily reflected changes at the time in the global conditions for capitalist expansion.

If there is no real evidence that policies for the spatial dispersal of non-agricultural forms of development were "inefficient" for national economic growth at that particular time, is there any evidence that they increase or enhance the chances of social "equity"? (Ireland may have been advantaged *vis-à-vis* its competitors for this sort of development in the earlier period, whereas nowadays, given the nature of the contemporary global economy, it might well be economically inefficient). Boylan has been unable to find conclusive evidence one way or the other, but he does identify some features of rural industrialisation during the 1970s and early 1980s which suggest that its impact on rural poverty, at least at that time, has to be seen as limited.

He points out that although it brought about an initial return of emigrants and a turnaround in population decline, this was not sustained for more than a decade or so. He suggests that the impact of the new companies in creating employment in rural areas has to be balanced against the fact that most of the profits they made left the locality and indeed the region. He notes that a large proportion of the new jobs were taken by members of farming households — particularly farm women — and that while this undoubtedly improved farm household incomes and the position of farm women, it may have further marginalised the non-farm poor in the rural localities involved, and helped to create a workforce which was relatively docile in accepting low wages, impermanence, and poor conditions of work (Ruane, 1978; Lucey and Kaldor, 1969; Harris, 1984). This raises a difficult policy issue: is it better to have jobs that could be deemed "exploitative" than to have no jobs at all? Even if welfare income were equal to the type of income to be gained from such work, we might still want to argue that people cannot be, nor can they feel, socially "included" if they do not have paid employment.

Boylan goes on to make a very interesting analysis of the fate of regional planning in Ireland in the more recent period. He suggests, first, that in the run-up to the creation of the Single Market in Europe, the Irish state increasingly emphasised its own need to develop policies to "facilitate what should essentially be market-led development", while leaving the problems of social and economic cohesion — that is, of planning for regional or spatial equity — as something to be dealt with by European policy. He cites the Culliton Report of 1992 as a particularly clear example of this line of thinking. Second, he argues that in the more recent period of proliferation of new strategies of "local development", the absence of any tradition of regional planning in Ireland has given rise to what he calls "the problem of the excluded middle". This is a situation in which a centralised state confronts a plethora of fragmented local development initiatives without having any broader models of how the spatial economy in Ireland might best be organised.

Boylan suggests that while this can be interpreted as failure on the part of state planners, there may be another and more cynical interpretation of it, which is that the rhetoric of local development is little more than an ideological smoke screen intended to allow state agents to preserve the greatest possible flexibility in deciding whether to support or disfavour particular economic initiatives from private enterprise. His analysis is reminiscent of earlier debates about the impact on Irish society of clientelist political power strategies (Gibbon and Higgins, 1974; O'Connell, 1982), which have also been seen as fragmenting, and setting in opposition to one another, people whose objectively similar disadvantaged social situation should have been a basis for them to organise collectively for change.

Overall, Boylan's analysis of the contribution made by spatial planning to the solution of poverty in rural Ireland over the past three decades or so is very pessimistic. For most of the time, he suggests, the Irish state has been negative towards the idea of planning for economic growth at a regional level, or even towards considering what sort of spatial distribution of population, employment and resources might be most usefully encouraged in Irish society. The assumption that regional planning produces inefficiencies for the national economy was never really challenged, while the argument for regional planning on grounds of equity appears never to have been given any real consideration. Rural industrialisation in the past had only a limited impact on the situation of the rural poor, while "industrial development in the envisaged future scenarios will bear an extremely tenuous connection to providing a solution for rural poverty". Nor does it seem likely that an increasingly service-work-oriented economy will be any more successful. However, there are some aspects of his argument that are worth further, brief consideration before we commit ourselves to acceptance of his pessimism.

It should be noted that, as in Chapter 3, the definition of poverty used in this chapter is basically that of "economic" or "income poverty". Boylan pays less attention to the impacts that spatial planning and industrial dispersion, or their absence, may have on social and political exclusion in rural areas. His discussion also focuses heavily

on the *spatial* implications of the State's industrial development
models, although he does also discuss the impacts on different occupational groups, classes and genders in the countryside. Despite his
criticism of the links between feminisation of the rural industrial
workforces in the 1970s and its docility, the potential effects of access to paid work and to companionship of other workers outside the
home in empowering rural women (Harris, 1984) may also be worth
considering.

Given the extent to which the IDA apparently opposed state support for industries which provided work for women rather than men
(O'Donovan and Curtin, 1991) as both unnecessary and undesirable,
any change in the marginalised situation of women as a result of the
rural industrialisation strategy could be regarded as doubly welcome.
It is also easy to play down the benefits of dispersing industrial jobs
into rural areas if those who take them up do so, as a number of
studies suggest, as a prelude to emigration or as a way of financing a
return to small farming and/or fishing at a later date; but this may
ignore the real assistance that small amounts of savings can provide
to the life chances of the very poor in either situation (see, for example, Nolan and Whelan, 1996).

A further issue which is particularly highlighted by his discussion
of state development policy over the period is the problem of the lack
of representation of the (rural) poor within the development policy-
making process: one could conclude from his account that the poor
have simply not been recognised at all, as a legitimate interest group
in relation to development policy. The problem of how the rural poor
can ensure that they are considered in state policy decisions is raised
by most of the following chapters, but is particularly clear in Chapter
6, on "Rural Poverty and Social Service Provision". Here, O'Shea examines the extent to which inadequacies in service provision to rural
areas act to exacerbate poverty and the experience of poverty in these
areas. He focuses in particular on four examples of service provision
— health care, education, housing and transport — seeing these as
particularly crucial, although by no means the only ones that could be
addressed.

Assessing Centralisation of Social Services

As in Chapter 5, this chapter shows how Irish governments have relied on arguments about efficiency and economies of scale to justify
centralising social service provision, even where this results in in-

equalities between rural and urban locations in terms of access to them. However, in some cases the claimed economies are only apparent because costs of dealing with the results of the absence of services are "externalised" from them — for example, the cost of moving elderly people into institutions and maintaining them there, when they are well enough to remain at home if the health and support services which they would need were available to them, is not calculated into the assessment of benefits to be derived from centralising the provision of public health nurses or other forms of medical care. In other cases, the impacts of centralisation may not be so easily costed in monetary terms, since they consist as much in lost opportunities (for education, for labour market access, etc.) experienced by specific social groups as in measurable reductions in their standard of living. As O'Shea puts it, inadequate service provision in rural areas can mean condemning many people to "a premature disengagement from economic and social life" — it generates social, economic and political exclusion.

Two particular issues are addressed in this chapter which could be usefully given further elaboration and discussion. The first of these is O'Shea's claim — a very significant one if accepted — that the problem described is not just a matter of failure by the Government to provide certain services equally to all citizens, it is evidence of a deeper failure, which is the lack of any government interest in or plan for the maintenance of rural social life. It would be unhelpful, in his view, for a study such as this simply to make recommendations that extra resources be put into rural health care, transport and so on; what is needed is "to probe the commitment to rural life itself" in contemporary Ireland.

The second issue raised is the relationship between spatial inequalities in access to social services, social inequalities, and poverty. O'Shea argues that although there are connections between living in a certain sort of area (particularly open countryside, villages or small towns) and having a high risk of being poor, poverty is "class-specific" rather than "location-specific" — in other words, we cannot identify particular places that are poor (or rich), but we can identify particular classes or social groups that are found in rural Ireland and that are at a high risk of poverty, particularly small farmers, agricultural workers, or unskilled manual labourers (many of whom are unemployed, underemployed, or retired) and their dependants. In his view, this means that policies which target specific locations for development or other sorts of intervention are unlikely to be able to solve the problem of rural poverty: since divisions within rural localities over access to resources and services are more significant than divisions between them, solving the problem of poverty demands that policies be targeted specifically at those within the rural area who are most at risk of poverty.

There may be some difficulty in holding both of these positions simultaneously. On the one hand it is suggested that the solution to rural poverty must involve the State being prepared not just to decentralise service provision but to "act as a catalyst for rural regeneration"; on the other, that the term "rural", and the whole concept of a division between "urban" and "rural", may actually prevent us from recognising who are really the poor in Irish society (Chapter 2 makes a similar argument). However, the contradiction is more apparent than real and indicates again how difficult it is to integrate spatial and social dimensions of analysis, even while recognising that both variables are of great importance for understanding poverty.

O'Shea, Boylan and Jackson and Haase could be seen as offering a similar conclusion from their different discussions: the absence of a developed policy in regard to population distribution and settlement patterns, the absence of any planning for regional or other sub-national allocation of development resources, and now the absence of any consideration of how service provision might be made more equal between rural and urban locations, effectively means that the Irish state has *no rural policy*. This means that people who live in the Irish countryside, and who are increasingly incurring costs by doing so, which they are having to bear without state help, will have either to be rich enough to carry these costs without suffering, or else, for one reason or another (age, lack of skills, lack of capital, responsibility for dependants etc.), be unable to move out despite the suffering which results. It may be that the majority of people in Irish society are content to see the countryside develop along these lines, but at least it should be recognised as a policy strategy rather than allowed to happen by default.

Chapter 6, however, can also be read as challenging or evaluating regional development and population settlement planning, *as an answer to the problem of poverty* in rural Ireland. O'Shea reminds us that the term "rural" primarily refers to a particular type of social structure, linked to a historical dependence on a certain pattern of agricultural production, and to particular processes of structural change which derived initially from changes occurring worldwide in the production of animals and crops and their industrial processing

into food. The spatial characteristics of "rural" as against "urban" derive from the social structural ones, rather than the other way
around. Therefore attempts to solve rural poverty should first tackle
structural inequalities rather than spatial ones. In other words, resources and services need to be targeted at those disadvantaged
groups who find themselves for historical reasons located within certain sorts of spatial areas, rather than targeted at certain sorts of areas which are defined, primarily because they have historically been
dominated by agriculture, as "poor".

Chapter 6 also, as mentioned earlier, raises the issue of who is to
speak for the rural poor. Since "the rural" is itself not an explicit object of state planning, it seems very unlikely that rural poverty will be
either, and given the type of people who are at most risk of poverty in
rural Ireland, it is difficult to envisage that they could successfully
demand state recognition on their own. O'Shea argues that we need
to adopt a new "philosophy" of social development, one that reinstates
"equity" with "efficiency" as an equally important value in evaluating
state policy, if we are to foster the sort of civic and social solidarity
which would lead others besides the poor to demand action on poverty. While this seems undeniable, it is not immediately obvious
where movement towards this type of philosophy might come from.
But the issue is important, and it is raised again in the last two chapters — Curtin's discussion in "Back to the Future? Communities and
Rural Poverty", which, among other things, assesses the community
movement in Ireland as a vehicle for those most in need in rural areas to establish their needs on the policy agenda; and Coyle's analysis
of "Local and Regional Administrative Structures and Rural Poverty",
which examines the potential of local government in Ireland to act as
civic leaders and promoters of rural and regional social solidarity,
even in the face of disempowering and fragmenting pressures coming
from the central state.

Community Movements

In Chapter 7, Curtin provides a comprehensive analysis of the issues
surrounding "community" and "community movements" in Ireland.
He demonstrates that "communities" are not *natural* elements in rural life. People are so used to hearing phrases like "the rural community", or claims that modern life is threatening a "loss of community"
in rural areas, that they tend to assume that it is "natural" for rural
people to address their problems through collective, communal forms

of mobilisation in a way which would not be so "natural" for urban people. Curtin, however, reminds us that communities are social institutions, and therefore that it makes sense to ask which circumstances and conditions are most likely to give rise to the construction of this institution, and which are least likely to do so.

While features such as the type of settlement pattern found in a rural locality, the population structure, the local culture and the value it places on recognising obligations to neighbours, etc., are all important conditions of the development of a community, Curtin points out that broader, macro-structure features are also relevant — such as the extent to which society in general has experienced the growth of social movements that emphasise community as a locus for action (for example, the emergence of the Green Movement with its injunction to "think globally, act locally") or indeed the extent to which the Irish or EU state targets regulations and funding towards a society which it assumes can meaningfully be broken up into a series of more or less discrete communities. It is only by recognising these social and institutional contexts that we can make sense of the recent revival of community and community action in an apparently inexorably modernising and changing rural Ireland.

Second, Curtin addresses the crucial question of whether the community development movement in Ireland, in the past or at present, has focused on the resolution of rural poverty. At first sight this may seem an extraordinary question to ask, since we are so accustomed to accepting the community development movement's own self-understanding as a movement that attempts to bring about development and improve levels of well-being in poor or underdeveloped rural areas. However, posing the question leads Curtin to make a distinction between what he sees as two distinct models of community development. One is a "consensus model", which assumes that since there is little social or economic differentiation within rural localities, raising the standard of living of "the community as a whole" must include raising the standard of living of those who are a bit poorer than the rest. It also assumes that members of a community share the same basic values and views on important matters. The other is a "conflict model": it starts from the premise that there is often competition between the needs of the poorest, and those of the better off, within a local area, and claims that "true" community development is marked by its primary concern with the needs of the local poor.

Differences in attitudes to the State are also central to this consensus/conflict distinction. The two models can be seen as two different concepts of reality — and also as two different strategies for action to solve local problems. Curtin uses the distinction to illuminate various features of contemporary development interventions in rural communities, arguing that Integrated Rural Development and LEADER Programmes and the 1994–99 National Development Plan tend to be based on a "consensus" model of the local rural community, while the recent Poverty Programmes and the PESP Local Area Companies, for example, in their desire to reach out to and include those outside the normal local power structure, are expressions of a more focused approach. Examining each of them in terms of their impact on the lives of the rural poor, Curtin reaches what many rural development workers would consider a very provocative conclusion — that "the evidence is inconclusive as to whether community efforts to alleviate rural poverty should be focused on the most disadvantaged or whether the gains to the poor are ultimately greater when the emphasis is placed on involving the 'whole' community and increasing the resource base and opportunities for all".

The two possibilities he outlines here resemble quite closely the debate in relation to national versus regional or local development in the period before EEC accession, which is critically addressed in some of the previous chapters, and his distinction between "consensus" and "conflict" models of the social world could probably be usefully applied here also. In the national/regional argument, the dominant position in recent decades appears to be that policies to strengthen the national economy should take priority over efforts to lift disadvantaged regions or areas in Ireland out of underdevelopment, on the "trickle-down" assumption that a strong national economy generates wealth which eventually translates into jobs, or (in a less market-economy-focused perspective) into improved social welfare for those in the areas that remain peripheral to economic growth. Most of our authors are suspicious of this argument — it would be interesting to discuss further whether there are factors operating on a local level which make it a more convincing argument than they seem to find it when it is applied nationally.

One of the particular strengths of Curtin's approach is the connection he makes between increasing interest in and concern about "local community", not just in Ireland but more generally in the European Union and also in the United States, on the one hand, and on the other the increasing globalisation of the economic and political structures that shape our everyday lives.

It is one of the most striking features of what sociologists and others are increasingly calling the "post-modern" period, that "the local" is routinely interpenetrated by "the global" — that within our local areas and local social relationships we live out lives that are constructed not just in terms of the work and production that we engage in, but equally in terms of our consumption, leisure and enjoyment patterns, by forces and tendencies that have to do with international economic factors as much as national ones. Local and global interpenetrate, as we have noted earlier, in the way in which international economic trends produce differentiation as well as homogenisation of national space — urbanising some spaces, ruralising others, de-urbanising yet others. But the local is tied crucially into the global in *cultural* terms too, as Curtin suggests: one of the ways, perhaps the main way, in which we respond to the globalisation of our daily lives is through a cultural reaffirmation of locality and its significance to us.

What this suggests, as indeed other earlier chapters do also, is that the production and reproduction of poverty in the contemporary world is not so much the result of a "failure" of our society, or of the international system of which it is part, to operate as it should, but that it is in fact one aspect of how that system operates. Readers may find that too harsh — a less stark position would be to say that any attempt to understand poverty, even if it starts at the local level, leads us inevitably to an examination of the workings of national and global society. This has been a central theme for the editors in conceiving and organising this book as a whole.

Local Government and Rural Poverty

The final chapter, Coyle's discussion of local and regional government structures and their relationship to rural poverty, continues the same theme. Coyle argues that in terms of structures of government and administration, globalisation tends to have contradictory effects at national and local levels — it presses towards a decentralisation of state power, as national states become less relevant to the workings of the international system, and at the same time it forces states to adopt stringent financial policies that weaken the local governments, which are being pushed into adopting more significant roles as the national states vacate them.

Coyle sees this as the context within which to examine local government structures in Ireland. However, she makes clear that Irish local government has been considerably weaker than local government in other European countries for a long time, and that its weakness, at least originally, had more to do with the determination of the Irish national government to centralise power in its own hands than with international pressures for financial rectitude.

Coyle argues that the weakness and failures of local government in Ireland have had very significant consequences for Irish society. Local authorities have tended to be seen by Irish people simply as organisations for delivering services to client populations, not as a "territorial authority representing a local community" which could express the will of that community in deciding on and shaping the form that economic, social and cultural development should take in the area. Even in terms of service provision, Coyle says, Irish local authorities are excluded from involvement in providing the "basic public services that constitute the fabric of social life" in a way that contrasts strongly with most developed countries in Europe. Only in relation to the provision of housing do Irish local government institutions play any significant role, and even here they are so constrained by financial dependence on the centre that their autonomy is severely limited. The absence of a strongly developed civic consciousness among Irish people, and of strong civic leadership, is linked, according to Coyle, to this fundamental weakness in our local government arrangements.

Coyle may perhaps underestimate the extent to which changes have been occurring in Irish local government politics in recent years. While the main political parties still remain relatively uninterested in local politics, unless as a stepping stone into national office, at least two of the smaller parties — the Green Party and Democratic Left — are explicitly committed to expanding local politics and both have done surprisingly well in local elections given their small support nationally. However, reform of local government structures which might allocate to local government some of the critical responsibilities and powers that Coyle sees as a characteristic feature of other European countries, though much promised, has not yet occurred here and may not do so within the immediate future. It may also be noted that Coyle's discussion does not conclusively establish that the presence of such decentralised local governments in other European regions actually does make a significant difference to the situation of the rural poor.

What can be said, then, about the implications of this issue for rural poverty? There are two answers to this imbedded in Coyle's analysis. First, she makes the point that community development work is increasingly required to occur "in partnership" with government — frequently with local government; but the absence of financial autonomy and lack of technical expertise generally found in Irish local government significantly reduce the extent to which it can play an effective role as a partner to the "voluntary" sector. This provides a further element to Curtin's discussion, in the previous chapter, of the extent to which we can expect community development and local partnership projects to be successful as ways of attacking poverty in local rural areas.

Second, Coyle clearly believes that even during periods when the national government is uninterested in tackling poverty, or when it emphasises ideological justifications for putting the resolution of poverty on the long finger — such as the "trickle-down" argument to which we previously referred — local authorities will continue to have a concern about poverty within their local area and continue to prioritise those sorts of development strategies which directly tackle poverty even if they do not immediately, or even in the long run, add enormously to average regional incomes or to measures of regional wealth. Her belief in this appears to derive from the claim that in other European areas local governments, in the person of the local mayor, for example, have played strong interventionist roles in relation to poverty in their area.

It is an attractive argument. But, at least in the Irish experience, there seems little reason to suppose that local government would be any more concerned about, or effective in reducing, poverty than national governments have shown themselves to be (support for this view could be derived, for example, from the 1994 NESC Report). It is possible that if, as Coyle suggests, local administrations really have the potential to be "real community governments", a more effective local government system might reduce feelings of alienation from politics, and reduce the degree of social and political exclusion felt by some social groups in rural localities. However, as Curtin warns us in the preceding chapter, it is not necessarily always the case that community organisation and representation empowers the poor.

Perhaps a more critical question that needs to be raised in relation to Coyle's argument is whether it is sensible at all to expect local government officials, elected or employed, to formulate and operate development models for their locality which run counter to the dominant model in use by the central state. Tucker's (1989) study of Glencolmcille, one of the few studies that exist of what appears to have been an attempt at a local level to follow a development strategy contradictory to that being promulgated by the Irish state, suggests a rather negative view of the chances of success of such attempts. Perhaps the best that could be expected of a reformed and strengthened local government in Ireland would be that it would provide some cushioning against disadvantage within the relevant locality for people whose existing precarious situation is a product of central state policies. This would reduce it largely to a local version of a central welfare authority, however, which is far from the radical vision of local government outlined in this chapter.

Having reviewed the main themes in the substantive chapters, it is important to identify some issues which remain unresolved. It is fairly clear that the aim of this study to balance a macro-structural approach to rural poverty with a focus on the subjective side of the issue — the way rural people experience poverty, and the way in which they respond, individually or collectively, to that experience — has not been fully realised. It will also be clear to readers that despite recognising the inadequacy of purely materialistic definitions of poverty, and specifically of poverty as measured exclusively in terms of income levels, the book has not been very successful in moving beyond such operational definitions of the concept. Attempts to relate "poverty as inadequate income" to "poverty as exclusion" in the lives of the poor in rural Ireland have not proved totally successful. This is not unique and it is recognised, by others who have worked in this field, as a particularly difficult issue to address. Finally, the intention to treat macro-structural factors as major contributing but non-determinant factors in relation to rural poverty has remained more at the level of a programmatic statement than a developed position — it is recognised that the poor can exercise some degree of agency in the way they deal with and react to social inequality, but it has not been possible to integrate this sufficiently into the model of how poverty is produced and reproduced, or, as the case may be, not reproduced, within rural families and rural social groups.

The editors recognise, therefore, that the study has not fully delivered on its initial promises of a political economy approach; but it is argued that it is a useful perspective and that some gains have been achieved. The chapters from the contributors have in fact established the usefulness of addressing "rural" as distinct from "urban" poverty — not in order to advertise inequalities in treatment between urban and rural in Ireland, nor indeed to minimise the issue of division and inequality within rural localities, but to establish that there are some specific examples of rural inequalities that would not be found in ur-

ban areas, because they proceed from different structural causes —
and of course, vice versa.

This has little significance on its own, perhaps, but it points towards something of considerable significance — namely, that to understand how and why rural poverty exists, it is not enough to concern oneself with examining the local characteristics of "disadvantaged" or "less developed" localities in Ireland. It is necessary to
try to trace how people within these localities continually find themselves disadvantaged — in some cases over a long period of time, and
in others quite recently — through their interactions with the wider
Irish society and ultimately with the international and global economic and political processes that heavily influence Irish society's
capacities for change.

In tracing those connections, one is repeatedly confronted by sets
of state policies for development and economic growth which, however
worthy their intentions, seem unable to do anything effective about
tackling poverty. So often they ignore the social position of the poor,
expecting them to be able to take advantage, in just the same way as
everybody else, of the new opportunities conferred by development
processes; or else, if they recognise their existence as a special group,
they tell them that they must wait until society is rich enough to afford to concern itself with their needs.

A problem with both positions is that they fail to consider the possibility that, in many cases, state policy itself is heavily implicated in
the creation of poverty. As Commins' discussion of Irish agriculture
shows, the model of development in use by the State (Irish and EU) is
itself, if not a cause of poverty, then at least an important contributing
factor to the deteriorating situation of small farmers. The point may
be broadened to include other sectors besides agriculture. The problem is that strong forces at the international level are operating to
increase inequality and the concentration of wealth throughout the
world's societies, and while states may respond to this by trying to develop domestic policies that will protect the well-being of their populations as much as possible, the extent to which they can alter the situation is quite limited. The extent to which they will even want to do so
may depend heavily on the degree of threat to their own legitimacy
posed by expanding and intensifying poverty among their citizens.

One way of addressing these issues may be through introducing
onto the state policy agenda a universal anti-poverty strategy which
would ensure that potential unequal impacts of any development policy
would have to be considered in advance of implementation. This is an

issue returned to in the final discussions of the book. However, it is the editors' view that, given the circumstances just outlined, the most important questions raised by the book may ultimately be the political ones — questions about how the poor can mobilise effectively, how they can be represented or have their voice heard in policy-making circles. These also will be addressed again at the end of this book.

References

Atkinson, A.B. and Barnes, A. (1989): *Poverty and Social Security*, London: Harvester Wheatsheaf.

Arensberg, C. and Kimball, S. (1968): *Family and Community in Ireland*, Harvard: Harvard University Press.

Bradley, T., Lowe, P. and Wright, S. (1986): "Introduction: Rural Deprivation and the Welfare Transition" in Lowe, P., Bradley, T. and Wright, S. (eds.), op. cit.

Callan, T and Nolan, B. (1988): *Measuring Trends in Poverty Over Time*. Dublin: Economic and Social Research Institute, Working Paper No. 7.

Callan, T., Nolan, B., Whelan, B.J., Hannan, D.F. with Creighton, S. (1989): *Poverty, Income and Welfare in Ireland*, Dublin: Economic and Social Research Institute, Research Series No. 146.

Commins, P. and Keane, M.J. (1994): *Developing the Rural Economy: Problems, Programmes and Prospects*, NESC Report No. 97, Dublin National Economic and Social Council.

Commission of the European Union (1988): *The Future of Rural Society*, Brussels: Commission of the European Union.

Culliton, J. (1992): *A Time for Change: Industrial Policy for the 1990s.* Report of the Industrial Policy Review Group, Dublin: Stationary Office.

Curtin, C. and Varley, T. (1991): "Populism and Petit Capitalism in Ireland", in Whatmore, S., Lowe, P., and Marsden, T. (eds.), *Rural Enterprise — Shifting Perspectives on Smallscale Enterprise*, London: David Fulton.

Ferge, Z. (1987): "Studying Poverty" in Ferge, Z. and Miller, S. (eds.), op. cit.

Ferge, Z. and Miller, S. (1987): *Dynamics of Deprivation: A Cross-National Study*. Aldershot, Hants: Gower.

Flynn, A. (1986): "Political Ideology: The Case of the Housing Act 1980" in Lowe, P., Bradley, T. and Wright, S. (eds.), op. cit.

Friedmann, H. (1993) "The Political Economy of Food: A Global Crisis" *New Left Review*, 197: 29–57.

Gibbon, P. and Higgins, M.D. (1974): "Patronage, Tradition and Modernisation: The Case of the Irish 'Gombeenman'", *Economic and Social Review*, 6(1): 27–44.

Goodman, D. and Redclift, M. (1986): "Capitalism, Petty Commodity Production and the Farm Enterprise" in Cox, G., Lowe, P. and Winter, M. (eds.), *Agriculture — People and Policies*. London: Allen and Unwin.

Goodman, D., Sorj, B. and Wilkinson, J. (1987): *From Farming to Biotechnology*, Oxford: Basil Blackwell.

Goss, K., Rodefeld, R. and Buttel, F.H. (1980): "The Political Economy of Class Structure in US Agriculture: A Theoretical Outline" in Buttel, F.H. and Newby, H., *The Rural Sociology of the Advanced Societies — Critical Perspectives*, London: Croom Helm.

Habermas, J. (1976): *Legitimation Crisis*, London: Heinemann.

Harris, L. (1984): "Class, Community and Sexual Divisions in North Mayo", in Curtin, C., Kelly, M. and O'Dowd, L. (eds.): *Culture and Ideology in Ireland*. Galway: Galway University Press.

Johnston, R.J. (1986): "The State, the Region, and the Division of Labour" in Scott, A. and Storper, M., *Production, Work, Territory — The Geographical Anatomy of Industrial Capitalism*, Boston: Allen and Unwin.

Knox, P. (1986): "Methodologies and the Poverty of Theory" in Lowe, P., Bradley, T. and Wright, S. (eds.), op. cit.

Leeuwis, C. (1989): *Marginalisation Misunderstood — Different Patterns of Farm Development in the West of Ireland*, Wageningen: Agricultural University.

Lowe, P., Bradley, T. and Wright, S. (1986): *Deprivation and Welfare in Rural Areas*. Norwich: Geo Books.

Lucey, D. and Kaldo, D. (1969): *Rural Industrialisation: The Impact of Industrialisation on Two Communities in Western Ireland*, London: G. Chapman.

Mormont, M. (1990): "Who is Rural? Or: How to Be Rural — Towards a Sociology of the Rural" in Marsden, T., Lowe, P. and Whatmore, S. (eds.), *Rural Restructuring*. London: Fulton.

National Economic and Social Council (1982): *A Review of Industrial Policy*, Report No. 64, Dublin: NESC.

National Economic and Social Council (1989): *Ireland in the European Community: Performance, Prospects and Strategy*. Dublin: NESC.

National Economic and Social Council (1994): *New Approaches to Rural Development*, NESC Report No. 97, Dublin: NESC.

Naylor, E.L. (1993): "Milk Quotas and the Changing Pattern of Dairying in France", *Journal of Rural Studies*, 9(1): 53–63.

Nolan, B. and Callan, T. (eds.) (1994): *Poverty and Policy in Ireland*. Dublin: Gill and Macmillan.

Nolan, B. and Whelan, C.T. (1996): *Resources, Deprivation and Poverty*, Oxford: Clarendon Press.

O'Connell, D. (1982): "Sociological Theory and Irish Political Research" in Kelly, M., O'Dowd, L. and Wickham, J. (eds.), *Power, Conflict and Inequality*. Dublin: Turoe Press.

O'Connor, J. (1973): *The Fiscal Crisis of the State*, New York: St Martin's Press.

O'Donovan, O. and Curtin, C. (1991): "Industrial Development and Rural Women in Ireland", in Varley, T., Boylan, T.A. and Cuddy, M.P. (eds.), *Rural Crisis — Perspectives on Irish Rural Development*, Galway: Centre for Development Studies, University College Galway.

O'Hara, P. (1994): *Women, Farm and Family in Contemporary Ireland*. Unpublished PhD thesis, Trinity College Dublin.

Ruane, J. (1978): "Rural Industrialisation and the Problems of the New Rural Proletariat" unpublished paper, Sociological Association of Ireland Conference, May 1979.

Townsend, P. (1979): *Poverty in the United Kingdom*, London: Allen Lane/University of California Press.

Townsend, P. (1987): "Conceptualising Poverty" in Ferge, Z. and Miller, S. (eds.): op. cit.

Tucker, V. (1989): "State and Community — A Case Study of Glencolmcille", in Curtin C. and Wilson, T. (eds.): *Ireland From Below*. Galway: Galway University Press.

van der Ploeg, J.D. (1993): "Rural Sociology and the New Agrarian Question: A Perspective from the Netherlands", *Sociologia Ruralis* 23(2): 240–60.

Williams, J. and Whelan, B. (1994): *The Dynamics of Poverty: Issues in Short-term Poverty Transitions in Ireland*, Dublin: Combat Poverty Agency.

2: Demography and the Distribution of Deprivation in Rural Ireland

John A. Jackson
Trutz Haase

INTRODUCTION

This chapter considers the place of demographic factors in an understanding of poverty and exclusion in rural Ireland. The exceptional
pattern of sustained emigration from Ireland has produced a tendency to attribute to outflow effects the main demographic imbalances in the population. This was highlighted in the report prepared
in 1958 by the Commission on Emigration and Other Population
Problems. It has, since that period, been taken for granted as a component of the cycle of disadvantage associated with the decline of sustainable rural landholdings and employment patterns and the growth
of disadvantage and demoralisation in rural communities especially
in the west of Ireland. Thus the history of Irish demography has been
characterised by both a net loss of population and the effects of this loss
caused by the selectivity of that migration process, leading to a relative
increase in the economically dependent population and — depending on
the differential emigration of men and women — gender imbalances.

However, the ideal of demographically balanced, self-sustaining
and economically viable communities may be a product more of ideology and structural functionalist theory, with its idea of a self-
sustaining system, than it is of actual and historical reality. That reality, stable as it may appear in the aggregate, is made up of enormous
diversity in detail. On either a larger world scale or a smaller local
scale, these imbalances are part of a broad dynamic process in which
it is recognised that there is no necessity for any particular area,
community or country to be continually in demographic balance.

The central question we are asking therefore in this chapter is to
what extent poverty in rural Ireland can explain weak demography
or to what extent poverty in rural Ireland is the outcome of weak demography. To this end the chapter is presented in five sections: the
first looks at why poverty in rural areas tends to be less visible than
in their urban equivalents. The second section examines some empirical data to trace the main movements in emigration and settlement
patterns over the past five years, as well as the resulting variations in
the composition of local populations. The third section presents some
considerations on possible indicators that might be used to analyse the
geographical distribution of poverty. The fourth section uses an analytical approach to determine whether the demographic changes are a
cause of poverty or whether these demographic changes are themselves
the result of the prevalence of poverty in these rural areas. The final
section speculates as to what may be equitable and feasible approaches to enable Irish society to maintain viable rural communities.

THE INVISIBILITY OF THE RURAL POOR

An adequate account of the extent and distribution of deprivation and disadvantage in Ireland, and particularly rural Ireland, is frustrated by the two main problems of defining poverty and locating the poor. Most of the extensive literature that has been produced on the subject over the past 30 years has taken a number of factors *associated* with poverty as the key indicators of disadvantage and used these to try to solve the distribution problem. Examples of these include the unemployment rate, social class, educational achievement, and the availability of certain household items or the lack thereof. This attempt has been hindered by the fact that it often has had to be based on aggregate data for large spatial units such as health board areas or planning regions which have tended to conceal or modify these effects rather than indicate them clearly. For example, a local incidence of 30 per cent unemployment or 5 per cent illiteracy can be masked by adjacent areas of relative advantage and thus be lost in any large population area. Social and economic characteristics of populations do not necessarily cluster conveniently in a spatial manner except in extensively class-divided societies. Indeed, there are considerable problems, as recent studies have shown, in defining social and economic characteristics according to area (Williams, 1993: 4–8.). Although the boundaries of District Electoral Divisions (DEDs), urban and rural districts, counties, regions and indeed nations may be inescapable units in relation to policy administration, they are, nevertheless, arbitrary limits in relation to the human activity that is being described within them. With the aid of computerised geographical information systems the mapping of objective social characteristics by area has become much easier and more sophisticated than in the past, but this fundamental limit still remains — the boundary is an arbitrary artefact and distortion may occur in the results because of aggregation, however small the designated area is. Even at the level of DEDs, while it is possible to isolate those factors associated with a risk of poverty, it is not always possible from available statistical sources to correlate a cluster of factors around particular families or households and their economic and social activities.

It is generally conceded that, depending on the choice of relative poverty line, some 20 to 30 per cent of the Irish population are in some sense economically poor. It has also been shown that the majority of these — or almost exactly two-thirds — live in rural rather than urban areas. Indeed, the proportion of households below the poverty line is largest in small towns and villages and smallest in Dublin

(Nolan, Whelan and Williams, 1994). And yet it is Dublin and the other cities that most people associate with conditions of poverty, mean streets and tenement blocks. In contrast, the countryside appears wholesome and content. Where are the poor here? Effectively they are invisible. This study puts forward six reasons for this invisibility, which are important in understanding the nature of disadvantage and social exclusion in rural Ireland.

Firstly, Ireland has a *residential pattern* in relation to the countryside which is unlike many other European countries, including Italy and parts of France, where the rural population, originally for reasons of defence, lived in a village or town and would go out from there to work in fields. The pattern in Ireland has been to locate residences on the land, and this has produced a scattered and isolated population with a number of centres, villages and small towns, which serve a wide, residentially dispersed hinterland. With the decline in the rural population and the consolidation of landholdings, this has often led to considerable distances between households and, in many instances, isolation for rural populations. This physical separation and isolation, reflected in the lowest population density in Europe, is one of the factors contributing to the invisibility of the rural poor. The growth of supermarkets in the larger towns and the decline of intermediate social centres such as the creameries have further exacerbated the invisibility of rural families, hidden up laneways or boreens and only revealed to the school bus or the postman.

A second factor is related to the *landscape as a consumption product* for tourism and the leisure needs of the urban population. The prettiness of the rural scene often belies the reality of what it depicts and from the point of view of the beholder many of the features of disadvantage such as old, cold and inadequate housing, isolation and separation from services and amenities and the reliance on outmoded forms of transport may appear as part of the "rural heritage" threatened by modernisation. From the tourists' view, as Slater (1993) observes, the rustic needs to retain the characteristic features of disadvantage in order to preserve the urban myth of superiority: "The ideological structure of the picturesque excludes the native people who actually live in the landscape, because they are seen as a source of disharmony" (*ibid.*: 23). Clearly this ideology of the urban and tourist gaze also excludes the evidence of poverty even if it were visible. In any case, the predominant image of poverty is, today, ideologically defined in terms of a blighted urban-scape "Roddy Doyle land"

and not a relatively green countryside. In a similar way in relation to rural England, Newby (1987: 24) argues that

> . . . ideas about the English countryside as a visual phenomenon and ideas about the English countryside as a social phenomenon have therefore merged together. A locality which looks right must, it is assumed, support a desirable way of life. In this way rural aesthetics and ideals about rural society have become closely intertwined.

A third and more substantial contributor to this invisibility of rural disadvantage is the *confusion between income and property*. The ownership of land by the farming class and the emphasis on the value of property, especially in the context of inflating urban and suburban land values, do not equate with what may be a very disadvantaged farm-income structure. Behind the farm gate and the tended acres of many small farm households is a concealed struggle to maintain their existence through subsidies and off-farm activity. This is evidenced by high rates of business collapse, debt and suicide. This economic desperation, while it may have supported the emphasis placed by this class on education for its children, has often concealed a life of struggle and misery for the adults caught in this situation themselves.

Declining family farm incomes, related to size of farm and system of farming as well as to region, show an index of viability of 53.6 per cent for full-time farms and 22.6 per cent for part-time farms where farm viability is defined as capacity to remunerate family labour at the average agricultural wage rate and generate a 5 per cent return on non-land assets. Taking all farms in their survey, Commins and Keane (1994) conclude that only one-third of all farms were economically and demographically viable in 1992. They define demographic non-viability as a farm where the holder is 55 years of age and where there is nobody under 45 years in the household. Thirty-one per cent of the farms defined as demographically viable by this measure did not satisfy the measure of economic viability (Commins and Keane, 1994: Table 6.13). A further 17 per cent were maintained through the non-farm occupation of the holder of the farm or spouse, and 19 per cent of farms were non-viable on all these measures. Indeed, these authors provide a striking contrast between the one-third of farms that are economically viable and which account for two-thirds of gross output, 70 per cent of family farm income, two-thirds of tillage acreage, 70 per cent of dairy cows, and the other two-thirds of farms, which depend on state transfers or off-farm earnings. As these authors indicate, while many of the farms in this latter category are no longer viable, "they view their assets in a different light than is implied in the concept of economic viability" (p. 55) placing a stronger value on property and the status and potential that it represents than on actual income. This tendency, of course, may be reinforced by the anticipation of future windfall gain as a result of urban or international "blow-ins" seeking secluded and, in their terms, relatively cheap sites on which to build, or old and "traditional" houses to convert and modernise.

Of course, the majority of rural residents are not farmers and not all rural residents are dependent upon the farm economy. Thus, a fourth factor is *the landless living in rural areas*. Although landholders are substantially more numerous than farmers, these landless include some who formerly provided farm labour and others who have gravitated to public housing outside the main urban complexes. In towns and villages, the housing estates established by county councils have been, to some extent, ghettoised by virtue of their location outside the central areas of small towns. The estate as a ghetto may mean that, in contrast to the town itself where all members live on the street or small complex of streets that makes up the town, the poor live somewhere else, invisible and apart from the town. In a similar way to that in which Travellers have been subjected to the NIMBY (not-in-my-back-yard) tendency when seeking halting sites, so also have those in local authority housing been relocated from town-centre streets to estates that are frequently marginal and effectively invisible to the townscape of which they form part. Two typical examples of this are the public housing areas in Skibbereen in Co. Cork and Rathdrum in Co. Wicklow.

A fifth aspect of this invisibility rests on the prevailing attitudes in Irish society toward the facts and realities of a highly stratified and differentiated society. There are strong *ideological and institutional constraints* within the community and parish ideology to prevent the recognition of objective differences in wealth and income opportunities. Whereas status differences are very precisely delineated, there is little tendency for these to crystallise in terms of class interest or to be expressed in such terms. The characteristic social structure of Irish rural society has been well described by Eipper (1986) in his study of Bantry in West Cork as a "friction of interests" by which social position is realised and reputation defined. The value of this model lies in its definition of class and strata as dynamic strategic elements rather than fixed layers. The idea of "friction" embodies this dynamic according to which class relations are experienced and acted upon within the parameters of structural constraints and the emerging conflicts between various actors with different interests. It allows for the cross-cutting and overlay effects whereby religious affiliation, commitment to sport, or other cultural factors may influence economically realised social position. One of the most significant elements here may be the degree to which people establish local "belonging", which is particularly important in relation to the changing population of the rural countryside.

Eipper's model could be elaborated in detail, of course, in any particular setting in relation to size of farm, the quality of the land, or the way in which it is farmed. The model has a further advantage in relation to pluri-activity and the diversity of economic activities in which a household may engage. This reality shows the importance of the retention of land as a base from which to operate, even when farming as such ceases to be the main economic activity in which the household is engaged. Class, in these terms, becomes a strategic framework within which economic relations of production and consumption are only part of the complex of available options. Even the poor may thereby retain respect.

The sixth and final factor is the character of Ireland as a *property-owning democracy*, with the highest proportion of homeowners in Europe, and the consequent scarcity of both public and private rented accommodation. This puts pressure on rural residents in relation to the need to own in order to belong and to have a place in the community. This has undoubtedly been a potent force in securing the status of the small farmer class and its development of pluri-activity, as Hannan and Commins show (1993: 97–99), where the possession and retention of land provides a framework for the development of alternative economic activities outside farming. It has, however, served to heighten the distinction between propertied and property-less in the countryside, while at the same time emphasising land and property as the basis for status in the community. The petit-bourgeois values of respectability and reputation, of carefulness and caution, further cloak the struggles of the poor in a mantle of discretion.

This invisibility of the rural poor is matched in urban areas by the phenomenon of "cognitive dissonance" where problems are defined "out of sight and out of mind". It should be noted that the wealthy also benefit from this concealment, as the community ethos of parish and village tends not to challenge or emphasise major structural cleavages, such as class.

DEMOGRAPHIC PATTERNS OF CHANGE AND SETTLEMENT

Notwithstanding the obstacles to the visibility of the rural poor, the single most important indicator of the persistence of deprivation in Ireland's rural areas has been the fact of continued emigration. Indeed, population decline has been the major issue in Irish demography since the Famine. The effects of emigration, which accounted for a decline from a population of eight million in 1841 to the present three and a half million, have characterised Ireland's demographic experience and set it apart from other European countries. Late marriage, high marital fertility, and a low rate of illegitimacy, in conjunction with emigration, helped to sustain a pattern in Ireland long after a low fertility pattern had developed elsewhere in Europe in response to population pressure (Coleman, 1992). The major losses throughout the period were from the rural western counties — a drain of population which led to the demographic distortion and demoralisation captured in books such as Brody's *Inishkillane* (Brody, 1973). Much attention was given to the consequentially poor demography in the *Report of the Commission on Emigration and other Population Problems* (Ireland, 1955). This report was especially significant in establishing the rural West as a region of special demographic disadvantage with very low ratios of females to males and relatively few persons of working age supporting the elderly and young. Indeed, the rural West was also associated with the additional disadvantages of remoteness and a physical topography which effectively cuts it off from the main centres and transport routes. As McCleery (1991: 146) writes in relation to the Highlands and Islands of Scotland, the same could be said in relation to the Irish rural West:

> Constrained by populations that are both numerically low and highly dispersed, remote rural areas invariably also demonstrate unfavourable population structures. In that it at once results from and contributes to marginality, the population condition of such an area is not only especially sensitive as an indicator of socio-economic health but it is also particularly complex to interpret.

Recent Migration Trends

Population decline continues to affect many of Ireland's remote rural areas, although it is no longer the case that such decline is associated only, or even typically, with rural areas. In the past decade, a number of urban areas have displayed very similar characteristics. Between 1986 and 1991, for instance, there occurred a population decline in 23 out of 34 county boroughs and counties, including the county boroughs of Dublin, Cork and Limerick. In Leinster, with the exception of Dublin, there was a decline in Carlow, Laois, Longford, Louth, Offaly, Westmeath and Wexford. In Munster, a decline was experienced in Clare, Cork, Kerry, Limerick, Tipperary North and South Riding and Waterford. In Connacht, this was the case for all counties apart from Galway County Borough, as it was for the three counties of Ulster.

In common with the experience of the rest of Europe, Irish cities are no longer simply magnets of attraction, but are becoming net exporters of people themselves. Recent work on Dublin, for example, shows a 53.3 per cent loss for the north inner city and 50.6 per cent for the south inner city in the period between 1961 and 1991 (Drudy and MacLaran, 1994: 10).

However, conceptualising emigration and settlement patterns in terms of county-level statistics may be of little actual use, and in fact may conceal more than it reveals. The reason for this lies with the particular type of population movements that have developed throughout Ireland: the thinning out of populations in both rural and inner-city areas and settlement in outer urban belts within commuting distances of the cities and towns. This development holds not only for the five major cities — Dublin, Galway, Limerick, Cork and Waterford — but also applies to Sligo, Dundalk, Drogheda, Athlone, Kilkenny, Wexford, Tralee and even places like Letterkenny, Donegal, Castlebar and Ballina, all of which are surrounded by vast areas that experience population decline.

It is interesting to note that this population movement is not a phenomenon characteristic of any particular region or province, but encompasses the whole of Ireland and appears to reflect structural changes in the organisation of society as a whole. These, in turn, may result from the location of jobs, changes in travel-to-work patterns, the increased availability of private transport, as well as the ready availability of new housing and planning permissions at the outskirts of existing population centres.

Figure 2.1: Population Change, 1986–1991

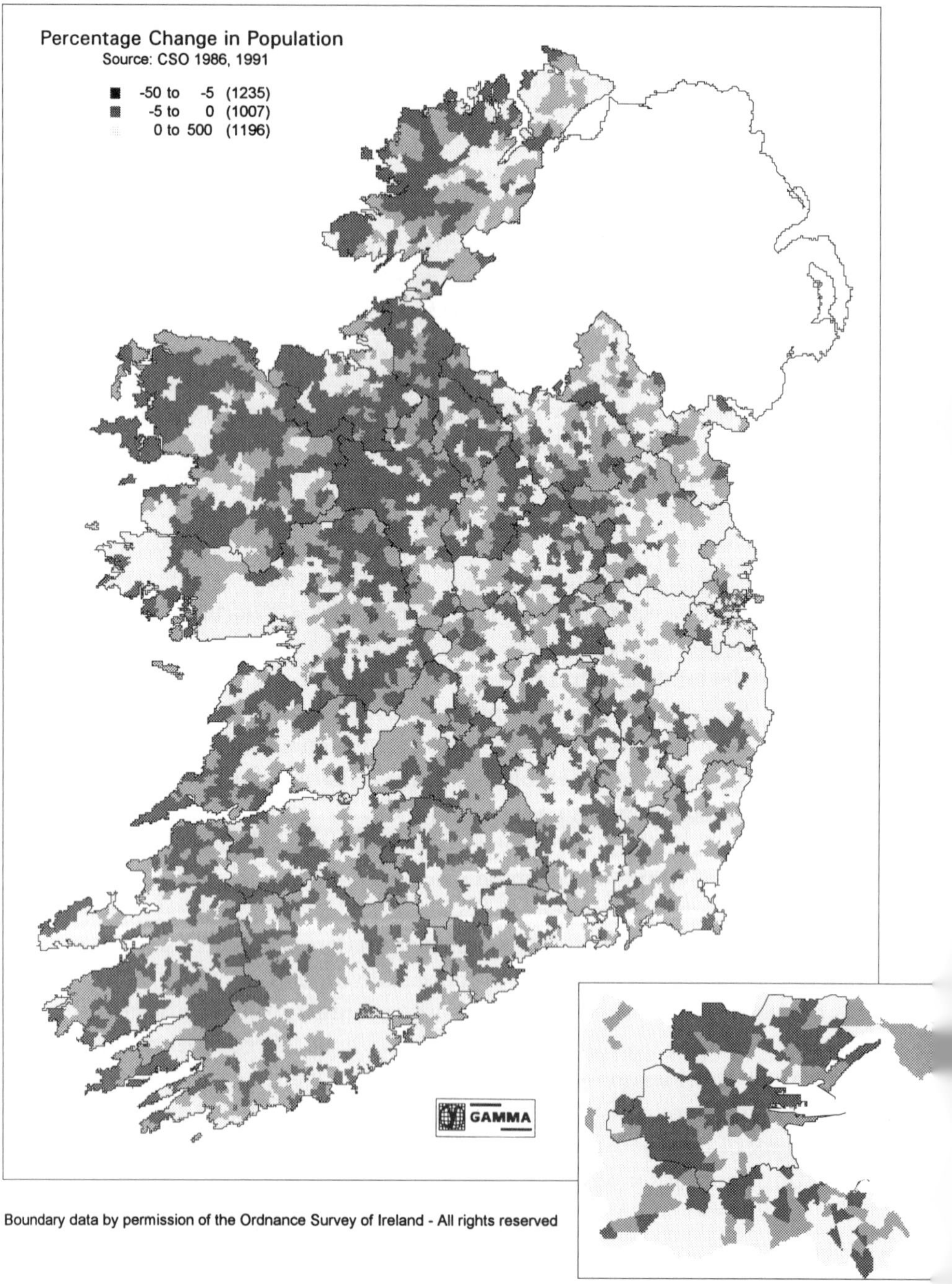

Percentage Change in Population
Source: CSO 1986, 1991

- -50 to -5 (1235)
- -5 to 0 (1007)
- 0 to 500 (1196)

GAMMA

The fact that this population movement results in net population losses for many of the northern counties — Leitrim (-6.4 per cent), Roscommon (-4.9 per cent), Mayo (-3.9 per cent), Longford (-3.8 per cent), Cavan (-2.2 per cent) and Monaghan (-2.1 per cent) — may first and foremost reflect the absence of any major population centre in these counties. In other counties, the movement from both urban and rural locations to the urban periphery is largely absorbed within a single, or at least neighbouring, counties.

Settlement Patterns

We have shown, therefore, that recent population movements have a common character throughout the whole of Ireland. Their social effects, however, are far from being unbiased, because of the selectivity inherent in this process. At a first glance, changes in the age dependency ratio among the populations at the level of individual DEDs seem to be arbitrarily scattered throughout the country. At closer inspection, however, the resulting distribution using the 1991 Census of Population shows that the cumulative effect of successive and continued selective migratory patterns has been the emergence of considerable regional differences in the proportion of family members who have to live off a single household income. Despite the increase in the age dependency ratios of the urban centres — shown in the map for Dublin only — the results for city areas are nevertheless profoundly different from the experience of overwhelmingly rural counties. In the latter, successive periods of emigration have led to the considerable thinning out of their core working-age populations, with a large and increasing proportion of dependants staying behind.

THE GEOGRAPHICAL DISTRIBUTION
OF POVERTY

It was pointed out at the beginning of this chapter that studies of the geographical distribution of poverty tend to depend on proxies that can be meaningfully employed to assess the relative likelihood of poverty in a particular area. Likewise, the methodological approach of the analysis presented here is based on a multivariate analysis of poverty surrogates from the Census of Population and builds on work by Williams (1993), and Haase (1993, 1995).

Figure 2.2: Age Dependency

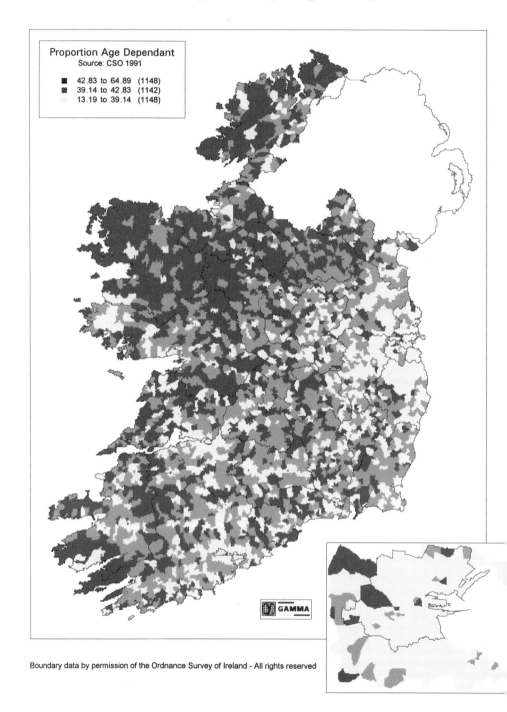

The basic consideration informing the work of these authors is that, although unemployment is one of the most significant factors associated with disadvantage, unemployment rates alone do not provide a sufficient indicator of underlying disadvantage in an area. Indeed, as will become apparent below, high unemployment rates are a predominantly urban phenomenon which, taken on their own, would introduce considerable bias into any nationwide study. One reason for this is the high level of emigration that persists in many rural areas, which reduces the prevailing unemployment rate. Statistics for migration are difficult to come by, and estimates are only available at the county level. However, as pointed out above, emigration tends to be selective in that it is concentrated among the working-age population, thus leaving behind a disproportionately large economically dependent population. Hence, sustained levels of out-migration can be identified from the age-dependency ratio — that is, those under 15 years of age and over 65 as a proportion of the total population.

The second reason why long-term adverse labour market conditions may assert themselves through indicators other than the unemployment rate lies with the peculiarities of small-scale farming. As pointed out above, there are strong social incentives why farmers, even if they do not derive a sufficient family income from farming, may nevertheless hold on to their economically unviable holdings. In such a situation, the unemployment rate is likely to understate the real extent of unemployment, as this is, at least in part, concealed by on-farm underemployment.

The analysis presented here builds on that of Haase (1995) and uses 13 indicators that have been shown to be strongly associated with the presence of deprivation. These are:

(1) The age dependency rate

(2) The proportion of lone parents

(3) The unemployment rate

(4) The percentage of those at work engaged in small farming (under 30 acres)

(5) The proportion of households with two or more cars

(6) The percentage of the population in the combined higher and lower professional classes

(7) The percentage of the population in the unskilled manual class

(8) The percentage of economically active persons with third-level education

(9) The percentage of the adult population leaving school at 15 years or below

(10) The percentage of the adult population leaving school at 20 years or above

(11) The proportion of permanent private households that are local-authority rented

(12) The proportion of permanent private households that are owner-occupied

(13) The average number of rooms per person.

As many of these indicators are correlated to one another, a factor analysis was undertaken to determine the independent, underlying dimensions of deprivation. This resulted in three dimensions being identified which account for 73 per cent of the total variation observed (Table 2.1). The first factor, accounting for 39.7 per cent of variation, is an indication of *social class*; the other two factors (accounting for 24.1 and 8.7 per cent respectively) are related to the distinct features of urban and rural deprivation: large proportions of people in local-authority housing, lone parents and unemployment are all distinctly *urban* indicators of deprivation, while the proportion of small farmers and the age dependency ratio are both distinctly *rural*. The proportion of households with two or more cars is loading almost equally onto both the urban and rural terms (obviously with an inverse sign).

The clear emergence of the overriding influence of social class in conjunction with two distinct but very clear indicators of urban and rural deprivation is of great interest, and concurs with the theoretical ideas present at the outset of the analysis. After assigning individual scores for the three factors to each DED, these were then aggregated to derive a single indicator for the overall degree of deprivation prevailing in each DED. Figure 2.3 shows the resulting distribution of relative affluence and deprivation throughout Ireland.

Interpretation

The distribution of deprivation, as measured by this analysis, clearly supports Nolan and Callan's (1994) assertion that it is a spatially pervasive phenomenon which affects almost every part of the country. However, there are differences in the degree to which disadvantage is clustered in particular areas, both urban and rural. In Dublin, the analysis fully confirms the known areas of deprivation. These are the north and south inner city, Coolock, Ballymun, Cabra, Finglas, parts of Blanchardstown, Rialto, Kilmainham, Ballyfermot, Cherry Orchard, Clondalkin, Kimmage, Crumlin, Walkinstown, West Tallaght, and pockets in Dún Laoghaire. In the urban areas outside Dublin, the main clusters of deprivation include parts of the four county boroughs of Galway, Limerick, Cork and Waterford and the towns of Drogheda, Dundalk, Sligo, Kilkenny, Wexford and Bray. In rural Ireland, disadvantage is most prevalent in Donegal and Mayo, but also extensive in the border counties of Leitrim, Cavan and Monaghan, as well as in Roscommon. In addition, significant pockets of deprivation are located in north Kerry and in Clare.

Table 2.1: Structure Matrix of Deprivation Factors Based on Multivariate Analysis of 1991 Small Area Population Statistics

Variable	Factor 1 Social Class	Factor 2 Urban Deprivation	Factor 3 Rural Deprivation
Labour Force with Third-Level Education	.90		
Leaving School at 20 or over	.89		
Rooms per Person	.80		
Leaving School at 15 or under	-.77		.66
Higher and Lower Professional Class	.73		-.62
Unskilled Manual Class	-.63		
Households Owner Occupied		-.91	
Households Local Authority Rented		.85	
Lone Parents		.78	
Unemployed		.77	
Proportion of Small Farming			.84
Households with 2 or more Cars		-.54	-.60
Age Dependency Rate			.56

Source: Haase, 1995.

Figure 2.3: Overall Deprivation in Ireland

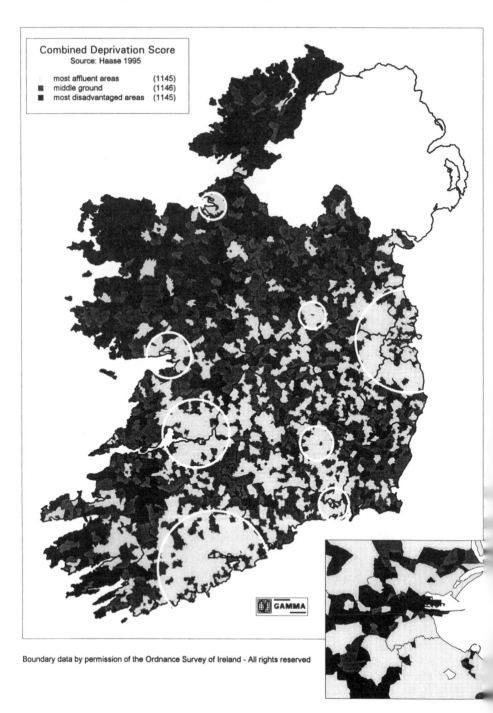

The second feature that is apparent from this map, and which concurs with our observation on population changes, is the extent to which the fate of rural Ireland is determined by urban factors. The interpenetration of the countryside by the urban shadow of the major centres of population could not be more striking. A pattern of relative affluence and disadvantage is evident, which forms concentric circles around the main centres of population. In the case of Dublin, this effect is visible in the form of an affluent belt stretching from Kells in a semi-circle which includes Kildare to the west and extends through most of east Wicklow to the south. Outside this arc, which can be described as an "urban fringe", there is a wide band of disadvantage stretching from Dundalk in the north to south Wexford and including much of the Midlands. In a similar way around Cork, the fringe circumscribes a wide arc around the city, stretching as far as Rathluirc to the north, Clonakilty to the west and Middleton to the east. As with Dublin, there is a wide zone of transition outside this in which the compensating effects of the urban process have not yet been felt. Similar but much less pronounced fringes and transition zones can be seen surrounding Galway, Limerick and Waterford.

Leaving aside the situation in Donegal and the western fringe of Mayo, Sligo and Connemara, a very substantial part of the country can be described in terms of this urban effect which has a number of features. Clearly, the urban fringe includes an increasing population who are commuting into the urban area and have benefited from some of the recent improvement in road and rail networks, which make it practical to live well outside the suburban ring and still be no more than an hour from the city. Many of these people have benefited from the opportunity to buy property at a much lower cost than inflated city prices and they may have benefited also from greenbelt provisions in the planning legislation to preserve some of the amenity values of their property in the face of future development. The areas concerned include a number of satellite communities that have attracted some industry and employment precisely because they are located near an urban centre, an airport and the range of cultural amenities the city offers. They include also agricultural landholders who, if their farms are large, have benefited from opportunities for intensive commercialisation of agriculture associated with a nearby urban market or, if they are too small to remain viable, have benefited from opportunities for off-farm economic activity in the city and/or the sale of sites for building development.

This process of urban extension is likely to continue. Its corollary — the depopulation occurring in the central areas of the cities — accounts, at least in part, for the significant areas of deprivation within the urban areas themselves. What these patterns clearly indicate is that one of the forces operating is the influence of land values on the life chances of the population. As the development of the urban fringe has continued, it has tended to worsen the situation of the propertyless and landless rural and urban population, as they have been forced to compete in a market inflated by affluent urban interests and a social structure and culture that is increasingly defined by affluent urban values.

Indeed, some doubt could be voiced about whether the traditional sociological distinction between rural and urban society is sustainable any longer. This has, in any case, been largely based on a series of misconceptions relating to an increasingly redundant theory of modernisation. The significant decline in the numbers engaged in agriculture, together with the encouragement of industrial location outside the larger urban areas, has led to a process whereby the populations of rural and urban areas increasingly resemble each other. Patterns of income earning have become diversified so that the economic activity of farming is increasingly related to off-farm earnings and pluriactivity and both urban and rural populations have experienced the consequences of industrial decline, down-sizing and the departure of multinational factories. These factors, in rural areas, have acted independently of the continued decline in agricultural labour brought about by growing concentration and industrialisation of food production, and the consequent decline in the number of farm proprietors. Factors such as media access, especially television, travel, tourism and the growing diversification of consumer products have contributed to the incorporation of the rural population into the global economy and society.

Nevertheless, the myth of rurality has an ideological strength that is used to perpetuate a sense of distinction between rural and urban where none may exist. A strong sense of region, urban prejudice and the balance of political forces and interests, such as the powerful farming lobby, emphasises the distinctiveness of the country and its needs against those of the cities. Equally, the concentration of population, government, financial, business and educational institutions and the media in the cities ensures that the message of urban interest in contrast to the rural is strongly sustained.

To the extent that the rural mythology is preserved by both political interests and ideological factors, it is reinforced by traditional and conservative forces in the society which tend to resist change in itself but equally continue to contrast what they see as the negative effects of change with a romanticised image of the status quo. The myth of the rural has been strengthened in Ireland as the significance of a distinctively rural economy has waned. De Valera's dancing maidens and valleys of happy, rustic toil, the self-sufficient, interdependent and co-operative farm economy and society depicted by Arensberg and Kimball (1968), the cultural revival and the special claims of the western seaboard as the "true Ireland" have all contributed to these myths. The commercial packaging of Ireland — and especially the rural countryside with its 40 shades of green — for the development of tourism has finally set the myth in concrete (literally, with a whole range of interpretative centres) with the result that the image of Ireland that is sold to the visitor as well as ourselves bears little relationship to the reality.

CAUSES AND CONSEQUENCES

In the previous two sections, it was demonstrated that out-migration from rural areas has remained a significant feature, but that this is hardly as striking as it was in the decade of the 1950s when sustained and heavy emigration co-existed with a high rate of marital fertility. The present decline in Ireland's rural population would seem to be part of a more general process across Europe whereby between 1950 and 1982 two-thirds of all those engaged in agricultural employment left the industry. This decline has been described frequently in terms of a "principle of circular and cumulative causation" as depicted in Figure 2.4 below, which is adapted from Drudy (1989: 127).

A cumulative cycle of disadvantage is set up whereby outward migration, itself stimulated by the lack of employment opportunities, leads to an unbalanced age structure and sex ratio which tends toward a low marriage rate and a reduction in natural increase, as well as adding to the economic disadvantages already present on the supply side. These factors in turn reduce demand for services and other amenities, thus stimulating further decline. This process may be further exacerbated by the additional threat to the linguistic and cultural identity of rural areas.

Evaluated by metropolitan criteria, the life chances the periphery can offer by comparison with the core are increasingly interpreted as being deficient. Such an unfavourable comparison often provides the critical pull factor that, combined with existing economic and social pressures already acting to push people out of rural areas, strengthens the motivation and generates the momentum for inexorable rural exodus (McCleery, 1991: 146–7).

Figure 2.4: The Principle of Circular and Cumulative Causation

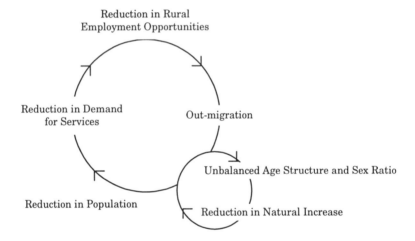

As was stressed in the previous section, this dynamic is no longer unique to rural areas, but increasingly affects many inner-city areas. On the surface, this similarity seems to be negated by the relative abundance of jobs in centralised services typically available in city-centre locations. However, it must be borne in mind that the majority of these jobs are unattainable for many of the local residents and that these centres often coexist with the greatest concentrations of unemployment.

This then calls into question whether the decline experienced by Ireland's rural areas is indeed specifically "rural" or whether wider, more fundamental forces of social and economic restructuring underlie this process. One of the fallacies of the demographic-decline argument is the implicit assumption that runs through the literature of an ideal model of a static, homogeneous unit replacing itself in a homeostatically balanced manner within the same area. In international terms and in light of the scale of mobility of human capital, these assumptions are less and less tenable. This chapter proposes instead a dynamic model of population interchange to describe the reality of rural (and urban) demography in Ireland today. If this model is adopted, there is no necessary reason why it should be assumed that rural decline is necessarily or inevitably the consequence of population decline. Just as certain cities have demonstrated the ability to turn around after decades of a downward spiral (take, for example, the cities of Glasgow, Berlin or Barcelona), so rural decline has been successfully counteracted in many areas throughout Europe. In fact, it could be argued that population decline may, in certain circumstances, be a necessary condition of *rural* regeneration.

While this argument questions most conventional policy thinking, it has the advantage of opening up some possibilities in the policy arena that have been closed for years, by the assumption that the property of the family home, protected as it is by the 1937 Constitution, is the pivot around which all else in Irish society revolves. This territorial imperative is deeply rooted in national thinking. Since land reform at the end of the nineteenth century, peasant proprietorship and the attachment to the land, to the family farm or, as in J.B. Keane's play, to *The Field*, dominates our imagination. This attitude to property is transported to the cities in the very high level of urban home ownership and the assumption that public housing is provided by a reluctant administration to accommodate merely the homeless or those made so by development. In contrast to many other European countries, housing is not treated as a public good with a much wider availability and function. Indeed, the long waiting lists for such public housing as does become available in Ireland indicates the level of priority that should be given to rectifying this imbalance.

These tendencies explain, at least in part, the strength of both private and public interests in Ireland in preserving a series of policies that provide disincentives to mobility and population decline even when they have, for the most part, been insufficient to stem the flow. Indeed, the fact of population decline has served to conceal the real nature of the rural restructuring that has been taking place. Most notably, the increased centralisation of government and government services, and the consequent weakening of the autonomy of local government, have served to reinforce clientelist politics and further to maintain the dependency of the rural population on gestures of support from Dublin and Brussels. Once we begin to question the assumption of natural immobility, the whole question of the cycle of disadvantage can be re-evaluated.

CONCLUSION

Poverty and social exclusion are the products of international, national and local forces which operate to structure the responses of individuals and families as social agents. As Marx wrote, people do not find themselves in situations entirely of their own choosing, nor are they entirely free to choose, as liberal theory suggests. Instead, people are the products of their pasts, sometimes victims and sometimes beneficiaries, but always living in the present and carrying into the future something of the circumstances that govern the situation in which they find themselves. Even within a single life, earlier choices, such as when to leave school, can be powerful determinants of adult opportunities and options. The cycle of social reproduction is limited by the options available, and the extent to which avenues are open depends on access to various kinds of resources.

Poverty and social exclusion tend to be reproduced in the structural shifts that occur both horizontally and vertically through time in the economic, political and ideological structures of Irish society. These shifts away from earlier modes of production, the decline of certain markets, and their replacement by modern alternatives, define the dynamic framework within which lives must be lived and choices reached. They reflect, and are reflected, in demographic factors, which, as we have seen, may add to the effects of exclusion the sense of being left behind as the rest of the world rushes by. It is in this way that the cycle of disadvantage depicted in Figure 2.4 develops what appears as an inevitable process of decline, as first emigration, and then other demographic effects, such as gender imbalance and ageing, take effect and contribute to economic and social decline.

Against this, the authors contend that the critical factors in the differential experience of participation in Irish society, both rural and urban, are the ownership of property, access to the labour market and access to what may be described as "state benefits". These different dimensions interact and, to a certain extent, are mutually reinforcing. In general, ownership of property may not only provide a means of gaining a direct income, as with land, but also carry with it fundamental conditions of entry for many schemes of support. This is particularly true in rural areas, as these schemes have been developed in relation to EU provisions directed at farm support for both land and stock. Even with the scaling down of the Common Agricultural Policy in line with the new GATT agreement, there are considerable supports available to those who are owners of land, whether farmed in increasingly mechanised and capital-intensive ways, or in alternatives to farming such as set-aside or farm tourism. In many of these schemes, and notably in those from the EU, there is a requirement for the applicants to provide matching funding. Even though part of this may be calculated in terms of inputs in kind, these are associated with either property ownership or capital acquisition which are usually denied to those who are neither owners of property nor earners in the labour market.

The reproduction of stratification in Irish society has depended to a large extent on the capacity of classes to retain access to property and to the labour market. State subsidies have been used effectively to this end, as demonstrated by O'Hara (1994) in her analysis of the educational success of the children of small western farmers who have benefited disproportionately from state support for low-income families. The decision to educate children for lives spent off the farm, to wish for children lives that do not imply the drudgery endured by their mothers in particular, has been related to a decline in the relative economic status and political influence of this class within the framework of the farm economy and, in cases of especially poor land, has also led where this is possible to pluri-activity. An example of the latter has been described by Duggan in her study of Carna (1994). In this area in Galway, she shows that despite attempts of the Congested District Boards to institute an economy based on agricultural production, this proved to be hardly viable in many instances. She shows also that it was the survival and resurgence of pluri-activity that provided a series of multiple alternatives for income that enabled the household as a unit to survive.

Somewhat similar examples are available from Newfoundland where the pattern of pluri-activity was also well established for both seasonal reasons and reasons of marginality. In an assessment of the situation before the banning of the cod fishery, the authors suggest that for those in work in these outpost communities

> . . . the wage is not being used in the way an industrial economy would use it — as the whole income on which one subsists. It is the start-up financial capital for a home production economy which permits people to subsist on lower cash flows than people in an urban-industrial economy could tolerate. . . .

What is vital to understand here is that this pluralist economy, with all its hardships, is still a better alternative for many people than to move away, abandon occupational pluralism and seek elusive jobs in the market economy. (Royal Commission on Employment and Unemployment, 1986: 111, 112)

Within the framework of rural restructuring, demographic factors play a part but, as the NESC points out, it is not the only part:

It is clear that population decline is but one, possible, element of the problem and is best not used as a definition of the problem. Indeed, depending on the severity of other problems, or the size of the geographic area chosen, population decline may not even be viewed as part of a rural development problem, let alone its definition (NESC, 1994, p. 5).

Poor demography is a consequence rather than a cause of changes brought about by shifts in the balance of the political economy of the country and countryside. Some of these stem from global market forces played out in local situations; some are the product of local adaptations and regeneration through pluri-activity or the reorganisation of industries such as forestry, farming or fishing.

These shifts operate at many levels and affect the lives of individuals in different ways. Some, like tectonic plates, gradually and very occasionally violently, overthrow the basic givens of the situation, the assumptions that have served several generations of small farmers about the values of land and property, the security of protection for their markets in milk and meat. Some operate to produce dynamics that have their own particular trade-offs — for example emigration and education.

Emigration has always been a more complex social process than simply a population loss from a given area. It is a strategy with evident costs but also certain actual or potential benefits. These benefits include remittances which can be used to sustain otherwise uneconomic structures and an expansion of networks and strategic resources which can be used to develop and enhance the life chances of other family members. Thus emigration presents the possibility of the elaboration at a family level of a geographically expanded web of pluri-activity among family members, which allows the potential of their intervention to be retained and drawn upon as circumstances dictate.

The second example, that of education, demonstrates ways in which, increasingly, relatively disadvantaged small farmers, especially in the west of Ireland, have managed to utilise the educational system to gain a significantly higher proportion of third-level places for their children than might have been expected (O'Hara, 1994). While this may have been achieved against a background of increasing strain and sacrifice on the part of their parents, the benefits for the children serve to demonstrate that in the longer term this is an effective strategy in response to the internationalisation of the labour market and the importance of educational qualifications as a prerequisite for an active stake in the global economy.

Because this is a dynamic process, there are, inevitably, losers as well as winners: those without resources such as land, educational qualifications or employment; those who are old, dependent and marginalised may have no effective stake which they can trade in against the new situation. More importantly, they may lack the incentives offered by the potential of long-term realisation to offset the lack of short-term gain. The cycle of disadvantage may lead to an active demoralisation which discourages participation in all activities. The reduction of strategic alternatives gives way at this point to a desperate cycle of survival against the odds, which suggests that no change in external circumstance is likely to have either immediate or lasting effect.

The restructuring of Irish rural society cannot occur without casualties and costs to individuals and communities. However, if we can use our resources more effectively to discover the causes of disadvantage, then the costs may not need to be borne disproportionately by those least able to absorb them. Moreover, it does emerge from this analysis that there are policy options that take a more differentiated, subtle and interactive view of the problem of rural poverty and disadvantage. For these to come to the fore it is not enough to rely on areal studies of the distribution of indicators of disadvantage, although these do clearly provide a necessary framework. Even at the micro-level, however, they can only provide broad indications of problem situations. In order to understand the actual experience of individuals and the strategies that they use to cope, more research is needed which will allow people to tell their own stories and relate the ways in which the objective structures of Irish society operate to facilitate or frustrate their best efforts. We have relied too long perhaps on the ability of observers from outside to describe the situation in which people find themselves and to provide rational choice models of their appropriate behaviour, without being aware of the complex, subtle, imaginative and enduring characteristics people themselves display.

This is in no way to suggest that disadvantage and poverty do not exist in rural society in Ireland. Rather, it is intended to stress the extent to which the problem of poverty and exclusion is embedded in a complex web of factors which are both historically specific and socially defined in terms of multiple and overlapping structures, local, national and international — social, political and ideological as well as demographic. The responses of individual social agents to these structures remain the dynamic element that defines the extent to which policies defined on a broad base of equity across national territories can adequately meet the strategic objectives of individuals caught in many different and very specific situations of disadvantage.

References

Arensberg, C. and Kimball, S. (1968): *Family and Community in Ireland*, Harvard: Harvard University Press.

Brody, H. (1973): *Inishkillane — Change and Decline in the West of Ireland*, London: Faber and Faber.

Coleman, D.A. (1992): "The demographic transition in Ireland in international context" in Goldthorpe, J. and Whelan, C.T. (eds.), *The Development of Industrial Society in Ireland*, Oxford: Oxford University Press.

Commins, P. and Keane, M. (1994): "Developing the Rural Economy: Problems, Programmes and Prospects", in NESC, *New Approaches to Rural Development*, Dublin: National Economic and Social Council, Report No. 97.

Commission on Emigration and Other Population Problems, 1948-54 (1955), *Reports*, Dublin: Government Publications (PR 2541).

Drudy, P.J. (1989): "The international–national–local interplay; problems and priorities in the development of rural regions" in Obrecht, L. and Moulaert, F., *Regional Policy at the Crossroad: European Perspectives*, London: Kingsley.

Drudy, P.J. and MacLaren, A. (1994): *Dublin; Economic and Social Trends*, Dublin, Centre for Urban and Regional Studies, Trinity College.

Duggan, C. (1994): *Economic Diversity on Smallholdings: a Study of Pluriactivity in West Connemara*, Dublin: Unpublished PhD thesis, Trinity College, Dublin.

Eipper, C. (1986): *The Ruling Trinity: a Community Study of Church, State and Business in Ireland*, Aldershot: Gower

Haase, T. (1993): *Identifying Prospective Areas for Inclusion in the Local Development Programme - A Methodological Outline*, Dublin: Working Paper, Combat Poverty Agency.

Haase, T. (1995): *The Designation of Disadvantaged Areas in the Local Development Programme*, Report to Area Development Management Ltd., Dublin, to facilitate the designation of areas under the Operational Programme for Local Urban and Rural Development (1994–1999).

Hannan, D. and Commins P. (1993): "The Significance of Small-scale Landholders in Ireland's Socio-economic Transformation" in Whelan, C. and Goldthorpe, J., *The Development of Industrial Society in Ireland*, Oxford: Oxford University Press.

McCleery, A (1991): "Population and social conditions in remote areas: the changing character of the Scottish Highlands and Islands" in Champion, T. and Watkins, C., *People in the Countryside*, London: Paul Chapman.

Newby, H. (1987): *Country Life. A Social History of England*, London: Weidenfield and Nicholson.

NESC (1994): *New Approaches to Rural Development,* Dublin: National Economic and Social Council, Report No. 97.

Nolan, B. and Callan, T. (eds.) (1994): *Poverty and Policy in Ireland*, Dublin: Gill and Macmillan.

Nolan, B., Whelan, C. and Williams, J. (1994): "Spatial Aspects of Poverty and Disadvantage" in Nolan, B. and Callan, T. (eds.) op. cit.

O'Hara, P. (1994): *Women, Farm and Family in Contemporary Ireland,* Dublin: Unpublished PhD thesis, Trinity College Dublin.

Royal Commission on Employment and Unemployment (1986), *Building on Our Strengths*, Final Report, St. Johns, Newfoundland: The Queen's Printer.

Slater, E. (1993): "Contested terrain: differing interpretations of County Wicklow's landscape", *Irish Journal of Sociology*, 3: 23–55.

Williams, J. (1993): *Spatial Variations in Deprivation Surrogates — A Preliminary Analysis,* Report to the Combat Poverty Agency, Dublin: Economic and Social Research Institute.

3: Agricultural Production and the Future of Small-Scale Farming

Patrick Commins

INTRODUCTION

For any category of household the "risk" of being poor is defined as the proportion of households in that category which is found to be "in poverty" — that is, below a given income level. The main determinant of a household's income is the employment status of its members, especially that of the head of the household. Studies of the characteristics of poor households (Callan et al., 1994) show that where the household head is unemployed or away from work because of illness there is a higher risk of being poor. These studies also show that households headed by a farmer face a risk of poverty well above the average. In 1987, 35 per cent of farmer-headed households had incomes which were below the "relative poverty line" of half of average national disposable income calculated on a per adult equivalent basis. Furthermore, as a proportion of *all* households which were below this poverty line, farm households accounted for a substantial share — 24 per cent — as compared with their representation in the national population of households — which was about 14 per cent.

Within the farming category the risk of poverty varies by the farm size of the household. Confining attention to households where the head was under 66 years and using a relative poverty line of 60 per cent of average income, together with a basic deprivation criterion, (Whelan, 1994) showed that the poverty risk varied from 7.6 per cent for farming households with over 100 acres to 28.4 per cent for those on less than 50 acres. Within a wider range of social class groupings, the under-50-acre farming households had the third highest percentage in poverty next to agricultural workers (38.5 per cent) and unskilled manual workers (47.9 per cent).

Most landholders have adapted quite rationally to market opportunities and constraints (Hannan and Commins, 1992: 84–7). Those on larger holdings have moved towards modern commercial farming, intensifying production and increasing output, frequently supplementing earnings from the farm by other sources of income. Others, on insufficient land resources, have taken up off-farm employment where the opportunities were available and their own job qualifications were adequate. Clearly, there remains an impoverished category of small-holders who are unable, for various reasons, to supplement farming income by non-farm earnings and are mainly dependent on state welfare payments. These now constitute one of the main recruitment bases for poverty in Ireland (Hannan and Commins, 1992: 104).

The purposes of this chapter are:

(1) To identify the main distinguishing features of small-scale farming in Ireland

(2) To trace the evolution of agricultural restructuring over the past three decades and explain the exclusion of categories of farmers from mainstream agricultural and other economic activity

(3) To review the policy responses to this restructuring and exclusion

(4) To assess the future prospects for the small-scale farming households and identify the policy options for reducing their risk of impoverishment.

CHARACTERISTICS OF SMALL-SCALE FARMING

The comparatively high incidence of farming households in the national population is related, in the first instance, to the historical and contemporary significance of agriculture in the national and rural economy, although the relative importance of farming activity has been declining in recent decades. In 1960 agriculture accounted for a quarter of Gross Domestic Product (GDP), for just over one-third of national employment and for half of the value of the country's exports. The corresponding proportions currently are 9 per cent, 14 per cent and 20 per cent, but these figures are considerably higher than those for the 12 EU Member States (where the proportions are 2.8 per cent, 5.8 per cent and 8.9 per cent respectively). In regard to agriculture's share of employment and GDP in the EU countries, only Greece exceeds the Irish figures.

National statistics of this kind obscure the high degree of rurality in Ireland as well as the significance of agriculture in the rural economy. The reason for this is that the inordinate size of the Dublin metropolitan area accounts for one-third of the population in the State. Thus, outside this single area, 60 per cent of the population live in rural areas (places outside centres of 1,500 persons or more) and the agricultural population accounts for about one-third of this rural category.

Apart from its dominance in the rural economy, Irish agriculture is characterised by family-operated farm units. In 1991, a total of 312,729 persons had undertaken some farmwork over a 12-month period (excluding casual, contract and relief workers). Of these, 96 per cent were family workers, and of these family workers, 81 per cent were farmholders or spouses of holders. Thus, although farm labourers may have a higher *risk* of poverty than farmers, their small absolute numbers mean that the *incidence* of their poverty nationally is much lower.

Poverty in farming households is inextricably linked to small-scale farming but small-scale farms are associated, in turn, with particular structural, demographic and regional characteristics. While the size of a farm is generally measured in map area — or, more precisely, the agricultural area used for farming (AAU) — a more useful measure of scale is economic size, as measured by European size units (ESUs). On this latter measure, a farm's various activities are reckoned on a common criterion by applying standardised economic coefficients, in the form of Standard Gross Margins, to the physical activity recorded on the farm on a per-hectare basis for crops and on a per-head basis for livestock.

The 1991 Census of Agriculture classified farms on an ESU basis. The average size for the country's 170,600 farms was 11.6 ESUs but 43 per cent of farms had less than 4 ESUs. At the other end of the size scale were farms over 16 ESUs, which accounted for 23 per cent of the total.

In general, small-scale farming is associated with cattle, sheep or mixed livestock production. By contrast, most large-scale farms are involved in dairying. Tillage is a relatively unimportant enterprise on Irish farms and also tends to be concentrated on the larger farms (Table 3.1). Small farms have poorer soils. Data from the Teagasc National Farm Survey show that whereas less than 1 per cent of farms over 40 ESUs are in Soil Group 3 (having a limited use range), the corresponding proportion for farms under 4 ESUs is over one-quarter.

The characteristics of the farmholder also vary by farm size (Table 3.1). The percentages of holders with formal training in agriculture increase progressively with the scale of farming, while the percentages of older farmers decline. Also, the older the age category among farmers, the higher the percentages of women farmholders. The proportions of farmholders with occupations other than farming decline consistently as farm size increases. Related to this, the total labour input on the smaller farms is lower than on the larger farms. Almost all farms over 16 ESUs had labour inputs equivalent to one annual work unit (AWU) compared to 44 per cent on farms with less than 4 ESUs.

Table 3.1: Characteristics of Farms and Farmholders in the State by Economic Size Class (ESUs), 1991

Type of Farm	ESUs					
	<4	4–8	8–16	16–40	40 +	Total
	Per Cent of Farms					
Dairying	2.9	13.6	13.5	61.8	69.4	24.4
Cattle	68.6	46.6	20.8	5.9	1.5	42.1
Sheep	7.2	13.3	12.6	6.5	2.1	8.8
Mixed livestock	18.1	21.1	21.6	14.2	7.5	17.9
Crops and livestock	0.8	2.1	3.8	5.0	5.7	2.5
Tillage	1.5	2.4	3.4	4.8	9.0	2.9
Other	1.0	1.0	1.3	1.7	4.8	1.4
	Per Cent of Holders					
Aged 65 years +	32.2	21.9	15.8	11.0	9.9	22.7
With formal training	3.8	10.3	19.1	32.4	42.6	14.6
With non-farm occupation	41.4	26.6	15.5	7.2	5.2	26.6
With one AWU	44.3	75.3	87.9	94.4	95.6	68.7

Source: Derived from Census of Agriculture 1991 (CSO, 1994).

Although differing in its regional manifestation, small-scale farming is widespread throughout the country — one-third of farms in Leinster and Munster combined and over 55 per cent of farms in Connacht and Ulster combined were below 4 ESUs in 1991. However, taking the average ESU per farm on a county basis, it is possible to discern four reasonably coherent gradations of county from the smallest farm counties of the north-west, to the larger farm counties to the south-east (Figure 3.1 and Appendix Table A3.1). Not alone does the size of farm increase progressively in the north-west to south-east direction, but the level of intensification also increases — as evidenced by the greater number of ESUs per hectare (Appendix Table A3.2). Just over one-third of the state's farms are in the six small farm counties but they account for only one-sixth of the total ESUs in the State.

Also associated with small-scale farming is the fragmentation of holdings into separate parcels. Although the differences between the groups of counties are not substantial, fragmentation on smaller holdings obviously means a splintering into pieces of more limited area than on larger holdings.

RESTRUCTURING IN THE AGRICULTURAL SECTOR

The contemporary pattern of agricultural structures and production is the outcome of several decades of economic and social adjustment in the rural economy. A series of interrelated transformation processes has had pronounced and differentiating impacts on regions and socio-economic groups. Unfortunately, pending the full publication of the 1991 Census of Agriculture and the 1991 Census of Population, it is not possible to get a complete picture of the changes that have occurred. There is also a problem in establishing a consistent statistical series because of changes in definition and methodology in the different enumerations. Nevertheless, the dominant trends, especially since 1960, can be discerned, as described below.

Technology

A major driving force in agricultural restructuring is technology, not just in terms of machinery, but, more recently, including biochemical and information technology. While some innovations in technology may be intrinsically scale-neutral, they are not neutral in their socio-economic impacts as their successful adoption may call for levels of knowledge, skill and management ability which are not randomly distributed among the farm population. Machine technology, however, tends to be scale-related, being associated with the larger production units. In 1993 the asset value of machinery on farms of over 100 hectares (ha) was over 13 times the value of that on farms of between 10 and 30 ha; moreover, a ratio of this order of magnitude prevailed for similar farming systems.

An analysis of the longer-term adoption and diffusion of farm mechanisation in Ireland has shown that there is a clear gradation pattern, whereby tractor ownership has extended north-westwards from some key clusters of early adopters in the east and south. This has resulted in changes in the distribution of farm sizes, tillage crops and the numbers of hired workers acting as important influences in dictating the uneven configuration of spatial patterns (Walsh, 1992).

Figure 3.1: Average European Size Units per Farm, 1991

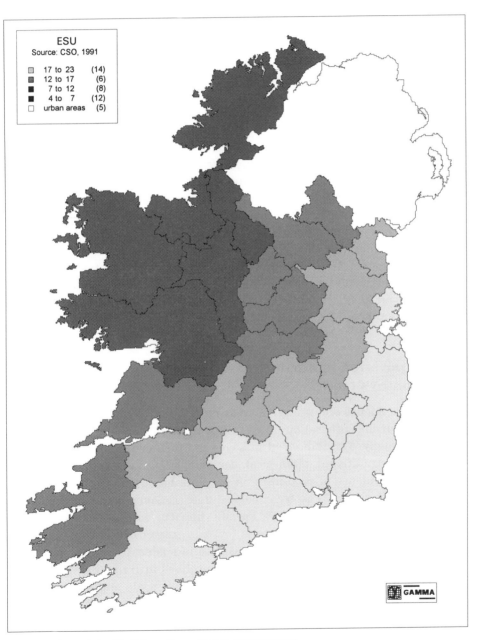

Rising Costs of Production

In association with the emergence of technologically-based agriculture, modern farming has come to depend increasingly on purchased inputs. This trend pushes up the cost of production, especially in years of inflation and high interest rates.

From the 1950s to the 1970s total net expenses (direct costs plus overheads) on Irish farms ranged between 35 and 60 per cent of the value of gross farm output, though remaining below 50 per cent for nearly all farm-size categories. Since 1980, costs annually have generally been above 60 per cent of output value. In 1993 the proportion was 66 per cent on the average farm nationally, but it was as high as 71 per cent on farms of over 100 ha. In absolute figures, costs on farms of over 100 ha were 14 times higher than on farms of between 10 and 20 ha, but, with their greater value of output, the larger farms were in a better position to absorb the higher incidence of costs.

Costs also vary by farm system, tending to be four to five times higher on dairy farms than on cattle farms. Dairy farms, however, have relatively high price supports and, with their numbers declining, their average volume of output has increased. By contrast, many farmers on cattle farms have remained outside the high-cost, high-output spiral, but, as will be shown later, their incomes are much lower than those of dairy farmers.

Incorporation in Agribusiness Systems and Global Market Systems

The consequence of farming's increasing reliance on purchased inputs is the growing integration of agricultural production into the industrial economy. Agri-industrial linkages are further intensified by the decline of traditional, often local, commodity markets and the more direct dependence of producers on markets based on centralised industrial processing. The technological and economic forces of capital accumulation have their own specific impacts on the agribusiness complex — for example, in trends towards greater concentration, oligopolistic structures, internationalisation of business and diversification of activities. Food processing co-operatives in Ireland clearly exemplify this trend in their increased economic scale and geographic range. Small farmer-owned co-operatives have been drastically reduced in number and replaced by much larger integrated and diversely capitalised organisations, some having made significant acquisitions in the EU and US.

Restructuring in agribusiness has knock-on effects at farm level. Large multiples in food distribution oblige processors to produce to their specifications as regards quality, delivery and presentation. They can exert pressures on manufacturing profit margins, which indirectly squeeze the revenues available to farmers. To stay in business, farmers must, in turn, carry out new investments (for example, in milk-handling equipment), change production practices or improve the quality of their products. In this way, modern farming has become increasingly implicated into a complex food chain in which the production component is subordinated to the needs of agribusiness (Tovey, 1991) and farmers lose a degree of control over production decisions (Shutes, 1991: 13). Those who are unwilling to respond to this trend, or are unable to do so because of inadequate resources, tend to become marginalised from mainstream agricultural activity.

Enlargement of Scale and Farm Consolidation

The relentless pressure to maintain economic viability in farming has obliged farm operators to enlarge the scale of the farm business by acquiring extra land and/or intensifying the scale of farming operations on their existing holdings. Between 1960 and 1980, holding numbers declined by 9 per cent, the decline in farms below 20 ha being only partly countered by increases in holdings above this size level. The trends since 1980 are not directly comparable with earlier years because of changes in the methods of enumeration at the 1991 Census of Agriculture. Part of the discontinuity is explained by the fact that the 1991 Census excluded farms whose area farmed was less than 1 ha, unless intensive agricultural production was undertaken on them. The more rigorous screening procedures used in 1991 would appear to have resulted in the elimination of over 30,000 of the smaller or more marginal units which were included in the coverage of EC Farm Structures Surveys during the 1980s (Central Statistics Office, 1994: 8). This "loss" of holdings would seem to be relatively greater in the north-west, which is, in fact, the area where the highest rate of holding consolidation had taken place between 1960 and 1980 (Hannan and Commins, 1993: 16–52). Thus, there has been an increasing disengagement from significant agricultural production by small landholders, and the resultant amalgamation of farms. Nevertheless, in the regions where this process has been most pronounced, the scale and intensity of farm businesses are still comparatively low, as we have seen.

Scale enlargement can be achieved by renting in land, but seemingly renting is predominantly used by the larger farms. In 1991, at national level, farms over 50 ha represented 11.5 per cent of all farms but accounted for 23 per cent of farms renting land and 51.1 per cent of the area being rented.

The enlargement of scale is clearly observable in the average size of herd or flock for the major livestock enterprises (Table 3.2). Pig production, in particular, which had been characteristic of small-scale farming, has now become a large-scale commercialised activity.

Table 3.2: Average Number of Animals per Farm for Specific Enterprises

Enterprises	1973	1981	1989	1991*
Dairy Cows	9.9	15.8	24.5	27.1
Cattle (Total)	28.4	30.8	35.3	45.6
Sheep	49.0	54.4	107.2	162.1
Pigs	29.0	102.0	400.2	453.8

*   Data for 1991 are not directly comparable with those of earlier years
Source: Agriculture and Food Policy Review Group (Department of Agriculture and Food, 1990); Census of Agriculture, 1991 (CSO, 1994).

Specialisation and Concentration of Production

The increasing average size of farm enterprises does not result solely from expansion in these enterprises per se, but also from contraction in the numbers of farms involved. Specialisation refers to the tendency for the numbers of farms having several enterprises to decline. Between 1973 and 1989, the numbers of holdings having dairy cows fell by one-half while cattle farms decreased by over one-quarter.

It will be clear from the above (especially from Table 3.2) that there has been concentration of production in a narrowing band of farm sizes. It is estimated that the top 20 per cent of Irish farms — in terms of farm income — account for 40 per cent of agricultural land, but produce 60 per cent of farm output. Again, this pattern of concentration has regional variations. Table 3.3 shows, for example, that in the small-farm counties dairy cow numbers have declined since 1960, and while the decline in cow numbers overtook all regions in the

1980s (under policy changes), the rates of decrease were not as large as in the small-farm counties. On the other hand, the small-farm counties increased their numbers of "other cows" and sheep, but, very significantly, the rates of increase were actually slower than for the other groupings of counties. So, even for what might be deemed the typical western farm systems, their rates of growth were surpassed by those in the rest of the country in the 1980s.

Table 3.3: Percentage Change in Livestock Numbers

Years	Dairy Cows*	Other Cows*	All Cattle	Sheep	Pigs	Crops
Large-Farm Counties						
1960–80	+105.2[†]	+2.4[†]	+55.4	-17.8	+0.4	-31.7
1980–91	-13.3	+83.4	+6.8	+188.2	+7.5	-2.2
Medium-to-Large-Farm Counties						
1960–80	+75.9[†]	+10.6[†]	+35.6	-42.3	-7.7	-57.8
1980–91	-16.2	+84.7	+1.5	+277.9	+58.1	+28.2
Medium-to-Small-Farm Counties						
1960–80	+59.01[†]	+56.2[†]	+43.2	-22.2	+38.5	-71.4
1980–91	-23.8	+95.2	-0.7	+204.6	+54.7	-62.3
Small-Farm Counties						
1960–80	-9.9[†]	+229.7[†]	+45.2	-22.3	+1.7	-58.3
1980–91	-36.7	+47.7	-10.4	+122.2	-14.4	-64.6

*   Including heifers-in-calf.
†   Estimated.
Source: Derived from Census of Agriculture (various years).

In the shifting regional pattern of agricultural production and with the different rates of change over the past decade, the small farm counties have lost their 1980 national share of all the major farm enterprises (Table 3.4).

The loss is most pronounced in respect of dairy cows, cereals, pigs and potatoes — enterprises that characterised the western economy of small-scale, mixed farming. Potato growing, in particular, has moved from the smaller to the larger counties. While the small farm counties in fact had increased their absolute numbers of non-dairy

cows and sheep during the 1980s, the rates of increase were not sufficient to allow the region to retain its national share of these enterprises. By contrast, the large-farm counties increased their share of
the major enterprises, except in the case of pigs (Table 3.4). Thus, it
could be said that farming in the small-farm counties has become
more specialised than in the larger-farm counties. However, this specialisation is not manifested in a focus on a reduced number of highly
commercialised enterprises, but in a regression to low-income cattle
and sheep farming.

Table 3.4: Changes in the Percentage National Share of Farm Enterprises(Numbers and Hectares by Categories of County)

Year	Dairy* Cows	Other* Cows	All Cattle	Sheep	Pigs	Cereals	Potatoes
Large-Farm Counties							
1960	34.7[†]	34.7[†]	31.0	28.9	49.5	50.6	23.0
1980	43.3	21.8	33.0	31.0	45.8	56.9	31.1
1991	46.3	23.2	35.3	33.0	39.0	58.1	45.8
Medium-to-Large-Farm Counties							
1960	20.6[†]	20.6[†]	21.8	13.4	15.8	20.4	15.0
1980	22.0	13.9	20.3	10.2	13.5	27.5	18.4
1991	22.8	15.0	20.6	14.2	16.8	31.4	28.5
Medium-to-Small-Farm Counties							
1960	24.4[†]	24.4[†]	24.3	13.8	23.9	13.9	25.3
1980	23.6	23.3	23.9	14.1	30.6	7.8	15.2
1991	22.2	26.5	23.7	15.9	37.4	5.7	4.8
Small-Farm Counties							
1960	20.3[†]	20.3[†]	22.9	43.9	10.8	15.2	36.8
1980	11.5	41.0	22.8	44.8	10.1	7.8	35.2
1991	8.7	35.3	20.4	36.8	6.9	4.9	20.8

*   Including heifers-in-calf.
†   Estimates.
Source: Derived from Census of Agriculture (various years).

Divergence in Farm Incomes

The spatial polarisation of farm production is inevitably reflected in the divergence of farm incomes. Data are not available for different regions over time, but information for farm-size categories and systems are sufficient to illustrate the trends. From the 1950s to the mid-1980s, and especially after 1972, the rate of increase in average family farm income was greater on the larger farms than on the smaller ones (Breen et al., 1990: 199). From the mid-1980s onwards, the higher rates of increase occurred in the medium-to-large farms (30–50 ha) rather than on the very large holdings. In this latter period, it appears that the type of enterprise on the farm rather than size of farm itself has become a more salient feature of high-income farming. Table 3.5 shows indices of changes in annual family farm incomes per farm for the years 1984–93. The tabulation excludes minor farming systems, but relates to over 90 per cent of all farms in the State. Clearly, there has been a growing income divergence between farms with a dairy enterprise and those relying mainly on cattle or sheep. Dairy farms, on average, are not quite as large as sheep farms but they have a higher percentage of the better soils. In 1993, incomes on dairy farms were over five times those on cattle farms.

In considering farm-income trends, a number of factors need to be taken into account. First, those farmers who are currently on low incomes are "survivors" from a larger cohort, many of whom have already withdrawn from farming activity, either partially or totally. Thus, the full significance of the economic marginalisation of smallholders is not revealed in the figures for farm-income trends on *existing farms*. Second, as against this, among the current "residual" farming population 27 per cent of farmholders and 37 per cent of holders' spouses have another gainful activity. There are also farm households where some income for household purposes may be available from the employment of other family members. Third, households may receive social transfer payments such as social welfare allowances (for example, pensions) and unemployment assistance. Fourth, gross incomes contain an element of subsidisation under agricultural policies, while they are also affected by state income transfers and taxation policies — factors which can influence the consumption levels of the farm household.

This last point is taken up in a later section (see Table 3.8). Here the reader's attention is drawn to the changing composition of gross household income in farm households over time.

Table 3.5: Index of Changes in Family Farm Income per Farm, by Major Farming Systems, 1984–93

	Farm System			
Year	Dairying	Dairying and Cattle	Mainly Sheep	Cattle
1984	100	100	100	100
1985	111	89	111	80
1986	95	80	93	69
1987	121	104	133	94
1988	162	151	156	113
1989	175	176	117	82
1990	142	147	138	105
1991	136	123	118	99
1992	171	153	130	128
1993	191	N.A.	126	142
1992 Characteristics				
UAA per Farm	30.3	38.0	31.1	20.3
% on Good Soil	49.4	44.3	35.9	35.3
Family farm income per farm (£)	15,336	13,466	4,844	2,943

N.A. = Not available.
Source: Derived from Teagasc National Farm Survey (various years).

Labour Decline and Multiple Income Sources

Historically, decline in the *total* farm labour force has been very much influenced by the relatively high ratio of departure among "relatives assisting" on holdings. In more recent decades, farm labour-force decline is caused more by the non-entry of relatives and assistants and the movement of farm operators to other employment, not necessarily by changing residence. This is reflected in a declining farmer-to-holding ratio, a trend which has been more significant on the smaller holdings (Hannan and Commins, 1993: 13–14). It is also to be seen in the fact that on farms under 50 acres (20 ha) non-farm-earned income accounted for 40 per cent of gross income in 1987 compared to approximately 25 per cent in 1973 (Table 3.6). Indeed, on farms below

this size, farm income is now the minor part of gross-household income when both non-farm earned incomes and State transfer payments are taken into consideration (1987 figures — see Table 3.6).
Even on the large farms of over 100 acres, non-farm incomes accounted for over one-fifth of gross household income in 1987. Perhaps
the most significant feature of the changing composition of farm
household incomes is that, in *absolute* figures, the non-farm incomes
earned by the households on the 100-acre-plus farms were marginally
higher than for the other farm-size categories. This is largely a result
of their different household structures and the presence of young
adult earners in the larger-farm households.

Table 3.6: Income Sources as Percentage of Gross Household Income of Rural Farm Households, by Area Farmed, 1973 and 1987

Year	<30 acres	30–50 acres	50–100 acres	100 + acres	Total
Farm Income					
1973	43.5	67.7	77.3	87.0	70.1
1987	20.3	35.9	59.4	74.0	54.2
Other Direct Income					
1973	30.3	20.0	17.2	10.5	19.1
1987	39.3	39.6	26.5	18.5	28.2
Transfer Payments					
1973	26.1	12.3	5.5	2.5	10.8
1987	40.3	24.5	14.0	7.5	17.6

Source: Derived from Household Budget Survey 1973, and 1987 (CSO, 1977;
CSO, 1990).

Viability of Farms and Farm Households

Given the restructuring process in the farm economy, as outlined in
the foregoing sections, a central question now concerns the contemporary viability status of many farms as economic units. The Teagasc
National Farm Survey assesses the economic viability of a farm as a
holding capable of:

(1) Remunerating family labour at the average industrial wage

(2)   Giving a 5 per cent return to non-land assets.

On this rather rigorous basis, and on using 1992 and 1993 figures, it was estimated that no more than one-third of the country's farms could be deemed economically viable. (This proportion will vary by a few percentage points on a year-to-year basis because of fluctuations in farm incomes.) In 1992, viable farms contributed 63 per cent of gross output and earned about 70 per cent of family farm income (Power and Roche, 1993: 6–39). However, two other factors need to be taken into account here. One is whether or not the farmholder and/or spouse has/have gainful employment besides farming. The problems of the non-viable farming category are reduced to the extent that they can draw on incomes earned from non-farm jobs. The second factor is that the viability of farming is also associated with the composition of the farm household and particularly its capacity to reproduce itself. The National Farm Survey regards farm households as "demographically non-viable" where the holder is over 55 years old and there is nobody else under 45 years in the household.

Based on these three criteria — economic viability, "other job status" and demographic viability — the 1992 National Farm Survey permits a breakdown of 159,000 Irish farms as shown in Figure 3.2.

While these figures must be taken as broad orders of magnitude, rather than very close estimates, they are sufficient to illustrate the scale of the low-income problem in Irish farming. This is represented by two main categories. One is the 32,000 households on economically non-viable farms (on the definition used), composed predominantly of older people, and in which neither the householder nor the spouse has an off-farm job. Further analysis of this category (Commins and Frawley, 1995) showed that their average family farm income in 1993 was approximately £2,400, of which direct farm-income payments (non-price compensatory payments and premia — see below) accounted for £1,100. The second low farm-income category is made up of the 48,000 households which are economically non-viable, and have no other employment, although having a "good" household demographic structure. Average farm income for this category in 1993 was £4,600, with direct farm-income payments making up £1,900 of this. By contrast, economically viable farms earned family farm incomes of £19,300 (in 1993), with direct payments contributing £3,450 of this amount.

Figure 3.2: Estimated Number of Irish Farms by Viability Classification, 1992

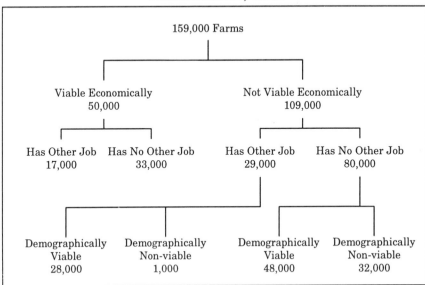

Note: The proportion of the economically viable category with demographically non-viable households was relatively small and therefore not shown separately.

Source: Derived from author's analysis of Teagasc National Farm Survey

This broad division of the national farm population is confirmed by a cluster analysis of two samples of farms — one in north-east Connacht and another in the perimeter counties of Dublin (Commins, 1994). In these regions three clusters of small-farm types were discerned as follows:

(1) Older farmers, mostly in their late sixties, many unmarried, on very small holdings, who were retreating into retirement or semi-retired status. Most had cattle and sheep, but a minority had only very limited levels of farm activity. Generally, these relied heavily on pensions and other transfer payments.

(2) Older than average farmers in their late fifties or early sixties farming full-time on medium-sized farms and with a certain commitment to farming, but with little use of modern practices and having static levels of production. Their ages, household composition and farm size precluded them from obtaining large

state income transfers. These farmed drystock but also accounted
for many of the smaller dairy farms.

(3) Comparatively young part-time farmers, having a moderate level
of farm production from cattle and sheep enterprises, but aug-
menting their farm incomes by other work.

Summarising Comment

Irish agriculture has undergone a severe process of economic rationalisation over the past three decades. The farm labour force has
been reduced substantially — from 377,000 workers in 1961 to
155,000 currently. The 1991 Census of Agriculture eliminated 30,000
holdings from the statistical record because of their minimal amount
of agricultural activity. The great majority of those who have quit
farming have left the smaller holdings. Were it not for this selective
outflow, the risk and incidence of poverty in agriculture would be
greater even than observed in recent studies. Despite these changes,
the structure that has emerged is not entirely appropriate for a modern commercial farming economy: many holdings are under the
threshold necessary to ensure future economic viability, and a considerable proportion of farm households fall below the poverty line. As
Scully (1971: 175) pointed out a quarter of a century ago, it is wrong
to assume that as farmers become fewer in number they all become
better off financially.

It is true that a considerable proportion of farmers have adapted
successfully to the treadmill of change. These have modernised their
businesses and concentrated on enterprises which allowed them to
capture the profits of generous price support policies (see below).

Also making a successful accommodation to structural change
were those who obtained other employment (Hannan and Commins,
1992), especially if they managed to combine off-farm work with
keeping sufficient numbers of livestock to draw down an increasing
amount of direct subsidy payments.

The process of rationalisation has uneven impacts on regions, reflecting the different mix of farm resources. The small-farm counties
of the north-west lost their national share of production for all enterprises during the 1980s. Even when these small-farm counties increased their production (for non-dairy cows), they did so at a lesser
rate of growth than in the large-farm counties of the south-east —
which had also claimed the growth in milk production. Consequently,
in the small-farm counties, the intensity of resource use per farm —

as measured by ESUs per hectare — is now little more than half of what it is in the large-farm counties. Simply stated, the traditional small-farm economy of the west and north-west has been severely disrupted and transformed in three decades.

POLICY RESPONSES

How have policy measures and development programmes related to this longer-term process of restructuring in Irish agriculture? Agriculture is influenced not only by policies, which by common understanding are deemed to be "agricultural", but also by a variety of more general economic and social policies. To answer the question posed within the limits of space available, it will be convenient to order the following discussion under six headings:

(1)   Market price supports

(2)   Structural and developmental policies

(3)   Direct income subsidisation

(4)   Diversification from conventional farming

(5)   Employment and rural development

(6)   State transfers and taxation.

Market Price Supports

A system of supporting prices received by farmers for certain products sold was introduced in the 1930s and expanded to include other products in later decades. The initial aim was to encourage production, but, over time, as output reached self-sufficiency levels, price supports took on a protective role, shielding agriculture from economic forces and helping to maintain farmer incomes and to slow down the loss of farmer numbers. EC membership in 1973 consolidated the national market support system but what had become an increasingly onerous burden on the Irish exchequer was shifted onto the European taxpayer under the Common Agricultural Policy (CAP) (Matthews, 1982).

The original design of the CAP envisaged that one-third of its budget would be devoted to structural measures — for example, to improve the structure of holdings, promote improved farming methods, support retraining, provide funds for capital investment and enhance farm viability. This ratio was soon abandoned and eventually whittled down to about 5 per cent as market support expenditure increased. One reason for this is that price supports were 100 per cent funded by the Community while structural measures had to be part-funded by member states. Clearly, higher product prices had far greater appeal to farmer organisations and political leaders than had non-price measures.

Of the total of Ireland's receipts from the EC over the past two decades, almost three-quarters came from the Agricultural Fund to support farm prices. In general, the allocations across commodities have been biased towards large farms and/or capital intensive operations, with a consequent widening of the gap in income and wealth between the small and large farms (Breen et al., 1990: 196). In particular, dairying, rather than drystock and sheep production, has benefited more directly and substantially from price supports. Income divergence was accentuated to the extent that farm profits became capitalised into land values, as happens when price guarantees reduce commercial uncertainties. Irish land values rose steeply in the 1970s and as the State withdrew from its involvement in land structuring activities (see below) small farmers with limited capital found themselves excluded from the land market.

The EC Commission had long recognised the negative aspects of price support policy but found it difficult to change matters, in particular because the social functions of the CAP provided an alibi often exploited by those opposing any serious effort to cut back on the indiscriminate support it granted (CEC, 1988). During 1983–91, under pressure of growing budgetary costs and increasing surpluses, the Community brought in more restrictive measures — such as marketing quotas — but when these proved inadequate to deal with the problems, even more rigorous reforms were implemented in 1992. These represented a significant step in switching from market price supports to other methods such as direct supporting of incomes and structural measures, but the impact of these reforms remains to be seen.

Structural and Developmental Policies

Generally, structural and developmental policies are taken as covering non-price/market measures but here the term is used in a restricted sense to exclude farm diversification and direct subsidisation (which are taken up separately below).

From the early part of the century until the 1970s, the State, through the Irish Land Commission, pursued a policy of structural improvement of uneconomic holdings, with special emphasis on the relief of acute land congestion in the western counties. The Commission had considerable powers to acquire land for the enlargement of small holdings, consolidation of fragmented holdings, and the creation of new holdings — sometimes for migrants from one part of the country to another.

In the 1970s, although the Commission's acquisitions amounted to 30,000 acres annually, the programme encountered difficulties. Acquisitions were slow and legally contentious; with the pool of large estates depleted, individual acquisitions yielded fewer acres and were of poor quality; and with too many applications for too little land the reallocations being made were still insufficient to bring uneconomic holdings up to standard size.

An Interdepartmental Committee on Land Structure Reform, reporting in 1978, recommended a system of controlling market transactions in a way that would channel land coming on the market to "priority land applicants" (IDCLSR, 1978). In a subsequent White Paper (WP, 1980) the Government accepted the principle of intervention in the land market in favour of "progressive small farmers". In the event, however, no policy action was taken. Despite repeated election promises and official declarations of intent to formulate new land policies during the 1980s, the issue was simply allowed to drift (facilitated by frequent changes of government or ministers), until overtaken by a new set of contextual conditions dictated by the over-production of agricultural commodities under the EC's price support policies. Land structure issues and especially the land needs of small farmers came off the policy agenda and farmers on uneconomic holdings were advised to turn to alternative enterprises or non-farm sources of income.

Currently, the nearest parallel to the Land Commission's redistributive policies is a subsidy scheme for eligible milk producers (those with quotas below 30,000 gallons) to help them to purchase milk quotas. This operates in conjunction with measures to restrict the outflow of milk quotas from disadvantaged areas. Priority categories of producers in these areas will have access to all of the quota that is offered for sale in their areas before it is made available elsewhere.

In regard to farm development policies Ireland's entry to the EC and the change-over to the CAP marked a definite relaxation of emphasis on "the small-farm problem". In the early 1960s, an Inter-

Departmental Committee was established "to consider and report on sound and practicable measures to deal with the special problems of agriculture in the western part of the country where small farms predominate" (IDCPSWF, 1962: 5). The Committee saw no single solution to this problem, but recommended some imaginative actions under structural policy, farm development and marketing policy, rural development programmes, and educational and social policy. Its proposals influenced a number of measures including:

(1) A Small-Farm (Incentive Bonus) Scheme, which encouraged participants to reach defined production targets

(2) A pilot areas development programme based on providing intensive support systems

(3) Other support schemes, which graded subsidies according to the scale of the farm business

(4) More intensive advisory services in the small-farm counties.

Following EC entry, national programmes for farm development were superseded by the EC-instigated Farm Modernisation Scheme (FMS) and its successor, the Farm Improvement Programme (FIP). The FMS categorised farmers as "commercial", "development" or "other", depending on their actual or potential capacity to generate a given target income and to attain viability. The most generous grants and advisory attention were devoted to the development category. However, Connacht and Ulster had a much lower participation rate for development farmers than Munster and Leinster. Between 1975 and 1982, almost 60 per cent of expenditure on the scheme went to the 30 per cent of farms classified as "commercial" or "development" (Kelleher and O'Mahony, 1984: 94).

In the FIP, introduced in 1986, the eligibility criteria were much more favourable to the inclusion of small farmers, partly because of the general shift away from any policies which exacerbated increases in production. At least much of the early investment under the FIP went towards improving working conditions on smaller holdings, but without directly expanding output — through new buildings, storage facilities and labour saving measures, for example (O'Hara, 1986: 54–5).

The remaining point to be made here relates to the provision of agricultural advisory services. Public funding restrictions have obliged development agencies to introduce charges for services. This has also resulted in a trend towards the privatisation of services and their supply by consultancy firms. These factors have disfavoured the small farmer, although, more recently, Teagasc (the national agricultural development authority) has established a service to enhance farm viability, for which it has received special allocations from the Budget.

Direct Subsidisation of Incomes

While price policies, structural policies and farm-development programmes were biased against small-scale farming, forms of direct income subsidisation leaned in the opposite direction. Recognising the deficiencies in the conventional system of price subsidies, the EC introduced regionally-specific programmes in the mid-1970s. Of most interest to Ireland was a directive which provided for policy measures to prevent large-scale population decline in areas of natural handicap. To compensate for such handicap, farmers in these "disadvantaged areas" receive payments directly (that is, not through the market), based on the number and type of livestock held. These "headage payments" have become a substantial component of non-price transfers in Ireland because of increases in the amounts payable and also the extension of the disadvantaged areas to cover 72 per cent of the country. Furthermore, under special livestock premia schemes, direct payments are also available to some farmers throughout the country. Between 1988 and 1993, total yearly direct payments to farmers under all headage and premium schemes doubled to £350 million and are expected to reach £600 million under CAP reform arrangements.

Coming to farm level, and using 1993 data, five observations may be made about the role of direct subsidies:

(1) For the average farm they amounted to 27 per cent of family farm income (Table 3.7).

(2) Their contribution to farm income varied widely by farm size and system, representing nearly 40 per cent of income on cattle farms (when both cattle systems were combined) and as much as 80 per cent on sheep farms.

(3) Other analyses (Commins and Frawley, 1995) show that increases in the absolute level of direct subsidies have not had a commensurate impact on the level of family farm income on cattle and sheep farms — their effect over recent years has been simply to maintain the level of subsistence incomes on these

farms and thus cover up a real decline in the conventional market income component of their earnings.

(4) As both the cattle systems together with the sheep system account for 65 per cent of all farms, it may be said that two-thirds of the country's farms depend on direct subsidies for over half of their earnings.

(5) As farms increase in size, the value of the subsidies also increases (Table 3.7).

Table 3.7: Average Direct Subsidy per Farm (£), by Farm Size and System and as a Percentage of Family Farm Income (FFI), 1993

System	< 10	10–20	20–30	30–50	50–100	100+	Hill	All
	Farm Size (ha)							
Dairying	161	302	728	1,020	1,965	4,493	1,010	879
% of FFI	5.0	3.5	4.8	4.8	5.6	6.6	14.0	5.1
Dairying & other	—	1,157	2,112	2,481	5,204	11,290	—	2,288
% of FFI	—	19.7	25.8	19.1	20.5	23.9	—	21.9
Cattle Rearing	442	1,284	2,671	3,196	—	—	964	1,339
% of FFI	54.8	47.5	62.1	59.6	—	—	59.2	52.3
Other Cattle	250	884	1,304	2,468	4,140	7,925	889	1,226
% of FFI	25.1	31.9	24.2	40.4	33.3	59.6	44.5	33.1
Sheep	1,257	2,263	4,348	7,597	10,259	15,156	4,877	4,682
% of FFI	56.5	71.3	76.9	75.0	67.3	91.0	110.7	80.4
All Farms	435	1,096	1,859	2,928	5,450	13,408	2,136	2,158
% of FFI	29.6	26.3	21.5	21.9	23.1	36.2	76.8	26.7

Source: Derived from Teagasc National Farm Survey 1993 (Power and Roche, 1994).

However, in relation to this last point, there are relatively few cattle and sheep farms in the large-size categories. Nevertheless, the conclusion must be that direct subsidies which are based primarily on a non-market or compensatory rationale — and which do help, in fact, to redress the distributive bias in market policies favouring large-scale producers — have their own regressive effects among their particular beneficiaries.

Diversification from Conventional Farming

"Diversification" refers to the diversion of resources from conventional production, to alternative enterprises on the farm. It excludes off-farm work. Various programmes (such as the Operational Programme for Rural Development and the LEADER Programme) support diversification as a means of adapting to restrictive policies and possible income losses in the established systems of farming.

There is very limited information on the types of farmers who are diversifying production, or on the characteristics of their farms. One study in Co. Wicklow found that diversification tended to be associated with both the large and the small holdings, and that alternative activities yielded a relatively low contribution to the household income (Kelly et al., 1992). A more significant finding was that those who diversified were comparatively young, at an early stage in the family life cycle and relatively well-educated.

While afforestation has historically been undertaken by the State, a number of programmes in the 1980s (the EC Agricultural Development Programme for the West of Ireland, the Operational Programme for Rural Development, and the Forestry Operational Programme) provide attractive grants to farmers for planting agriculturally marginal land. In response, private-sector tree planting increased substantially over the decade.

The available research evidence on the pattern of private afforestation is limited, but reveals interesting contrasts between the small-farm and large-farm counties. A survey in the north-western counties (Kelleher, 1986) showed that most of the land planted privately in that region was accounted for by investment companies rather than farmers. Also, those farmers who did plant had larger than average holdings on which they afforested small parcels of marginal land. A more extensive analysis by Hannan and Commins (1993) found that there was a marked regional differentiation in the patterns of applications for afforestation grants. In the west and north-west the applicants tended to be forestry companies, landholders other than farmers (such as retired persons) and part-time farmers. In the Leinster and Munster counties, applications came disproportionately from full-time farmers. Paradoxically, landholders in commercial farming counties show more interest in tree-farming than do low-income farmers in the counties of poor agricultural land. This study concluded that, while there were sociocultural and attitudinal barriers to forestry among smallholders, there were also basic inconsistencies between the various income-support measures and the incentives to diversify farm-based economic activity. The gradual extension over time of a range of policy measures serving agricultural development, commodity price maintenance, diversification of farming, and income-support purposes has resulted in a situation where the impacts at the point of the intended beneficiaries can be mutually contradictory. In particular, there can be a conflict between measures which meet the short-run income and welfare needs of the farm household and the longer-term needs of resource development.

The most common mode of diversification in recent years has been farm tourism, but, for a number of reasons, this can provide only a partial solution to the problems of low-income farming. In particular, rising expectations for improved standards of accommodation, together with more rigorous eligibility criteria for grant payments (for example, the need to have higher minimal levels of facilities), mean that larger capital investment is required by the farm household. Of course, agri-tourism would not be appropriate for older persons or for those not living in areas of tourist interest.

Non-Farm Employment and Area-Based Development

It has already been seen how *farming* incomes show increasing disparity over time between large farms and small farms. However, the opposite trend is evident in the case of *gross* household income and *disposable* household income, as analyses of returns from Household Budget Surveys show for the period 1973–87 (Table 3.8). The influential factors here are the contributions made to the economy of small-farm households by non-farm-earned income, together with the operation of the taxation system (see next section). During 1960–80 dependence on non-farming occupations and income sources increased at a far greater rate in the north-west than in the east and south (Hannan and Commins, 1993: 15). In particular, farming areas near towns which benefited from a policy of dispersed industrialisation experienced a substantial switch to part-time farming, in contrast to the more remote districts.

Table 3.8: Index Changes in the Components of Household Incomes, State Transfers and in Household Composition in Rural Farm Households, 1973–87 [1973 = 100]

	Acres				
	<30	*30–50*	*50–100*	*100–200*	*Total*
Household Income Components					
Farm Income	310	293	388	439	482
Non-Farm-Earned Income	934	1,076	798	889	912
Total Direct Income	541	472	456	485	559
State Transfers	1,032	1,090	1,287	1,535	984
Gross Income	669	548	502	512	605
Direct Taxation	1,224	1,475	1,345	2,834	1,613
Disposable Income	642	518	481	479	575
State Transfer Components					
Children's Allowances	762	618	709	940	796
Unemployment Benefit/ Assistance	1,023	797	1,277	2,665	797
Old Age/Retirement Pensions	1,379	1,269	1,680	1,554	1,314
Average No. of Persons in Households					
Under 13 Years	99	67	75	102	89
Over 65 Years	103	99	127	127	107
Total Household Size	96	88	93	99	97
Unemployed	163	208	1,643	4,067	322
Retired	111	76	237	215	163
In Full-Time Education	100	85	101	111	106

Source: Derived from Household Budget Survey 1973, 1987 (CSO, 1977; CSO, 1990).

With the economic recession of the 1980s and the increasing competition for, and mobility of, international capital, it has not been possible to replicate the 1970s model of rural industrialisation. Imported capital and enterprise and the diffusion of job opportunities to rural areas favoured the employment of rural workers as *employees* — that is, without the need for capital investment on their part. Two factors have altered this pattern of employment creation. The first is that a disproportionate amount of new business establishments are going to the most urbanised regions (Hart and Gudgin, 1994: 367–80). The second is that the new programmes of rural development are based on the promotion of schemes, which require co-financing by private entrepreneurs who come forward with development proposals. In this way, development programmes tend to consolidate the asset base of those who already have a stake in the local community (in property or capital).

Taxation and State Transfers

As already noted in relation to Table 3.8, direct taxation, which increased more rapidly on the biggest farms, as well as non-farm earnings which rose faster on the smaller farms, helped to narrow the gap in disposable incomes across farm sizes. Interestingly, however, the rate of increase in state transfers rose steadily as farm size — and farm income — increased. This may seem inequitable, but a number of factors help to explain the trend, as can be seen from Table 3.8:

(1)   Although average household size declined on farms of all sizes during 1973–87, the rate of decline was least on the farms of over 100 acres.

(2)   The increase in the numbers of children under 13 years and the numbers at school were highest on the largest farms.

(3)   The increases in the numbers of persons over 65 years, and among those who were retired, were highest on both categories of farm size over 50 acres.

(4)   The numbers unemployed increased directly as farms got bigger.

Clearly, the pervasive influence of high unemployment has had its impacts on farm households where there are adult family members.

Thus, the households on the bigger farms are larger in size and more varied in composition and in income sources than those on small farms. Related to this, increases in pensions, unemployment benefits and — to a lesser extent — in children's allowances, have all been at a faster rate on the larger holdings but have had to be spread over a greater number of persons.

Summarising Comment

The macroeconomic forces of agricultural rationalisation have been accentuated by the regressive distributional impacts of commodity price-support policies, especially within the CAP. Such policies emerged in a context of concern about the inadequate level of farm incomes and, while most producers benefited to some extent, the larger-volume producers gained most. It has been noted that price-support policies frequently create powerful vested interests, making the reform of such policies politically difficult (FAO, 1987: 137). Farmers and governments have not been enthusiastic about structural or development policies and these never became as significant a feature as intended in the CAP. Irish land policy achieved some re-distribution of land, but the State withdrew from this activity in the 1970s. Basically, policies did little to alter the inter-farm inequalities of marketed output, which are rooted in differential access to the means of production.

On the other hand, state policies of rural industrialisation did much to generate local employment opportunities in the 1970s. However, the recession of the 1980s and the changing character of industrialisation, especially its transnational mobility, have made it difficult to replicate the pattern of industrial development in the 1970s. While there is growth in service employment, it is more pronounced in the commuting areas of urban centres and away from the remote small-farm areas. Policy responses to the small-farm problem now hinge very much around direct income subsidies, incentives for maintaining the environment, and forms of rural development based on maximising the economic value of local resources.

THE FUTURE: PROSPECTS AND POLICY OPTIONS

As noted above, many features of agricultural modernisation, development and restructuring dictate a pattern of change, marked by growing economic divergence between categories of farmers and between regions of the country. To some extent, this process of polarisation in farm incomes has been modified by non-farm incomes and by the differential impact of taxation. In assessing whether past trends will hold for the future, it is necessary to understand the dynamics of past agricultural adjustments and to gauge the likelihood of their continuing to influence structural change.

At this point, therefore, it would be helpful to make explicit the conceptual framework and interpretative perspectives which have underlain the analysis up to this point (see Commins, 1990).

Conceptualising Agricultural Transformation

Basically, the contemporary economic and social composition of Irish agriculture is the outcome, however much unintended, of a confluence of factors consisting of:

(1) The macroeconomic and technological forces of the market economy

(2) The role of the state and public policies

(3) The differing capabilities of individual farming households to establish "coping strategies" in face of the constraints and opportunities in the environment.

The fundamental logic of capital in agriculture — as for capital in general — is accumulation, evident in its continuous drive to increase returns to units of capital, land and labour. A particular difficulty for agriculture is that it must pursue this aim in conditions of inelastic demand for food. Capital in the agricultural sector is also limited in the extent to which it can penetrate primary production — because of the unique features of farming (for example, its subservience to nature, its extensiveness in space). However, industrial capital has permeated selective parts of the production chain, especially in adding value to farm products. Thus, although farmers as individual producers occupy an indispensable link in the food chain, the control over the conditions of production has been moving towards capital external to farming (Lewontin and Berlan, 1986). A declining share of what the consumer pays goes back to the producer. These pressures force out the economically uncompetitive farmer.

In the market economy, the state has a two-fold role. To generate its own resources, it must ensure the continuity of capital accumulation in general (and not just in agriculture). It also must promote the political acceptance and the legitimacy of the conditions under which accumulation can continue. In practice, then, the state in the capitalist economy has a set of "propellant" policies and also a set of "palliative" measures. In agriculture, the former are manifested, for example, in state support for technical innovations and in incentives to increase productivity. The latter are evident in "compensatory" measures, or in schemes which institutionalise the non-productive, consumption, environmental or public-good functions of land and farming.

In pursuing its roles of defining and defending the public interest, the state has a certain amount of autonomy from civil society. Bureaucrats and politicians may set the policy agenda based on "objective" assessments of requirements for the common good. But, there are two constraints on the state's autonomy. One is the tendency for interest groups to invade the policy-making arena with their claims on the state's resources. In fact, the state may even shape the configuration of policy-influencing groups — for example, by the manner in which it accords recognition, or otherwise, to partners in negotiation arrangements. In the case of agriculture, the more commercial farmers generally have the stronger voice in this regard. The other constraint arises from the fact that, increasingly, individual states are enmeshed in wider international networks. Specifically, in the EU context, Ireland's control over agricultural policies has been considerably reduced. Taking these factors into account, policies may be seen less as *solutions* to problems than as the *outcomes* of bargaining processes among diverse interests with unequal influence.

At the micro level of the farm household, the central elements needed to cope successfully with agricultural restructuring are market capacity — capital, land and skills — and access to life chances. But, these elements are influenced, in turn, in selective ways by both economic forces and state action.

Continuities from Past to Future

With this interpretation of the dynamics of agricultural restructuring in mind, it is possible to trace continuities between past transformations and the adjustments likely in the medium-term future.

Up until the 1940s, and even into the 1950s, the small-farm economy, concentrated in but not confined to the western regions, was effectively reproducing itself and its associated social structure (Hannan, 1972). From the 1960s onwards, technological developments penetrated Irish agriculture, inducing reductions in the marginal costs of production and increases in the scale of farm businesses. Large farms benefited most from this process because their owners could more easily adjust the scale of output to an optimal level. Often, the fixed costs of new technologies are too high to make it worthwhile for small-scale producers to adopt them (Breen et al., 1990: 195)

The major policy interventions in the post-1950 period were price supports. Moreover, following EC entry, the allocation of price supports across products has been biased towards commodities requiring large acreages and/or capital-intensive operations (Breen et al., 1990: 196). Rising farm incomes spurred increases in land prices, especially during the 1970s, and the State withdrew from land structuring activities. National policies, which had focused on the development of the small-farm sector, were displaced by EC schemes that favoured those with the better resources. The deleterious consequences of mainstream policies were countered, to some extent, by compensatory payments and Smallholders' Unemployment Assistance — measures which kept many farm households from falling below the poverty level, despite the regressive element in direct subsidies. In addition, taking up off-farm employment has been one of the most successful "survival strategies" adopted by smallholders (Hannan and Commins, 1992: 103). However, international recession and the mobility of enterprise capital have made it difficult to sustain the momentum of rural industrialisation.

On the experience of agricultural restructuring over the past three decades, it is difficult to envisage any significant shift in the underlying structural causes of economic marginalisation in agriculture. To alter these factors, public policy would have to pursue such a degree of regulation and control of the economic system as to make that course of action politically unrealistic. Intervention, on the scale necessary, would also mean rejecting much orthodox economic theory which endorses the dominant restructuring paradigm. The orientation of policy is in the opposite direction — towards deregulation and the free market. The CAP reforms and GATT Agreement have taken major steps towards a more market-orientated and globalised agriculture. Individual farm survival will depend, even more than in the past, on the market capacity of farmers to be efficient and competitive.

Some current trends confirm that the "shake-out" is still proceeding. Dairy herd numbers, which fell from 68,000 to 43,000 between 1983 and 1993, are expected to fall to some 28,000 herds by 2005 (Fingleton, 1995). Expectedly, the smaller-sized herds are accounting for the major share of this decline. Students currently entering training courses in agriculture come predominantly from the larger farms. The take up of non-conventional farm enterprises appears to be selective, in that they attract the younger farmers with capital, skills and enterprise (Commins and Keane, 1994: 133).

Policy Options

While, realistically, policies may not eliminate the structural causes of poverty in the farming community, they can offset the more negative consequences of structural change and have greater effect than before in reducing the risk of poverty. Essential to any approach along these lines is the more precise targeting of specific sub-groups and tailoring of responses to their particular needs.

The priority category would appear to be those 30,000, or so, farm households composed mainly of older people on low incomes. Lessons from the EU Programmes to Combat Poverty, especially the experience of "Poverty 3" in north-west Connemara (Harvey, 1994), point to the effectiveness of an integrated approach to improving basic living conditions, through actions in health care, personal social services, housing repairs and local transport schemes. Providing these in a district requires concerted action, involving a number of statutory authorities and their working with community organisations in a single partnership. Within this framework, it should also be possible to explore the feasibility of matching retiring farmers with younger farmers, so as to increase the movement of land to the latter while improving the living conditions of the former.

The other major category of concern are those on uneconomic holdings with no other source of employment. The 48,000 households in this category are likely to include a number of sub-groups. One such sub-group comprises those who could readily increase their farm incomes by improved farm practices. Studies of farm management (for example, Power and Roche, 1994) note the wide ranges in production costs and the scope for controlling costs in livestock management by relatively simple improvements in farming methods. The 1994–99 Operational Programme for Agriculture, Rural Development and Forestry provides for a "farm viability service" to focus on smaller farms with viability problems, who must increase the efficiency of their farms. This is a commendable initiative, although its effectiveness remains to be seen, given that the public financial commitment to the proposed service is 3 per cent of the overall public expenditure in the Operational Programme. (By contrast, the corresponding figure for compensatory headage payments is 57 per cent.)

For a second sub-group of non-viable farms, the main option lies in alternative farm enterprises. Studies of farm diversification (Cawley et al., 1995) show that the most realistic option for many is farm forestry, given its high level of financial support, combined with ease of management and absence of marketing problems. However, these studies also noted that while there have been improvements in the institutional resources allocated to the promotion of alternative farm enterprises, this activity was still of secondary importance for the majority of organisations concerned. In the specific case of forestry, for example, one of the obstacles to its promotion was the limited agency provision for reaching out to some categories of the potential clientèle of landholders, especially those who have been excluded from the "target groups" of the conventional farm advisory services. There is need for a much higher level of personal interaction between low-income farmers and the advisory system (Commins and Hannan, 1993: 191).

Some small-scale farmers — because they have assets and manual skills — can be enabled to start an alternative business, but again, these are likely to need training, technical assistance and specially devised funding arrangements. Experiences from the "Poverty 3 Programme" in urban Limerick and from some LEADER projects indicate that available supports can be "packaged" specially and tailored to local circumstances, to allow small-scale entrepreneurs to get a start in business (see, for example, Harvey, 1994: 31 and Thorne, 1995: 3). An important factor in this context is close personal contact between agency and client.

Another key ingredient in enterprise development is training, not in a formalised and structured sense, but in terms of personal development, capacity-building, engendering confidence and self-esteem, and developing skills in negotiation and communication.

As the conventional agricultural training courses continue to cater mainly for young people from the larger farms, the inheritors of small-scale farms will require multi-skills training to prepare them to earn a livelihood in other forms of employment besides farming. The report of the Committee on Rural Development Training (1993) recommended the establishment of a Certificate in Rural Enterprise to prepare school-leavers for multiple employment. The Operational Programme for Agriculture, Rural Development and Forestry provides for such a qualification to be delivered, by arrangement, among a number of vocational training agencies. It will be important, however, that this kind of training is located in places within reach of the more disadvantaged farming communities.

From the data presented earlier, it is quite clear that many households on small-scale farms would be poverty stricken without supplements to the income earned from farming. This is recognised in the fact that, as noted above, over half the public (national and EU) financial outlay under the Operational Programme will be absorbed by compensatory headage payments. In fact, almost 80 per cent of the national expenditure in the Operational Programme is taken up by such payments. However, there is now a question as to the willingness of the EU to continue to pay direct farm-income supports, on the basis that these are properly a member state responsibility and, thus, Community financing should be phased down over an agreed time scale. Payments to "redundant farmers" may be difficult to defend politically except in a context where general social welfare policy addresses the problems of those economically marginalised (Sheehy, 1994). Any restrictions in these payments would make it all the more necessary to target the available funds to those most in need.

Notwithstanding the rhetoric of EU declarations about combating social and economic exclusion, progress with Community social policy has been difficult — even contentious. The main policy measures have an urban-industrial bias, being concerned very much with the conditions of workers and their employment. While substantial resource transfers come to Ireland under the Structural Funds, these are primarily aimed at narrowing regional differences — that is, the gaps in average income between member states and between regions (Nolan, 1994: 293). Some Community initiatives such as Horizon and NOW are more directly concerned with excluded groups but, as with anti-poverty programmes, their local projects are comparatively few in number.

Farming communities, however, have an advantage in EU policies to the extent that criteria other than market principles or narrow technical or economic rationality are being invoked, such as the need to maintain minimum population levels in rural areas, or to protect the environment. Specifically, farmers may expect greater EU recognition of their role as providers of public goods in the form of managed landscape and an enhanced natural environment.

Overall, the point of these last remarks is to affirm that the primary responsibility for dealing with the question of low-income households in Ireland will rest with national governments. Responses to the low-income problem in farming, will have to be framed within a strategic approach derived from a well-articulated national policy to reduce the risks of household poverty.

Appendix

Table A3.1: Counties Classified by Average Farm Size, ESUs and AAU, 1991

County	Average Economic Size (ESU)	Average Farm Size hectares (AAU)
Large-Farm Counties		
Waterford	22.6	39.5
Kilkenny	19.8	37.8
Wexford	19.6	35.5
Cork	19.3	31.8
Dublin	19.2	32.6
Tipperary South Riding	19.0	34.4
Carlow	17.4	36.6
Wicklow	17.1	38.1
Medium-to-Large-Farm Counties		
Meath	16.8	33.9
Tipperary North Riding	15.8	32.5
Limerick	15.6	27.5
Kildare	15.3	37.8
Laois	14.4	30.8
Louth	14.3	28.0
Medium-to-Small-Farm Counties		
Offaly	11.8	29.3
Kerry	11.3	26.5
Westmeath	10.3	28.8
Monaghan	9.1	16.7
Cavan	8.8	19.2
Clare	7.7	26.2
Longford	7.3	22.0
Small-Farm Counties		
Galway	6.9	19.7
Donegal	6.1	20.5
Roscommon	5.7	20.0
Sligo	5.5	19.1
Mayo	5.1	16.2
Leitrim	4.0	18.8
Total State	11.6	26.0

Source: Census of Agriculture, 1991 (CSO, 1994).

Table A3.2: Selected Characteristics of Agriculture in Different Categories of County, 1991

Characteristic	Large-Farm Counties*	Medium-to-Large Farm Counties†	Medium-to-Small Farm Counties‡	Small-Farm Counties**
Per Cent of Farms				
Below 2 ESUs	16.3	21.4	26.4	34.6
Below 10 ha	18.3	22.8	25.1	31.8
In 3 or More Separate Parcels	22.0	19.4	19.0	25.3
Specialist Dairy	36.0	30.8	29.6	9.4
Specialist Beef	25.1	36.7	49.0	51.6
Specialist Sheep	7.9	4.8	4.8	14.1
Specialist Tillage	6.6	5.8	0.8	0.6
Mixed Livestock	16.4	16.4	13.3	23.0
Mixed Crops/Livestock	5.6	4.2	0.9	0.8
With Rough Grazing in Use	29.2	17.3	31.8	41.0
With Holders over 65 Years	18.1	19.4	20.9	28.6
With Holders Having Other Gainful Activity	21.1	27.0	26.6	30.2
Average No. Per Farm				
Hectares	35.8	31.8	24.1	19.1
ESUs	19.3	15.4	9.5	5.6
ESUs per Hectare	0.54	0.48	0.39	0.29
Separate Parcels of Land	1.9	1.8	1.8	2.1

* Farms over 17.0 ESUs on average.
† Farms of between 12.0 and 16.9 ESUs on average.
‡ Farms with 7.0 to 11.9 ESUs on average.
** Farms with less than 7.0 ESUs on average.
Source: Derived from Census of Agriculture 1991 (CSO, 1994).

References

Agriculture and Food Policy Review Group (1990): *Agriculture and Food Policy Review*, Dublin: Stationery Office.

Breen, R., Hannan, D.F., Rottman, D.B. and Whelan, C.T. (1990): *Understanding Contemporary Ireland*, Dublin: Gill and Macmillan.

Callan, T., Nolan, B. and Whelan, C.T. (1994): "Who are the Poor" in Nolan, B. and Callan, T. (eds.), *Poverty and Policy in Ireland*, Dublin: Gill and Macmillan: 63–77.

Cawley, M., Gilmor, D.A., Leavy, A. and McDonagh, P. (1995): *Farm Diversification: Studies Relating to the West of Ireland*, Dublin: Teagasc.

Central Statistics Office (1977): *Household Budget Survey 1973*, Dublin: Stationery Office.

Central Statistics Office (1990): *Household Budget Survey 1987*, Dublin: Stationery Office.

Central Statistics Office (1994): *Census of Agriculture, 1991*, Dublin: Stationery Office.

Commins, P. (1990): "Rural Restructuring in Advanced Societies: Transformation, Crisis and Responses" in Marsden, T., Lowe, P. and Whatmore, S. (eds.), *Rural Restructuring: Global Processes and Their Responses*, London: David Fulton, Publishers: 45–76.

Commins, P. (1994): Data from files, unpublished, Dublin: Teagasc.

Commins, P. and Frawley, J. (1995): "The Structure of Irish Farms in 2005", paper to Agricultural Research Forum, University College Dublin.

Commins, P. and Keane, M. (1994): *Developing the Rural Economy: Problems, Programmes and Prospects*, Dublin: National Economic and Social Council, Report No. 97, Part II.

Commission of the European Communities (1988): *The Agricultural Situation in the Community 1986 Report*, Brussels.

Committee on Rural Development Training (1993): *Strategy for Rural Development Training*, Dublin: Teagasc.

FAO (1987): *Agricultural Price Policies : Issues and Proposals*, Rome.

Fingleton, W.A. (1995): "Structural Changes in Dairying in Ireland and in the EU — Actual and Projected", (unpublished), Dublin: Teagasc.

Goodman, D., Sort, D. and Wilkinson J. et al. (1987): *From Farming to Biotechnology*, Oxford: Basil Blackwell.

Hannan, D.F. (1972): "Kinship, Neighbourhood and Social Change in Irish Rural Communities", *The Economic and Social Review*, 3(2): 163–88.

Hannan, D.F. and Commins, P. (1992): "The Significance of Small-Scale Landholders in Ireland's Socio-Economic Transformation", in Goldthorpe, J.H. and Whelan, C.T. (eds.), *The Development of Industrial Society in Ireland*, Oxford: Oxford University Press: 79–104

Hannan, D.F. and Commins, P. (1993): *Factors Affecting Land Availability for Afforestation*, Dublin: Economic and Social Research Institute.

Hart, M. and Gudgin, G. (1994): "Spatial Variations in New Firm Formation in the Republic of Ireland, 1980–1990", *Regional Studies*, 28 (4): 367–80.

Harvey, B. (1994): *Combating Exclusion*, Dublin: Combat Poverty Agency.

Interdepartmental Committee on the Problems of Small Western Farms (1962): *Report*, Dublin: Stationery Office.

Inter-Departmental Committee on Land Structure Reform (1978): *Report*, Dublin: Government Publications.

Kelleher, C. and O'Mahony, A. (1984): *Marginalisation in Irish Agriculture*, Socio-Economic Research Series 4, Dublin: An Foras Talúntais.

Kelleher, C. (1986): "Forestry and Farmers", in *The Changing CAP and its Implications*, Rural Economy Research Centre, Dublin: An Foras Talúntais: 188–213

Kelly, C.E., Ilberry, B.W. and Gilmor, B.W. (1992): "Farm Diversification in Ireland: Evidence from County Wicklow", *Irish Geography*, 25(1): 23–32.

Lewontin, R.C. and Berlan, J. (1986): "Technology, Research and the Penetration of Capital: The Case of U.S. Agriculture", *Monthly Review*, July-August, 21-34.

Matthews, A. (1982): "The State and Irish Agriculture" in Drudy, P.J. (ed.) *Ireland: Land Politics and People*, Cambridge: Cambridge University Press: 92–113.

Nolan, B. (1994): "The EC and Combating Poverty" in Nolan, B. and Callan, T. (eds.) *Poverty and Policy in Ireland*, Dublin: Gill and Macmillan: 293–307.

O'Hara, P. (1986): "CAP Socio-Structural Policy : A New Approach to an Old Problem" in *The Changing CAP and Its Implications*, Dublin: Teagasc: 34–49.

Power, R. and Roche, M. (1993): *National Farm Survey, 1992*, Dublin: Teagasc.

Power, R. and Roche, M. (1994): *National Farm Survey, 1993*, Dublin: Teagasc.

Scully, J.J. (1971): *Agriculture in the West of Ireland*, Dublin: Stationery Office.

Sheehy, S.J. (1994): "The Future of Direct Payments to Farmers", paper to Agricultural Economics Society of Ireland, 24 January.

Shutes, M. (1991): "Kerry Farmers and the European Community: Capital Transitions in a Rural Irish Parish", *Irish Journal of Sociology*, 1: 1–17.

Thorne, B. (1995): "The Challenges and Benefits in the local development approach from a practical viewpoint", paper to Seminar on Local Development, University College Galway; September.

Tovey, H. (1991): "Of Cabbages and Kings: Restructuring in the Food Industry", *Economic and Social Review*, 22 (4): 333–50.

Walsh, J.A. (1992): "Adoption and Diffusion Processes in the Mechanisation of Irish Agriculture", *Irish Geography*, 25(1): 33–53.

Whelan, C.T. (1994): "Poverty, Social Class, Education and Intergenerational Mobility", in Nolan, B. and Callan, T. (eds.) *Poverty and Policy in Ireland*, Dublin: Gill and Macmillan: 130–148.

White Paper (1980): *Land Policy*, Dublin: Stationery Office.

4: Natural Resource Development and Rural Poverty

Hilary Tovey[1]

[1] Thanks are due to Andy Conway and Carol Conway who brought together much of the statistical information on the current state of Irish natural resource exploitation used in this chapter.

INTRODUCTION

Natural resources and natural resource exploitation are central elements in rural life. Some studies of rural areas go so far as to suggest that the term "rural" should be confined to describing activities which involve people who either live from or use the natural environment. For example, writing about the experiences of the Third EU Anti-Poverty Programme and, specifically, the Forum project, located in North Connemara, which was supported under this programme, Byrne et al. define "rural development" as "a set of strategies intended to improve the well-being of those who not only live in rural areas, but also depend on the rural environment to provide them with a livelihood" (Byrne et al., 1993: 238). In their view, the purpose of a rural development programme is to "attempt to develop alternatives in rural communities so that people can continue to live in rural areas and *sustain a living from the natural resources* at their disposal" (Byrne et al., 1993: 238–9; emphasis added).

Such a definition would mean, if it were accepted, that rural development planning should not concern itself with those who live in rural areas but earn their income elsewhere, or with those who work in industries that only locate in rural areas because of the access this gives them to certain sorts of labour. It may not be desirable to limit the term so tightly, but the approach of Byrne et al. can still be useful. It prompts the question as to what is happening currently to natural resources in Ireland and how they are being used or developed; even more importantly, how this is affecting the ability of rural people, especially the poorest among them, to survive and to make a living in rural areas.

This chapter addresses those issues. It is not a comprehensive study, but simply tries to bring together material which allows an examination of some natural resource uses which seem of particular significance in rural economies at present: specifically, aquaculture, mining, forestry and tourism. Examining forms of resource exploitation like these takes on particular importance given the widespread agreement that agriculture — seen for so long in Ireland as the quintessential way of sustaining a rural livelihood from natural resources — can no longer solve problems of poverty and unemployment in rural areas.

A great deal of significance has been attributed to some "new" forms of resource use — for example, tourism — as part of a strategy for rural diversification and integrated rural development. It is expected that their development will enhance wealth generation and increase employment in rural localities. However, this chapter argues that the gains from rural resource development do not automatically go to rural people, or, within rural populations, to those groups most in need of them. Resource development may produce changes in the ownership of the rural environment, or in the forms through which it is worked, which benefit some groups far more than others. It may also be associated with the rise of new claims to ownership of the rural, symbolic as well as material, and of new claimants — for example, urban-based conservationist or recreational interests, for whom what matters is the survival of rural space, rather than of rural people.

Thus, although this chapter is primarily concerned with issues of economic change and development in rural areas, it must also address the impact on these areas of the growth of environmentalism in Ireland in recent years. The two are interlinked in many ways, not least through the increasing use by politicians, policy-makers, and environmental organisations of the idea of "sustainable development" as a concept of particular relevance and importance to future programmes for Irish rural development.

RURAL DEVELOPMENT AS RESOURCE DEVELOPMENT — THE CONTEXT

The Revaluing of Rural Resources

Up to the mid-1980s in Ireland, rural development as a whole tended to be subsumed into agricultural development (O'Hara and Commins, 1991). Supporting and developing farming was taken as identical to, or a precondition for, supporting and developing rural society. This resulted in part from the ideological dominance of what has been called a "productionist" model of development within EU and Irish agricultural development policy.

Productionism took for granted that progress in the agricultural economy in Europe could be measured in terms of ever-increasing levels of farm output, on the same or a declining land area, through the adoption of industrialised and science-based methods of production. Its proponents also took for granted, especially during the economic boom of the 1970s, that if productionism made agricultural workers surplus to requirements, this unwanted labour could move without much difficulty out of agriculture into industrial employment. This would both ensure a plentiful labour supply for expanding industry and allow land relinquished by surplus farmers to move into the hands of the most "progressive", or most productionist ones.

The productionist model is recognised nowadays as having contributed considerably to marginalisation and poverty among agriculturally dependent households. Productionist policies in agriculture have been instrumental in making possession of or access to capital, rather than to even highly skilled labour, the key to farm success. In addition, it is now widely accepted that productionist agricultural policies helped to lower the quality of food produced in Europe, and had some very negative impacts on the quality of the rural environment, both visual and ecological. Arguably, however, the most important factor impelling policy-makers to reconsider EU agricultural policy generally and the direction that it was taking was the mounting financial pressure on the EU budget, which resulted from trying both to support productionism and manage the social and political tensions which resulted from it (Deverre, 1995).

The period since the mid-1980s is often described as a "post-productionist" era. In some respects this is misleading — as Commins notes (Chapter 3), the forces driving commercial farming towards ever-increasing output and the continuous adoption of new technology have not been removed. Rather, the term indicates the public acceptance within the EU in the past decade that food surpluses must be curtailed, that fewer and fewer farmers are actually needed to produce a sufficient level of food output, and that if employment is to be maintained in rural areas it must be predominantly outside conventional agricultural production.

As Commins' discussion shows, "post-productionism" is working itself out on the ground in Ireland as a continuing tendency towards the concentration of conventional food production, both socially and spatially. In the east and south-east of the country, there are areas of capital-intensive commercial farming where productionism continues as before, held in check if at all by the imposition of production quotas on certain lines of production. In other areas, particularly in the west and north-west, farmers withdraw or semi-retire from production, relying on welfare payments to live; or they look for ways of combining income from farming with off-farm income earned by themselves or by other household members; or they switch farm production to take advantage of environmentally oriented farm supports, or diversify their farm enterprises into lines which do not involve producing more of those farm goods that are already in surplus — as in deer farming, for example, or in non-food-based products such as providing leisure or recreation services on the farm. The varying opportunities offered for any of these "survival strategies" in different rural locations result in an increasingly uneven and differentiated patterning of rural space.

A second feature of the "post-productionist" policy era has been the re-emergence of "the rural", as opposed to the purely agricultural economy, as a management problem for the state. Since the publication in 1988 of the EU Commission document on *The Future of Rural Society*, policy-makers have accepted that the needs of rural society are not the same as those of farmers, and that rural development cannot be assumed to be achieved through agricultural modernisation. Indeed, it has become evident that in many rural areas the survival of farming itself increasingly depends on the vibrancy of the broader local economy and the opportunities for non-agricultural earnings it can offer to farm household members. But what sorts of employment can be created in rural areas, particularly in an era in which it has become untenable to assume that surplus labour of any sort can easily be absorbed by industrial development? Or what, indeed, should be "the function" of the rural within society as a whole at this late stage of the development of capitalist society?

Marsden et al. (1993) suggest that the move towards "post-productionism" can be seen as a set of changes in the way in which rural issues and problems are now understood in European societies. They describe this as a shift "in the axis of debate . . . from a concern with the competitive efficiency of agriculture and other land uses versus the extent and continuance of rural deprivation, to the potential for agricultural and rural diversification versus different forms of environmental protection and regulation" (1993: 175). We could say, therefore, that there are several features of the new orientation towards the rural, and rural development, which are highly significant for our concerns in this chapter. They are as follows:

(1) A renewed interest in the economic potential of rural, as opposed to just agricultural, resources

(2) The emergence of new interests around the rural environment, sometimes competing with, sometimes complementing the interest in rural resource exploitation

(3) As will be discussed later, a decline in the political will to incorporate poorer rural groups into the prosperity generated by rural resource development or at least to protect them from the worst effects of exclusion from it.

The growing interest over the past decade in developing the rural economy in a multi-sectoral rather than single-sectoral way is not only the product of changes in thinking among social and economic analysts and policy-makers, even if this is how it is commonly explained in the available literature. It also should be linked to processes occurring within an increasingly globalised economic system. Marsden et al. suggest that the economic recession of the 1980s, which produced a crisis of accumulation for capitalism, pushed the holders of large capital within Europe and internationally to look for new opportunities for profitable investment. It made them reassess resources and spaces which were previously thought of as unprofitable or unproductive. In this context, rural space has taken on a new economic importance. It is still (if not as strongly as in the 1970s) the location of a type of workforce which is often particularly attractive to international corporations; it is the site of resources required by, or more easily exploitable as a result of, advances in science and technology; and it is the site of consumption goods — living space, a clean environment, recreation, education — sought by an increasingly urban, affluent middle-class society.

Again, it is important to note that the resulting processes of change within rural areas are highly uneven. Some rural localities have become incorporated into an international tourist, mining or fishing economy, for example. Others have attracted national or regional business investment, others again new forms of state management and regulation, while some have become more marginal to national economic life than they had previously been. There is no single concept of change — for example, "urbanisation" — that can summarise the total pattern. Rural places are becoming more differentiated from each other than before; locality, and the features and resources found within specific locales, have become more significant in shaping, through their interaction with international and global capital, the development process in rural areas.

Natural Resources and State Development Policy

This international revaluing of rural space and natural resources from the 1980s on coincided, in Ireland, with other significant shifts in general state development policy. The main one has been described as a change in emphasis from creating jobs to creating wealth, or, as Brunt has summarised it, "[E]mployment creation was no longer the sole objective of policy. Instead, policy should focus on maximising net domestic value added which would itself induce additional employment through its multiplier effects" (1988: 31–2). A similar point is made by Byrne et al. (1993) when they complain that much of what passes for rural development, in contemporary state programmes and initiatives, is in fact concerned only with economic development, in the sense of wealth creation. In their view, "rural development" must also mean social change, for example, reconstituting local power structures so as to distribute favourable life-chances more evenly across the local population.

A second important shift, mentioned by a number of contributors to this book, is the decline in commitment to any sort of regional policy or management of economic growth so as to maximise equality of participation in it by different areas of the country. This has been a feature of Irish state policy-making in recent years. In this context, it has been easy for the state to present the exploitation of natural resources as one increasingly important way of improving "the nation's" total assets. Rural resource exploitation has been part of the turn towards "looking to our own" in state development rhetoric — a response to negative experiences with multinational corporations, which closed down their Irish operations during the 1980s, and which has been able to gloss over the abandonment of direct state intervention into providing jobs. Instead, state advisors adopted the thesis that expanding the nation's wealth must eventually spill over into the creation of employment or self-employment, even if this is primarily in services rather than in production, and not necessarily located in the same place as the wealth-creation process itself.

Thus the renewal of interest internationally in rural spaces and rural environments has been seen primarily as an opportunity for national wealth creation, rather than rural or local development. This is not peculiar to the Irish State — Marsden et al. (1993) describe the British state's approach to rural development in the same period in similar terms, and suggest that it is probably true of European states in general — but can be expected to have particularly critical effects in the Irish case given the historical distribution of the population and the symbolic importance attached to rural society.

The "trickle-down" theory of development through which the above approach is justified has been the subject of considerable attention and research. A recent, detailed examination of its validity as applied in the UK has been carried out by a team of economic experts under the auspices of the Joseph Rowntree Foundation. Their conclusion is that in the absence of even minimal state intervention to manage the process of wealth creation and the distribution of the benefits that accrue from it, inequality increases and a growing proportion of the population may find themselves permanently excluded from any prospect of employment. The researchers offer a strong warning about the consequences of allowing this to continue. "Regardless of any moral arguments or feelings of altruism," they say, "everyone shares an interest in the cohesiveness of society. As gaps between rich and poor grow, the problems of the marginalised groups which are being left behind rebound on the more comfortable minority" (Joseph Rowntree Foundation 1995: 8). Part of the problem of the rural poor, however, is that they may be unable or unwilling to create the sorts of problems for "the comfortable minority" which might be experienced as seriously threatening to the cohesion of society. Their continued presence within the rural environment may itself be increasingly regarded as unnecessary or illegitimate.

Rural Environmentalism and Sustainable Development

Earlier we suggested that a feature of the context within which rural development is being undertaken today is the emergence of important new interests around nature and the rural environment. The past decade has been marked by some important changes in the perception of and attitudes to the countryside of significant groups within Irish society (Tovey, 1993). The increasingly urban distribution of the population has been accompanied by the emergence of urban dominance in terms of cultural prestige and symbols of status. One important expression of this has been a challenge to the automatic right of farmers' organisations and other agricultural interests to represent themselves as the spokespersons for and guardians of rural Ireland. At the same time as economic activity in rural areas is increasingly the result of intervention by external interests, rural Ireland is becoming the object of competing claims to symbolic ownership (Mormont, 1987) by external groups concerned primarily with consumption of the rural environment, including both conservation and tourism.

The environmental movement has probably been the most vocal and public of the new claimants to rural Ireland. Environmental experts and members of environmental organisations tend to be drawn predominantly from an urban middle class whose claim to authority rests on their status as knowledge users and producers (scientists, historians, physical planners, lawyers, engineers), and who are able as a result of this authority to lay claim to management rights over the countryside in a way that may bring them into direct conflict with its material owners and exploiters. Within Ireland, the main material owners targeted by environmentalist discourse have been the farmers and farming organisations. There have been conflicts around other forms of natural-resource exploitation, such as in mining or fish-farming, but these are not prominent in environmental discourse and often they have bypassed the formal environmental movement in Ireland.

To what extent are concerns about protection of the rural environment compatible with the claims of the rural poor to a better livelihood? Irish environmental discourse about the rural environment has been dominated by conservationist ideas. To that extent, the environmental movement here has focused on the rural as nature, rather than as rural society. But recently there has been a gradual movement towards a discourse of "sustainable development" amongst both environmentalists and politicians. This offers, on face value, a way of reconciling the interests of both developers and conservationists (Murdoch, 1993). It concedes that there is still a need for development in rural areas, and that demands for conservation should not be allowed to prohibit this entirely, while at the same time insisting that development should not be of a kind which permanently or significantly damages the rural environment, and often demanding this in the name of the rural poor themselves who are most dependent for their livelihood on access to undegraded natural resources.

There are, however, growing doubts about how meaningful the concept of sustainable development is (Redclift, 1991, 1992; Murdoch, 1993; Martell, 1994). Some of its critics argue that its current fashionable status owes more to the way that it allows environmentalists access to the circles in which economic policy and national development plans are shaped and decided than to any insights that it might contain about how development should actually proceed. Both "sides" in an environmental conflict find the term attractive, O'Riordan has suggested, because developers "now realise that under the guise of sustainability almost any environmentally sensitive programme can be justified", while "environmentalists abuse sustainability by demanding safeguards and compensating investments that are not always economically efficient or socially just" (O'Riordan, 1988, quoted in Murdoch, 1993: 226).

Contrary to what is often taken to be the case, allowing a discourse of sustainable development to dominate development planning for rural areas in Ireland may in fact further disadvantage poor people in rural areas. As O'Riordan hints, it tends to be used in ways that run counter to the needs of social justice. The concept of sustainable development is widely perceived to draw attention to the need for equity *across generations*. It appeals to the concerns of parents about the future of their children or grandchildren, rather than to more abstract conceptions of equity and fairness within contemporary society. Notably, the most quoted definition of sustainable development comes from the Brundtland Report (1987) and speaks of "development which meets the needs of the present without compromising the ability of future generations to meet their own needs".

Although the Brundtland Report is, in fact, also concerned with equity *within* generations, particularly as between inhabitants of developed and underdeveloped societies, that aspect is much less often recognised or emphasised by environmental organisations and representatives. Their emphasis is primarily on the physical and ecological sustainability of a proposed development — that is, the extent to which it will deplete or destroy natural resources on which we depend to maintain current standards of living. This can adapt itself to concerns about economic sustainability over time, but is much harder to reconcile with concerns about access for specific social groups to an acceptable standard of living now and in the future. Redclift (1992) has pointed out that in less-developed rural economies contestations about the environment, and resistance to its conservation or monopolisation by others, are often social and political struggles for survival, because in these situations it is the destruction or at least the exploitation of the environment which creates value. Others criticise "sustainable development" as a top-down management process, which is in danger of becoming "another instrument of first-world domination, for it will restrict the poor's resource base in the name of environmental protection" (Kousis, 1993: 4).

There are, of course, strong reasons for maintaining extreme care in regard to the sorts of development that we accept as suitable to natural resources in rural areas. Murphy argues that capitalist corporations inevitably degrade the environment in which they operate, since the profits they make do not only come, as Marx thought, from exploiting their workers, but also from exploiting the environment. "Surplus value and profit come into being in the process of production, not only through the unpaid labour of workers but also by not paying the costs of waste reduction, waste purification, and resource renewal, that is, by degrading the natural environment" (Murphy, 1994: 111). The environmental degradation caused by economic growth has been treated by economists and accountants as "external" to the system and hence largely left unpaid by those who produce it. It thus becomes a social cost, borne most heavily by those whose environment is the most degraded. Murphy argues, like Redclift (1984) and others before him, that as environmental pressures have been brought to bear on producers in the Western World to deal with the pollution they produce, they have responded by shifting the problem to the Third World. Instead of changing their production processes to avoid polluting (which would make their products unacceptably expensive to consumers), they locate the most degrading parts of the production process in peripheral countries which have not implemented such severe environmental controls, or which are so desperate for jobs and revenue from industrial development that they are willing to accept high levels of pollution as well.

Similar analyses can be and have been made about the location of some industrial production or resource extraction processes in the rural peripheries of Western countries (Allen and Jones, 1990). They suggest that in assessing the impact of various forms of resource exploitation on rural poverty we must pay close attention to their environmental effects. However, relying on a discourse of "sustainability" may be of very little assistance in deciding whether or not to accept rural development of this sort, because as developed so far, the discourse is fatally ambiguous when it comes to determining first, what "sustainable" economic practices are, in a rural economy, and second, how they can be implemented, assuming that it has been possible to identify them.

To identify sustainable, as against unsustainable, economic practices, it would be necessary to be able to define "natural resources" and agree on their limits. This is effectively impossible since it would require knowing in advance what sort of technological and scientific developments will happen in the future. But in any case the decision about sustainability cannot be left for scientific determination alone. Kousis (1993) shows how a decision to exploit the potential for geothermal energy on the Greek island of Milos, which, in terms of the Greek economy as a whole seemed to fit perfectly with sustainable development aspirations, mobilised determined local resistance because of the ecological damage that it was causing. She comments that "if sustainable development is . . . truly [to] realise its full potential . . . it should foster local control over resources, participation in decision making and empowerment of the local people, especially the under-privileged and marginalised" (1993: 4). Politics, as well as science, is involved in defining what is "sustainable" at a local level.

This raises the second issue: to implement sustainable development, it is not enough just to develop ways of measuring environmental impacts to ensure that resources are not becoming depleted or that wastes are not too large to be assimilated by local ecosystems, and so on. Changes would be necessary also in existing institutional and political structures, so that they become more likely to enforce or reinforce sustainable practices. In other words, it is necessary to think in terms of major social change, not just implementing limits on resource use. Achieving sustainability may well demand more state intervention, more regulation of ownership and of the social forms used in developing specific natural resources, more use of various sorts of market support and incentive — none of which seem likely to be very acceptable in the current policy context for rural resource development. If Murphy is right in identifying environmental degradation as a central source of profit in capitalist economies, bringing about the required changes will be challenging indeed.

NATURAL RESOURCE DEVELOPMENT IN RURAL IRELAND

Our review of the development of natural resources in rural Ireland, as mentioned earlier, covers only four examples — aquaculture, mining, forestry and tourism. There are other examples which could have been examined — peat extraction, gravel quarrying, wind or water-powered electricity generation, deep-sea fishing — and this does not pretend to be an exhaustive discussion of the issue. Even in the examples that are reviewed, the availability of information is not always ideal. Much of it has been taken from official statistics and economic projections, and although we have tried as far as possible to draw on sociological case studies to illustrate the development processes in action, this has not always been possible.

Each of the four discussions follows roughly the same structure. First, the current situation or level of development in the case concerned is examined, along with state policy in regard to further exploitation. This is followed by a discussion of how ownership of the resource concerned is structured and how it may be changing over the course of the resource development, linked to an analysis of the main methods or means of exploitation being used. Following that, we try to identify some of the employment impacts for local populations, particularly in relation to class and gender characteristics; and we conclude with a brief discussion of the ecological effects of the development, as far as it is possible to identify these, again particularly in regard to how these affect the existing livelihoods of the local people.

In putting together these portraits of resource development policy and practices, our central concern has been not the contribution that natural resource exploitation can make to rural development per se, but its implications for reproducing or challenging poverty and inequality in the Irish countryside. This issue will be addressed more fully in the last part of the chapter, but it is worth noting here that most of the existing material on the examples selected is concentrated on the first of these concerns and has relatively little to say about the second.

Aquaculture[2]

Aquaculture, or "fish-farming", is one of the new uses of rural space and the natural environment to have attracted much interest from multinational capital from the late 1980s onward. It is estimated to produce around 15 per cent of the world's seafood supply at present, and has been regarded in the Irish situation for some time as a form of economic development particularly suited to rural areas in the west, with the ESB and Údarás na Gaeltachta taking specific initiatives to encourage it. Irish aquaculture is dominated by three main sectors — salmon, trout and shellfish production — and is seen as still relatively underdeveloped, particularly the shellfish sector.

Farmed salmon production increased in Ireland from 100 tonnes in 1982 to 9,300 tonnes in 1991. Competition from producers elsewhere, especially in Norway, led to a fall in prices on world markets in the late 1980s and early 1990s, but in the past couple of years, with world output falling, production in Ireland is once more profitable.

Trout farming can take place in the sea or in inland waters. The sea-farmed trout are produced in much the same way as salmon, and nearly all sea-farming takes place along the west coast. Freshwater trout production, at around 710 tonnes in 1990, was double the output

---

2   Material in this section is based largely on O'Connor, R. et al. (1992) (and on private communications from R. O'Connor) and on EURADVICE Ltd. (1992).

from sea-trout farms, but trout production generally has grown much more slowly in Ireland than salmon production, and most of it is sold on the domestic market.

Farmed shellfish include mainly oysters and mussels, but also some clams, scallops and abalone. Their present sales value is around £6 million annually. Two species of oyster are grown here: the native oyster, which is regarded as a choice market item both in Ireland and on the Continent and which commands high prices, mainly because of limited supplies; and the Pacific oyster which is not yet subject to any major disease and is therefore much easier to grow under controlled conditions, but which is in ready supply already on the Continent. Mussel farming can be done either by bottom culture, which consists in dredging seed mussels, usually from offshore beds, and transferring them to shallow areas within a harbour to grow to maturity, or by suspended culture where the seed mussels are collected in settling areas and grown to market size in different areas suspended on long lines or from rafts. Suspended mussels cost more to produce, but they contain more meat and thus fetch higher prices. Both are sold for either fresh production or processing. Of the other species currently being tested, scallop and abalone production are still at the experimental stage, while clam production, concentrated mainly off the Sligo coast, is expected to increase substantially over the next few years.

Ownership, Employment and Work Processes

According to O'Connor et al. (1992), 802 people were employed within the salmon and trout-farming industries in 1990. Of these, 511 were full-time workers. The part-time hours available were small, with 291 people sharing the equivalent of 37 full-time workloads or "person-years". It has been estimated however (*ibid.*) that each person-year in aquaculture generates a further 1.26 person-years of work in related or indirectly induced employment, which would have brought total employment from finfish farming in 1990 to 1,240 person-years.

The organisation of work in shellfish farming is quite different from that in salmon and trout farming. Shellfish production occurs in a large number of small enterprises — at present there are around 200 shellfish enterprises in the State, employing about 1,000 people on a whole or part-time basis, amounting to some 450 person-years of work. Whereas salmon-farming is a capital-intensive industry, and appears to be increasingly open to penetration by foreign capital, shellfish operations tend to be small-scale enterprises carried on by local people, many of whom also have other operations. The majority of the labour used is that of the enterprise promoter, and the employment combines well with inland fishing or small-farm activity. Co-operative forms of organisation are much more likely to be found in shellfish than in finfish farming. According to Duggan (1994), this is not because there are particular features of the production process which make co-operation between shellfish workers more "natural" — it has more to do with historic characteristics of the struggle to retain control of shellfish resources in local hands, or, as in the cases described by Curtin (1993), with deliberate attempts by anti-poverty groups such as the Forum Project in north Connemara to develop the area's natural resource base in a way that improves the economic situation of the unemployed and underemployed people in the locality.

Ruddy and Varley, also writing on aquaculture in north Connemara, note the clear distinction that exists between the two principal types which are found there:

> High profit margins and high capital requirements have meant that salmon farming here, as elsewhere, has come, despite long production cycles and high production risks, to be predominantly controlled by large-scale private investors. In contrast, mussel farming in north Connemara would appear to be inherently more accessible to local people in terms of capital and expertise requirements, as well as more compatible with part-time work patterns and co-operative structures (Ruddy and Varley, 1991: 77).

The two main finfish farms in the area on which they report appear to be moving towards the use of a full-time labour force, gradually dispensing with workers who are also involved in farming or are in other ways pluri-active. This essentially also means dispensing with female workers since in both farms the workforce is predominantly male and only in one of them is there a significant presence of women, concentrated in the part-time/casual sector of the workforce. They claim that a significant proportion of the production of farmed salmon is financed in Ireland, as also in Scotland, by Norwegian capital; and that the industry exhibits fairly clear trends towards concentration in production, with the three largest finfish companies in Ireland at the time (when around 16 farms were in operation) accounting for 60 per cent of output. In the north Connemara case, 60 per cent of one of the main salmon farms is owned by Tiedemanns, a Norwegian tobacco manufacturers, while 80 per cent of the second has been bought by Bradán Mara Teo which at the time was a subsidiary of the Irish tobacco manufacturer Carrolls.

Ruddy and Varley (1991) note that finfish farming in the area began in a form (of "domestic commodity production" or self-employment) not dissimilar to that used now by individual mussel producers. Since finfish farming has expanded and gone through a path of transformation into capitalist production, is the same likely to happen to mussel farming? Or can mussel farming survive in the way that it is currently organised — small-scale and egalitarian, using individual producers grouped together in a co-operative relationship? They suggest that a number of factors have been involved in salmon farming's expansion into capitalist production: the high level of capital needed to establish production in what is an intensive and still a high-risk form of production; the role of the state, which in the case of finfish farming, unlike earlier interventions to develop other natural resources such as peat and forestry, has encouraged private capital to play the leading development role and has provided generous grants and tax incentives to the industry; and the existence of large-scale international capital seeking diversification into new investment outlets and for whom finfish farming, with its rapid technological advances, state supports, and anticipated high profit margins appeared as a very attractive opportunity.

Mussel farming on the other hand has been fairly unattractive to outside capital so far. It has had low or stagnant profit margins, and relatively little assistance or support from the state (while at the same time being apparently subjected to a tighter régime of state inspection than finfish farmers are). But Ruddy and Varley (1991) point out that mussel producer co-operatives in the early 1990s were reaching a situation where they would have to decide whether they could continue with the existing level of output, or would have to expand production. The co-operative they studied had decided in fact that production levels would have to be increased substantially, even if only to allow them to pay for the employment of a full-time manager; but this was likely to demand investments of capital unavailable to the co-op members, which meant that the co-operative would have to try to negotiate relationships with external sources of capital which would still allow it to maintain effective control of the mussel farms involved.

Ruddy and Varley suggest that whether or not such relationships could be established, the decision to increase output could be fateful for the co-op membership. To produce more and to ensure the sort of all-year-round supply that external markets require, the workers may find that they can no longer treat their mussel farming as part-time work intended to bring in additional income: all or nearly all of them may have to become full-time if they want to remain in the co-op. Over time, too, the members are likely to go through a period of differentiation and concentration, with the eventual emergence of a small number of large-scale farmers employing wage labour in working their shares of the overall operation. The apparent differences, then, between finfish and shellfish farming in terms of their mode of organisation and the ownership of the productive resources may not be very long-lived, particularly in the absence of deliberate efforts to support co-operative forms of organisation among mussels producers. Overall, Ruddy and Varley suggest that small-scale domestic forms of production — usually praised as the most distinctive feature of the Irish rural way of life — are gradually disappearing in all sectors of the rural economy:

> What is happening in north Connemara aquaculture — where small and large-scale enterprises co-exist but where the underlying trend is toward the larger scale — would seem to mirror a dominant tendency in development based on natural resources in Ireland (Ruddy and Varley, 1991: 77).

Neither Duggan nor Curtin offers such a pessimistic analysis of the future of small-scale shellfish farming. Duggan emphasises the centrality of pluri-activity to the household economy in coastal areas such as this. She suggests that shellfish co-op members (who regarded themselves, in her account, clearly as fishermen and not farmers — not even fish farmers) limit and resist any incorporation into commercial production which reduces their flexible movement between resources and in particular which demands substantial capital investment by the household. Her study suggests that local workers will continue to place a high priority on local control of resources, and are increasingly adept at mobilising environmental justifications for support for this form. Curtin points out that co-operatives vary greatly in their organisational capacity and effectiveness, and that, while some may never get the commitment or loyalty from their members that they would need to develop further, others appear to be quite successful in establishing a strong basis for continuing "endogenous development".

Environmental Impacts

Besides offering development assistance for aquaculture, the Irish state is also involved in regulating the industry through a system of licensing. Applications for licences for salmon farming in particular have provoked considerable resistance from local groups. These objections are often on visual amenity grounds, but also on the grounds of interference with existing local livelihoods because licensing a farm could lead to their exclusion from local bodies of water taken over by the fishfarmers, or because of water pollution, or the spread of disease or infestation to wild fish which are necessary to the local tourism economy, for example. Over time, problems like these may turn out to be as important in constraining the growth of the finfish farming industry as world competition or falling prices on international markets.

Shellfish production appears to generate less resistance, at a local level, partly because of the smaller scale and reduced environmental impacts of the enterprises (shellfish farming does not affect water quality and does not use chemicals for disease or pest control), and partly because as noted above the industry has generally so far been retained strongly within local hands, individually or in co-operative associations. This supports Redclift's suggestion that in rural or peripheral societies, environmental contests generally have more to do with sustaining or protecting local livelihoods than with conservationist or amenity concerns. There is considerable scope for misunderstanding between locals and members of formal environmental organisations if this is not recognised in drawing up resource exploitation policy.

Mining

Ireland is already a fairly major producer of zinc and lead: it accounts for 17 per cent of Europe's zinc and 9 per cent of European lead mine production (MINFO, 1993). In addition to existing productive mines, prospecting in recent years has uncovered other potential sites for mining both base metals and gold. After the discovery of gold in Northern Ireland in 1983, a surge of exploration activity occurred in the Republic: between 1982 and 1988, the number of gold-prospecting licences issued rose from 5 to 300. The result is that four separate districts are now known to contain gold (although they may not necessarily be developed as active gold mines): the Avoca district in Co. Wicklow, Clontibret in Co. Monaghan, Connemara, and south Mayo.

The most prominent new mining location for lead and zinc is at Galmoy, Co. Kilkenny. There is also a more recently discovered site at Lisheen, Co. Tipperary, 8 km south-west of Galmoy, where Ivernia West plc and Chevron are currently undertaking detailed costing and planning of production facilities and are preparing an environmental impact assessment and a planning application.

The mining industry as a whole accounts for 3 per cent of total industrial output and 1.75 per cent of total exports (Dhonau, 1992). Mineral-based exports have a value of about £250 million annually. Mining directly employs about 1,000 people (about three-quarters of these are employed at the most successful mine operation in Ireland, Tara Mines in Co. Meath), and 200 further jobs at least are anticipated at the proposed mine at Galmoy. This mine will also produce around 350 temporary jobs during its construction.

There is surprisingly little information available on government policy in regard to mining. Mention of mining is notably absent from all national planning documents from the period 1987–99, and one might conclude that there has been little change in state thinking about minerals developments since the 1981 NESC Report on Minerals Policy. Certainly, a prime concern about developments in this sector is their potential for expanding the economy as a whole. A 1993 statement by the then Minister for Transport, Energy and Communications said: "It is my belief that the very significant potential contribution of our mineral resources to the national job and wealth creation effort should be exploited to the full" (Cowen, 1993). The need to protect the environment has been recognised as a possible constraint on mining in recent statements, although the general belief appears to be that technological improvements in the industry are making it increasingly compatible with environmental concerns (Cowen, 1993; Treacy, 1993).

Structure of Ownership, Employment, Work Processes

Curtin and Shields describe mining globally as an industry dominated by multinationals. They argue that mining development can be seen as a particular form of dependent development in peripheral economies, in which multinational corporations exploit mineral resources across the global periphery through their capacity to control the capital, information and technology required for their extraction. "The outcome of dependent development of mining may thus not only be the extraction of profits and the exploitation of labour but the destruction of a locally finite resource" (Curtin and Shields, 1988: 109).

Dependent development perspectives see the local state as participating in this process by offering incentives to multinational capital to invest in local resource exploitation. In Ireland, for example, tax legislation gives allowances to promote the development of exploration and mining. Exploration costs are allowable to companies for tax purposes, justified on the grounds of the expensive nature of exploring and establishing a mine and on the grounds that the mining industry, in contrast to most other industries, is not grant aided in any way.

The suggestion that mining in Ireland is foreign-owned and controlled is contested by another study (Dunnells and Hitzman, 1992), which suggests that, of the prospecting licences being worked in 1990, covering over 25,000 kilometres, more than 50 per cent were controlled by Irish companies. However, the ambiguities associated with ownership and owners' nationality are evident in the Tynagh case described by Curtin and Shields. The controlling company at Tynagh, Northgate Exploration Ltd, was created by five Irish emigrants to Canada who in 1958 bought out, reorganised and renamed a Canadian public company Kirk-Hudson Mines Ltd. Despite having Irish directors then, Northgate was a publicly quoted company registered on the Toronto Stock Exchange, and its long-term planning was based in Canada and linked to the evaluations of it made by its Canadian shareholders, and the readiness of Canadian financial institutions to support it. In fact, Northgate was not large enough to undertake the costs of developing the mine at Tynagh on its own, so it brought in a further financial consortium, including two British firms and three European smelting corporations, in return for giving away first preference on Tynagh's concentrate production through most of the mine's productive life. It would seem to be quite problematic to infer from the owners of prospecting licences the eventual ownership of the ore and the extraction process.

Research on employment effects from mining development offers some contradictory conclusions. According to the Green 2000 Advisory Group, the development in Ireland of a significant mining industry has resulted in the creation of new skills, and the jobs associated with them are well paid — a 1990 industry survey showed that average wage earnings were over £19,000 per annum (Green 2000, 1993: 205). Other commentators argue that the skills are highly specific, and the employment created is "typically unrepresentative, favouring young men over women and older workers" (O'Dowd, 1990: 15). There is also some concern that the high wages and salaries paid in the mining

industry may inhibit other firms offering less well-paid jobs from locating in the vicinity of a mining operation.

Curtin and Shields' description of the workforce in the Tynagh
lead and zinc mines, during the 1970s, gives us a detailed picture of
employment and the labour process, at least in this specific case. They
also suggest that employment at the mine led to the creation of skills
among a section of the labour force, but point out that actual mining
work employed only a minority of workers:

> For the majority at Tynagh, work took place in the mill, stores, of-
> fices, laboratory or garage. A striking feature of the mine was the
> range of jobs it gave rise to (Curtin and Shields, 1988: 116).

A major distinction was made between underground and overground
work; then, within these categories, further distinctions were made
between (underground) development, production and service workers
— only the first two of these would have been regarded as skilled
workers, while service workers included general labourers, drivers of
mobile equipment, pumpmen etc. — and (overground) between relatively unskilled maintenance crews, machinery operators and general
labourers, on the one hand, and, on the other, technical staff employed
in the laboratory, and clerical staff.

These distinctions were reinforced by shift-work patterns, and by
variations in pay scales and bonus systems, while there were also divisions between farmers and non-farmers in the work force and most
of the workers did not live in one single settlement. "The workers did
not form nor did they see themselves as forming a single community,
in the sense that mining communities are structured elsewhere"
(*ibid.*: 117). One result of this was that there was little solidarity
across the workforce, and "in the early years of production and despite poor working conditions and far from abundant pay packages,
there was little industrial trouble at the mine" (*ibid.*). Thus, despite
what seems from the outside to be the skilled nature of their work,
mining workers in rural Ireland may be vulnerable to similar forms
of exploitation as new workers in other industries that have been established in "greenfield' sites.

A question raised by mining development is the length of life of
the jobs created, and whether the state should accept being involved
in promoting short-term as against long-term employment. The life of
a mine is dictated (barring other complications) by the size of its ore
body. For example, the copper mine at Gortdrum, Co. Tipperary, com-
pletely exhausted its ore supply in only eight years (1967–75), al-

though this seems to have been somewhat exceptional. According to the Green 2000 Advisory Group, of the seven significant mines opened since 1960, only one lasted for less than 10 years and three are likely to continue for more than 20 years (1993: 203). This might still hardly be regarded as "sustainable" employment. Concern about duration of employment depends on whether one is looking at the situation from the point of view of boosting national employment statistics, or from the point of view of maintaining opportunities for work in a specific rural area. As long as new ore bodies continue to be found, national employment statistics will not suffer from short-duration jobs, but this is of little comfort to a particular rural locality, where closure of the mine means that workers may be left with specific skills for which there is no local market.

Local Employment and Environmental Impacts

Mineral resource development thus brings to local economies the danger of a boom/bust scenario, whereby the temporary prosperity in the area, while the mine is in production, is followed by drastic depression when the mine expires. In addition to the unemployment caused by the mine closure, all those in the area who have become accustomed to a periodic payroll injection into the local economy may be affected and the effects of closure may spin over into the local economy as a whole. As O'Dowd points out, the boom atmosphere "will only persist while the mine is actually in operation, unless careful parallel development is planned" (1990: 16).

The problem may be exacerbated if other industries have been discouraged from locating in the area because of the presence of mining, and, even more so, if the introduction of mining into the area has had very negative impacts, because of its environmental effects, on existing agriculture or tourism enterprises. Curtin and Shields describe how the operation of the mine at Tynagh over 20 years from 1962 to the early 1980s resulted in widespread pollution: "On the closure of the mine, it was estimated that at least 2,000 acres of the adjoining land had been made unusable and unproductive" (1988: 120). They emphasise the major inequalities in power and influence that exist between local landholders and a multinational corporation supported by state development policy, which even affected the capacity of local farmers to take recourse to the law. Those farmers who did not simply sell out and leave their land have faced great difficulties in securing any compensation from the company.

In some cases, mining development can have considerable spin-off effects for the local economy. For example, it is estimated that for each person employed at Tara Mines in Co. Meath, 2.5 people are in part maintained in employment in related industries or in services (Robinson, 1991). The Green 2000 Advisory Group (1993: 203) suggests a more conservative estimate of between one and two additional jobs for each direct job. However, the impact in terms of job creation seems likely to depend heavily on the nature of the locality within which the mine operates — in the case of rural areas rather than small towns, for the reasons suggested above, it may be negative rather than positive. Moreover, the employment generated by further processing down the line is limited. The underdevelopment of smelting facilities in Ireland — which for a number of reasons, including environmental ones, seems likely to continue — means that metal concentrates have to be shipped out of the country for smelting, mining and manufacturing of the final product. Encouraging the development of mining, to this extent, is encouraging the continuation of economic dependency relationships through which raw materials are exported from the less-developed periphery to the more developed core countries. This is reinforced when, if the mining companies are themselves foreign-based or foreign-backed, even the profits themselves may leave the country to be repatriated abroad.

If mining development is to have any use as part of a rural anti-poverty strategy, a number of conditions need to be established: ways need to be found of retaining ownership of the natural resource as far as possible in local hands; the development of the resource needs to be planned in ways that ensure that it will interfere as little as possible with already existing forms of livelihood in the locality; access to jobs needs to be kept open for those local people most in need of the work; and "parallel" development planning is needed to ensure that the locality develops alternative employment before the mine is exhausted.

Forestry

Ireland is reckoned to have the most favourable climate in Europe for the production of timber. Yet, in the mid-1980s, with 4.8 per cent of the total land area under forest, it had the lowest proportion of afforested land for any European country except Finland (Kelleher, 1986). By 1995, forests had increased to about 6.5 per cent of the land area of Ireland, of which about 85 per cent was originally in state ownership and is now vested in Coillte. The low level of planting, and the pattern of ownership reflect the fact that, historically, forestry policy was framed within the objective of maintaining as many people as possible in agricultural employment, given the endemic nature of unemployment and emigration from rural areas. As a result, only land that was not suitable for agriculture was considered for afforestation. Moreover, since the income from afforestation would be negligible for the first 15–20 years, the state had to undertake the major role in planting.

However, these policies have changed dramatically in recent years (see also Chapter 3). Since the early 1980s, EU policies have been improving assistance to forestry in order to encourage the diversion of land from agriculture. Under the Community Support Framework for Ireland, 1989–93, funding of nearly 65 million ECUs was made available to support forestry, which the 1989 Programme for Government had identified as potentially very significant for economic growth. A Forestry Operational Programme was established, whose objective has been described as "To contribute to the generation of wealth in the Irish economy by utilising available and suitable land and human and financial resources to the best advantage in creating new, and developing existing, forests" (Kearney et al., 1993: 1). Since 1989, grant aid for planting has no longer been restricted to marginal or non-agricultural land, forestry premia are paid annually on planted land and planters other than the state have been encouraged to move into afforestation. The rates of planting by different interests in recent years are shown in Table 4.1 below.

Table 4.1: Forest Planting in the State, in hectares, by Type of Planter, 1989, 1990, 1991, 1992, 1993

Planter	1989	1990	1991	1992	1993
Coillte	6,412	6,706	7,986	11,500	11,000
Private					
Farmer	3,660	3,988	7,978	5,308	6,786
Other	4,837	5,159	3,302	4,170	2,384
Total	14,909	15,853	19,266	20,978	20,170

Source: Forest Service, Department of Energy, private communication.

Structure of Ownership and Participation

Table 4.1 shows a noticeable increase in afforestation since 1990, and in participation by farmers themselves since 1991. This is a major change from the mid-1980s when, as Kelleher noted (1986: 194), Irish farmers tended to be much less involved in forestry than farmers in other European countries, and when it seemed that, even in those counties most suited to forestry and least able to provide farmers with reasonable incomes from agriculture, external investment companies and other private business or professional people were doing most of the planting. Her study showed that in Leitrim, for example, where nearly 400 hectares (ha) of land had been planted up to September 1986, 9 per cent had been planted by farmers and 82 per cent by insurance and other companies moving into forestry as a long-term investment location for their funds. In Leitrim, Cavan, Sligo and Monaghan taken together, in the same period, less than a quarter of the land area afforested was planted by farmers, while over half was accounted for by investment companies.

Kelleher argues that farmers were reluctant to turn over land to trees, partly because of a perception that only "waste land" which was no good for anything else should be given over to forest, and they generally perceived that only very small portions of their farm fitted this description; but more importantly because they saw the returns from forestry as too long-term, because they could not envisage surviving without an annual income from the land while waiting for the trees to mature, or because the initial costs of preparing ground and planting etc., were too high.

Changes in the system of grant-aids and income payments since that period seem, therefore, to have had a strong effect in encouraging farmers to plant. Currently, farmers who plant land in disadvantaged areas of the State are allowed to keep their entitlement to animal headage payments, and land suitable for agricultural use has also been deemed to be eligible for afforestation aids as part of a strategy for maximising incomes from land use. Annual premia have helped to solve the income problem in the early years of growth. In 1994, grants and premia were increased by about 50 per cent overall, and even more in the case of better quality land in less disadvantaged areas of the State, reflecting the EU policy goal of speeding up the removal of land from food production. The result has been a big increase in afforestation by farmers, to the extent that since 1990 they have planted more land than have private forest-development companies.

Low stock rates in much of Irish farming suggest that large quantities of land, up to perhaps a million ha, could be released to forestry without seriously affecting the viability of livestock farming. Farmland could still be stocked at less than 1.4 livestock units per hectare, which is the extensive production criterion that entitles farmers to the extension premium. In general, therefore, it would appear that forestry is compatible with continued farming and is particularly suited to farmers in the more disadvantaged areas of the country. However, two problems are still evident in relation to farmer participation in afforestation.

One is that the average area on which farmers are applying for afforestation grants, at around 10 ha, is less than half that of investment companies or non-farming individuals (at 25 ha). It is generally estimated that at least 20 ha is the minimum viable area for those who expect to realise all or most of their income from forestry. In encouraging farmers to plant less than this, it could be argued that the State is more concerned about the interest of the timber-processing industry than about the farmers.

Small farm woodlots can have both commercial and environmental benefits. For example, they can provide a locally produced and renewable source of domestic fuel. About 2–4 ha are enough to meet the fuel needs of a domestic dwelling house, so there may be a place for small-scale farm forestry as a supplier of fuel-wood either for the grower's own household or for local consumption. However, this raises the second problem, which is that the farmers planting relatively small areas of land, and receiving state support for this, are not in fact the farmers who are most in need of such additional household resources. Hannan and Commins (1993) investigated grant applications for afforestation in the early 1990s and found that the sort of farmer most likely to become involved in afforestation is in fact the larger, more commercial farmer, in areas of the country where incomes from agriculture are under less pressure anyway. Small farmers whose land is of poor agricultural quality and who live in those areas of the country, particularly the north west, where the retreat from full-time farming has been most dramatic, reveal much less interest in diversifying into forestry, and this is most true of those who are most dependent for a living on social welfare payments.

Hannan and Commins point out that this is, to some extent, a result of contradictions in the outcomes of different policies in regard to land use and mobility — changes in early retirement schemes, the possibility of payment for "nature management" on the farm, in the

level of headage payments and so on, can all discount the effect of incentives to forestry at particular times. It also may be related to differences in the way that different types of landholder perceive and
feel about their land: developed commercial farmers may find it easier to identify a part of their land as relatively unproductive and suitable to be turned over to trees, than a farmer with a smallholding of
generally poor quality land. The point remains, however, that as a
way of meeting income needs of the poorest in rural areas — or at
least, the poorest owners of land — afforestation policy may be rather
ineffective as operated at present.

The state forest programme, which is managed by Coillte Teo,
continues to play an important part in maintaining levels of new
planting. Coillte also has a long-term aim of ensuring that an internationally competitive processing industry is developed in Ireland,
and of developing itself into a broadly based forest-products business.
It is only in recent years that a state agency has become directly involved in wood processing — previously, wood produced in state forests was generally sold for processing to private companies, and indeed it seems likely that this will continue to be the case in the future, despite developments towards processing within Coillte itself.

Employment and Environmental Effects

Studies of the likely employment and other economic benefits to follow from afforestation are few, which is understandable considering
how recently interest in these issues has developed in Ireland. Most
of them depend on synchronic data in order to draw diachronic infer-
ences — such as in the study by Kearney and O'Connor (1993), which
compared the different sociodemographic situations of two rural
areas — one with a stable population, the other with a declining one
— and argued that at least part of the difference could be attributed
to the presence of mature forestry in the stable case, and its absence
in the other. Or else these studies make predictions about employment based on calculations of the labour required for forestry operations in places where mature forest already exists. These suggest
that, in the early years of production, forests produce fairly low levels
of employment. However, this may suit those who are planting trees
in combination with reducing their workload in farming, or who already have alternative employment of a relatively undemanding sort.
Once forests mature, their contribution to employment should increase markedly. It is estimated that a million ha of mature forest
could yield somewhere between 30,000 and 40,000 person-years of

employment. This is based on the assumption that a forest mature enough to sustain a steady rate of clear felling and replacement planting would maintain the equivalent of employing one person full-time for every 23 ha, if processing is included, or every 35 ha if processing is not included.

The existence of processing plants within the locality is thus rather important — particularly if we are concerned about the creation of jobs for those who do not possess resources in the form of land, as well as those who do. It is acknowledged that if processing plants do not exist within a reasonable commuting distance, the employment multiplier effect of forestry is quite low, and in circumstances where local landholders are in the process of switching from agriculture into forestry, areas may lose some of their long-term or permanent residents. Experience in Scotland suggests that, for these reasons, widespread afforestation can have significant repercussions on the social fabric of some localities.

On the other hand, timber processing has the capacity to be a very polluting industry, particularly if the processing includes paper or pulp manufacture (Richardson et al., 1993). It is also evident that afforestation on its own can dramatically change the appearance of landscapes, can affect the quality of water resources and the habitats of local wildlife, and can increase the sense of isolation of individual farmsteads or homes. If poorly planned, for example where there is insufficent diversity in the species planted and the continuous land area afforested is very large, it can cut across attempts to develop alternative forms of employment in the locality, in tourism, fishing and recreational pursuits. In particular, water which becomes heavily shaded and acidified as a result of being bordered by dense pine forest can become inhospitable to fish and quite rapidly destroy a well-established local economy based on angling. If well planned, for example to allow the inclusion of walks and nature trails, games reserves and so on, forestry can be an asset to local tourist development; but it is worth noting that women tourists may be reluctant to take advantage of such facilities, and people of both genders often dislike the sense of enclosure that comes from a forest environment.

Control over the afforestation process, therefore, through use of the grant-aid system or planning-application systems, would seem to be essential if the exploitation of local natural resources to produce wood is not to have a negative impact on the local economy as a whole. At present, afforestation proposals for areas of particular landscape or amenity importance are submitted to the county councils concerned for discussion. Particular guidelines are set down for tree planting in designated sensitive fishing zones and compliance with these and other guidelines set down by the Forest Service is a condition of receiving grant aid. In other areas, however, only plantings of over 200 ha require planning permission from the relevant local authority, including a formal Environmental Impact Assessment. Given the reservations set out above, this size limit is, arguably, set too high.

Tourism[3]

Tourism internationally is growing at the rate of 5–6 per cent per annum, and some argue that by the end of this century it will be the largest single source of employment in the world (Urry, 1992; O'Connor et al., 1993). To give us a sense of the scale of the industry, Urry writes:

> There are 400 million international arrivals a year (in 1989). This compares with merely 60 million in 1960. There are between three and four times that number of domestic tourists worldwide" (1992: 1).

It is no wonder, in this context, that the development of the tourism industry is given considerable importance by the Irish state.

Tourism has been an important influence on both the economy and the culture of Ireland since the nineteenth century. Over the past eight years, the number of tourists visiting Ireland doubled, and in 1995 was expected to equal the size of the indigenous population. At present, tourism accounts for nearly 7 per cent of GNP and for over half of export earnings from the services sector; total foreign earnings from tourism in 1994 were just under £1.5 billion. As industrial and agricultural employment continue to contract and with the general shift towards a service-based economy in Ireland, dependence on tourism will continue to increase. Britain still accounts for over half of tourists here. About one-quarter of them come from continental European countries, while about one in eight comes from North America. The most rapidly increasing group in recent years has been those from continental Europe.

---

[3]   Data sources for this section are mainly Bord Fáilte, CERT, CSO and Government Publications.

State policy, as set out in the Operational Programme for Tourism 1994–99, sets ambitious targets in terms of increases in revenue (to £2,250 million in 1999) and in "job equivalents" (from 91,000 to 120,000). It hopes to encourage change in the seasonal shares of overseas visitors, spreading out the tourist period over more of the year, and, particularly, reducing the numbers who come at peak times (from 30 per cent to 25 per cent) and increasing visitors who come just before (May/June) and just after (September) the peak. The Operational Programme envisages an investment of £125 million on marketing, to extend the season and develop new markets as well as expanding sea and air access.

Spatial Distribution and the Structure of Ownership

There is practically no official information available on the structure of ownership in the Irish tourist industry. The best that can be done here is to look briefly at the spatial distribution of Irish tourism, and at the forms of tourism provision encouraged or supported by the tourism authorities in Ireland.

Unlike in some other countries, the Irish tourism industry affects all regions of the country and is not dominated by the capital — or at least, not obviously so; data on the final destination of tourism earnings are very inadequate. Official statistics reveal that in 1993, when Dublin's share of the total population of the State was 29 per cent, this was the same as its share of foreign-exchange earnings from tourism in that year. It had a lower share of domestic tourism revenue, at 16 per cent. The North-West (Donegal, Sligo, Leitrim, Cavan and Monaghan) had around 9 per cent of total tourism employment at that time, matching its share of total state population, while 17 per cent of employment was located in the South-West (Cork, south Kerry in particular). However, during 1995, Dublin experienced relatively strong growth in demand for tourism services, probably as a result of an increase in the number of visitors coming for short-stay visits, particularly from Britain, and also the introduction of direct US flights into Dublin Airport.

It is also the case that "rural Ireland" plays a significant part within Bord Fáilte's overall marketing and development strategy: "Ireland must develop an image as an uncrowded, relaxed island, of great scenic beauty, with a distinctive heritage and culture, a friendly welcoming people, high-quality facilities and a superb, unspoilt environment for outdoor activity" (1994: 3). As well as a focus on the environment, Bord Fáilte's development plans emphasise development of accommodation, natural and cultural amenities and special-interest activities, and also transport facilities for visitors and basic public services to cater for numbers, during peak periods, at up to twice that of the resident population in many remote areas. The hope is to encourage tourists first to visit rural areas and then, once there, to stay longer by having a wide range of activities of interest. O'Connor (1993) argues that tourism is not a static phenomenon. In addition to often quite rapid changes in the origins of visitors to Ireland, there are changes in the nature of international tourism which affect the destination choices visitors make. These have been summarised as a shift from "the tourism of modernity", equated with mass tourism, to that of "post-modernity", equated with the pursuit of niche markets (O'Connor, 1993: 82), which in turn is often associated with a rise in "rural tourism". The image of Ireland marketed by Bord Fáilte, already that of a land of great beauty and with a "pre-modern" (that is, agriculturally dependent, non-urban) economy and society, is well-suited to incorporate a growing international interest in "rural tourism" into marketing strategies and packages.

However, it must be asked to what extent this marks a commitment by Bord Fáilte to encourage tourism promotion by rural people, or is simply an exploitation of rural space and other amenities for consumption by tourists visiting the State as a whole. It is necessary to distinguish between the promotion of touring in rural areas, which may not involve any contact with, or economic returns to, the inhabitants of those areas, and the promotion of rural tourism. Yet the term "rural tourism" is itself rather vague. Rural tourism has been promoted in recent years in Ireland for two reasons: first, because it is seen as a significant solution to the problems of underdevelopment and poverty experienced in many rural locations in Ireland; and second, because it is often presented in the literature as a sort of "soft" tourism, one that can bring economic growth into a rural locality but without bringing in the environmental and other forms of destruction associated with mass tourist development. Proponents of rural tourism claim, for instance, that it is careful of both the social and the natural environment, that it is more attuned to values than to profit, that it relies on "small and slow developments by local interests. Farm economies are strengthened and retained rather than replaced. Existing buildings are re-used rather than being replaced by new buildings. . ." etc. (Lane, 1988, quoted in Byrne et al., 1993: 234). One may suspect that this sort of designation of rural tourism is more prescriptive and utopian than descriptive, and this is discussed further below. For the moment, this section concentrates on discussing the first claim, that rural tourism offers a way out of poverty in under-developed rural areas.

The sort of "rural tourism" claimed to be most effective as a way of attacking rural poverty is usually described as "agri-tourism", or, in other words, the involvement of farm households or farm family members in the provision of bed and breakfast and other tourist amenities to visitors. The adoption by Bord Fáilte of the idea of agri-tourism occurred relatively late, in comparison with some other European countries with similar rural problems to those of Ireland. Quinn and Keane (1991) say that although the agricultural advisory service (then ACOT) began to promote the concept of a more diversified tourism, including farm tourism as well as conventional hotels and so on, for rural areas in the 1980s, it failed to persuade Bord Fáilte to take up the idea. Bord Fáilte's attitude changed only in the late 1980s, after considerable pressure from Macra na Feirme, and the publication of a Price Waterhouse report on Irish tourism which "recommended the development of special-interest tourism along the lines of Israel, Austria and England" (Quinn and Keane, 1991: 191). In 1989 the board appointed an agri-tourism product manager and, recognising that establishing the idea of rural tourism clearly in specific foreign markets would be crucial to its future success, in 1990 it produced, in English, French and German, a "branding brochure" called *Irish Country Holidays* (1991: 196).

More recently rural and agri-tourism have been given a strong boost from the importance which has been attached to them by groups involved in LEADER, INTERREG and other EU-supported rural initiatives. LEADER groups in particular have identified the development of rural tourism as a practical response to the decline in agricultural employment and in the population of rural areas through out-migration. They have high expectations about it as a potentially very significant way of diversifying the economy of rural areas and increasing local economic activities. This can be seen from the fact that the LEADER initiative in Ireland devoted 43 per cent of its funding to tourism development under LEADER I (although it should be said that this was not peculiar to Irish LEADER groups). In contrast, only 16 per cent was spent on developing small and medium enterprises and craft enterprises.

Employment and Forms of Enterprise in Rural Tourism

Are the expectations that rural tourism can make a significant impact on rural poverty well-founded? It is useful to look first at what information is available about employment in tourism overall. A 1992 manpower survey (CERT, 1993) identified 156,639 people working in various sectors of the tourism business, sharing between them some 91,000 full-time-job equivalents. Permanent employment in tourist-related enterprises was highest in "licensed premises" (94 per cent), intermediate in "hotels and guesthouses", and lowest (at 59 per cent of workers) for "leisure services outside leisure centres". These would include many rural tourist jobs, for example, as guides at important monuments, rangers in national parks, or in local interpretive centres. Women were more likely to work in this sector than men (the ratio of male to female employment was 42:58) but, as is so often the case, women were clearly under-represented at management levels where the ratio was 59:41. This was despite an increase in the proportion of women who were described as being in management positions, from 30 per cent in 1988 to 41 per cent in 1992.

The involvement of women in rural tourism is particularly affected by the development of farmhouse accommodation or agri-tourism. Farmhouse tourism could be expected to give women tourism workers much better conditions of work and control over their work. It appears from official estimates to be still very underdeveloped: in 1993, there were 630 farmhouses registered with Bord Fáilte, which between them provided 2,761 rooms and 5,522 bed spaces. It has been estimated that, on average, 3 per cent of overseas visitors spend an overnight stay in such farmhouse accommodation. However, this conceals a much larger unregistered sector about whose economic impact and work relationships little is officially known.

Sociological studies shed a bit more light on the phenomenon. A study by Quinn and Keane (1991) of the development of agri-tourism in Ballyhoura (a collection of parishes in the centre of Munster straddling the Cork-Limerick border) focuses closely on the question of who benefits from this type of local economic development. They note that "Policy-makers, community leaders and state agencies all appear to accept that agri-tourism has an important part to play in rural development". However, "The academic literature that reflects the experience of agri-tourism to date does not fully support that view" (Quinn and Keane, 1991: 199). There is some evidence from elsewhere to suggest that the encouragement of farmhouse tourism helps to reinforce social inequalities among farmers, since only the better-equipped households, and those with enough capital to risk investing some of it in the provision of visitor facilities, can afford to take part. Quinn and Keane's own study suggested, encouragingly, that this was not the case in the particular area they deal with: here, there was a surprisingly high rate of participation by the very smallest farms (0–30 acres). Nevertheless, for three-quarters of the participating farm households, the income they got from tourism contributed 5 per cent or less to total household income, and in general the farm families they studied were not very optimistic about agritourism as a way of providing sufficient employment to family members to deter them from emigrating from the area in future.

Byrne et al.'s paper on rural tourism (1993) also presents the results of a study of participation in, and benefits from, the development of tourism in a local rural area — in their case, the north Connemara region, which was the site of one of the projects funded by the third EU Anti-Poverty Programme. Their study suggests that claims that rural tourism is an answer to the economic problems of rural areas, and that it is "non-intrusive" on either local social relations or local culture, both need to be subjected to critical evaluation.

They focus particularly on the involvement of rural women, rather than simply farm households generally (as in Quinn and Keane's study) in farm tourism, and on the possible problems and benefits that these women may experience. But they are also concerned about whether rural tourism is, in fact, a type of rural development that is open to participation from the poorest households in the local population. As Byrne et al. show, the north Connemara area is one that contains a substantial amount of poor households: the majority of people are engaged in agriculture as their main occupation, but holdings are small and land poor, and most survive only through headage payments, unemployment benefits and other welfare payments, along with whatever other income sources are available locally in fishing, non-agricultural wage work, bed and breakfast and other small enterprises, and so on. The local housing stock and transport infrastructures are both in poor condition. Byrne et al. comment:

> It seems clearly unreasonable to expect many people in this economic predicament to develop tourist enterprises unaided. It may be therefore that purely market-led tourism, whether it is a "rural" version of tourism or not, excludes from participation those who lack resources, both material and cultural (1993: 245).

However, 21 out of the 121 households studied in the area were, even if only minimally, involved in tourism, and they can be examined further to see what sort of involvement is possible to such low-income households in such conditions.

Only eight of the 21 households, in fact, have been able to set up their own tourism business, in the form of bed and breakfast enterprises. The other 13 contain members who work in the hotel industry as waitresses, cleaners, kitchen assistants, receptionists and chefs, all on a part-time seasonal basis. Chefs and receptionists are "comparatively well-paid" but the take-home pay of the others is very low, and, in general, working conditions are poor and the hours very long. Byrne et al. conclude:

> It is difficult to assess whether this level of participation in the tourist industry is a precursor to further entrepreneurial development or whether it merely provides opportunities for some members of low-income households to engage in labour-intensive activity for minimal returns. Working as a waitress during the summer months does provide an injection of cash into a household short of capital. Whether it is an effective ingredient required to assist other members to set up their own business, though, is highly debatable. It seems more realistic to assume that additional income earned in this manner is a haphazard benefit of tourism (1993: 246).

The eight households which have been able to set up independently, if in a very limited way, share some characteristics which distinguish them from their neighbours. They are situated on already established tourist routes and they tend to own their own homes, either outright or on a mortgage. They tend to be better educated, and to come from households in which, while like their neighbours they have to engage in a range of activities to generate household income, one partner, usually the man, has a source of regular income either as an employee or from self-employment. "It would seem that a regular source of earned income may be a prerequisite for poor households setting up their own business" (Byrne et al., 1993: 248).

All of the bed and breakfast businesses are run by the woman of the household, with some help from other family members — there are no employees. The enterprises bring in incomes of from £500 to £2,000 a month while the season lasts (typically for four months from June to September). Few plan to expand — for example, by building on extra rooms — because they cannot afford the cost. Similarly, none are registered with Bord Fáilte, for reasons which range from being unable to afford the costs of registration and inspection, to fear that their premises would not meet the required standards, "a wariness about having to pay income tax and a general fear of losing welfare and health benefits if they became 'official'" (Byrne et al., 1993: 249). Byrne et al. stress that the economic context in which households in this area live cannot be ignored, and that while these eight households do show that people can participate in farmhouse tourism, even from very low starting points, they are also very exceptional in terms of the 121 households studied in total. Most households in such an area could not take advantage of opportunities for new economic activities like this unless they had some very strong support, such as from a community-based organisation: "Without this, those whose economic situation is closest to entrepreneurship are likely to benefit from tourism to the exclusion of weaker sections of the society" (*ibid.*).

Duggan's (1994) study of a west-Connemara Gaeltacht community found that the economic activity of women was important for the income of over half of the households in the area, and in most cases this came from farmhouse tourism, particularly the hosting of language students. In some cases earnings from language tourism were extremely significant: she discusses one case where the income derived was equal to half the income that the household derived from fishing and up to four times what they derived from farming. Duggan too is very interested in the impact of this work on women in the locality. She argues that women in this community exercise almost total control over tourism activities, in the sense of both being responsible for providing the services and of "owning" the rewards. Involvement in tourism has also, she argues, helped to give value to the domestic domain — maintaining a high-quality home is now recognised as a source of high status in the area, and it is a source of status for women in the area, who have generally lacked any basis for status in the past.

Duggan also notes the barriers to entry into agri-tourism — in particular, the high standard of accommodation needed if a house is to be accepted by the sending organisations as suitable for hosting language students. Generous grants from Údarás na Gaeltachta have helped considerably in overcoming these.

Tourism and the Rural Environment

Environmental and "sustainability" concerns are central issues for all of the types of natural resource use discussed in this chapter, but for none more than tourism which treats the very characteristics of the countryside itself — its landscapes and its space — as amenities for visitors and hence as key resources for exploitation. We noted earlier that rural tourism is often promoted on the grounds that it is a "soft" or "environment friendly" type of tourism. Interestingly, Bord Fáilte's Tourism Development Plan for 1994–99 puts considerable emphasis on sustainable development tourism, defining this as "sustainable in terms of a quality environment . . . in terms of developing profitable enterprises [and] . . . in terms of enduring job creation" (1994: 1).

Whether in fact the tourist industry could ever be considered "sustainable" in environmental terms is strongly challenged by Urry (1992). He points out that international tourism has

> profound environmental consequences. These stem first from the fact that tourism is very much concerned with in a sense visually consuming that very environment; second, from the enormous flows of people carried on many different forms of transport which enable tourists to gaze upon often geographically distant environments; and third, from the various transformations of the environment which follow from the widespread construction of tourist attractions and from the incredible concentrations of people into particular places" (1992: 1).

Even if "soft" tourism is able to avoid bringing some of the worst consequences of mass tourism into a rural locality (which may be questioned), from the point of view of global resource conservation it can only add to the already existing "unsustainability" of the industry.

In Bord Fáilte's understanding of it, however, sustainability is related not just to environmental quality, but also to profit and to a certain type of employment. We have already noted that much tourism employment, although it may be "enduring", is not necessarily full-time or permanent. Bord Fáilte also places community involvement high on its list of distinguishing features of sustainable tourism. Rural and agri-tourism are often seen as particularly needing the involvement of the "whole community" and as suitable, therefore, for organisation through the community co-operative form. Bord Fáilte suggests that communities become committed to tourism development when there is local participation in decision-making and when tourism development contributes to local environmental, social and economic goals. Therefore, every opportunity should be taken to promote local shops, pubs, cafés, craftworkers, accommodation, bus services, entertainment and events, all of which will help to sustain the living community. Quinn and Keane (1991) strongly support this approach, arguing that community involvement is essential if the attractions and amenities offered in a rural area are to be developed enough to keep visitors in the area for any length of time. For example, maps, signposting and parking facilities need to be provided; walks, pony trails and other local attractions may need to be created and this may necessitate co-operation at least between adjoining landholders whose land is involved; "product suppliers" have to be organised and co-ordinated so as to combine into a single package for visitors the various elements available locally.

Beyond this, however, there is a further sense in which "the tourism product depends on the whole community. Tourists must be made to feel welcome in shops, post-offices and pubs" (Quinn and Keane, 1991: 205). Given the desire expressed by so many visitors from abroad to meet Irish people when they holiday here, there is a sense in which the "package" that locals have to make up and sell to tourists includes the people themselves. They are being encouraged literally to commoditise their own social relationships (Tovey, 1994).

Byrne et al. (1993) argue that although "soft" rural tourism is thought of as non-intrusive and praised for not destroying the local culture and ways of life, change is in fact unavoidable when large numbers of people are encouraged to come into and visit a rural area. The presence of tourists, they suggest, helps to transform the previously "exotic" or "pre-modern" ways of thought and speech, which attracted tourists in the first place, into the "modern", "industrial" thoughtworld which the visitors bring with them from their more politically and economically powerful societies. Even more dangerously, the tourism interests who are promoting a rural area will nearly always try to reorganise it in order to persuade the visitors that what they are seeing really is the authentic "pre-modern" rural Ireland — inevitably, in the process, "using signs of past-ness rather than restorations of artefacts which actually existed in the past" (Byrne et al., 1993: 154) (cobbling what would have been a mud road, for example) because these signs are universal and can be readily grasped by the visitor from another culture.

Bell (1995) and Slater (1995) also suggest that tourism can have the effect of transforming the rural landscape into images that the tourists are already expecting to see. In doing so, it persuades even the local inhabitants to share the tourist perspective — particularly when the tourism traffic is from rich and powerful urbanised societies, to relatively poor rural peripheries whose inhabitants are already uncertain of the continuing value of their own way of life. This does not necessarily always happen, even in rural tourism; some forms of this, such as language tourism, for example, may increase the value of elements of local culture through the evidence it provides that they are valuable and valued beyond the rural locality itself. But in many cases, tourism can be a form of neo-colonialism, simultaneously exploiting and undermining the "difference" of the colonised.

Rural tourism is inextricably linked with both the conservation and the creation of "heritage". Bord Fáilte's measures for promoting sustainable and community tourism, for example, include positive initiatives to help conserve "heritage properties" such as the "Irish Country House" (understood as "the Big House" rather than the small dwellings of the farmers and farm workers of the past), and a set of guidelines for conserving the physical environment in the face of pressure from visitors or from leisure and recreational development. Bramwell and Lane (1993) suggest that rural tourism can provoke strong tensions between the forces of rural development which seek to reverse rural decline, and the forces for conservation, which may seek to fossilise the countryside. While this may happen, it is equally likely that in the process of promoting rural tourism as a solution to the economic difficulties of some rural areas, "development" becomes synonymous with "fossilisation" and the creation of the theme park.

Byrne et al. conclude their discussion of rural tourism in north Connemara by saying that it "is certain to erode much that is indigenous and precious to an area and is therefore an option with great costs: we must be sure that it is worthwhile" (1993: 255). It is salutary to set this statement alongside much of the promotional literature from official sources which recognises few if any costs to this strategy for rural development. If our concern is with poverty and inequality in rural areas, and not just with the use of rural resources to generate economic growth, we would want to be certain that it does not exclude from participation the very poorest households in rural areas. The evidence on this, so far, is still quite uncertain.

CONCLUSIONS

The different processes involved in natural resource exploitation in rural Ireland are complex, and the data that it has been possible to find on the four cases discussed here are, in many ways, incomplete or unsatisfactory. At this stage, then, any conclusions drawn can only be tentative.

We argued at the start of the chapter that the trend towards natural resource exploitation in Ireland in recent years should not be placed only in the context of changing EU and Irish state policy towards rural development, and particularly towards agriculture. While these changes have obviously been important in stimulating a fresh look at the possibilities that rural and local economies offer for economic growth, it is also important to recognise that what gets defined as "a possibility" depends on what capital, and especially international capital, defines as worth investing in. What appears as a "natural resource", in other words, is not "natural" but social or socio-economic — it exists as the object of a mix of ideological, financial, and technological interests as these are brought to bear on rural space.

Of course, the fact that Irish natural resource extraction is of interest to global capital is not necessarily a reason for saying that it is inappropriate to Irish rural development. The experience of foreign-led industrialisation in Ireland 20 years earlier, when the sort of labour force, rather than natural resources possessed by Ireland, was attracting the interest of multinational companies, has taught us that if the state is prepared to intervene, even to a limited extent, and to manage the way in which industries are spatially distributed and socially integrated into the economy, some benefits can be derived from this type of development strategy. In a similar way, recognising that contemporary resource exploitation is part of a global development process in which Ireland is largely a dependent participant, it can be argued that there are grounds for maintaining as strict controls over the process as possible, to ensure two things in particular: that access to the opportunities and rewards that it creates remains open to the poorest rural households; and that some transfer of skills, capital or initiative occurs that will encourage a parallel process of endogenous development in the locality.

However, in the 1970s, despite heavy reliance on external capital, state policy-makers were still prepared to allow a role to the state in managing the social forms and impacts of economic development. In the 1990s, and in regard to rural resource exploitation, this seems much less clear. Certainly the review of development policies and practices in the four cases discussed above suggests that addressing the problems of excluded groups is not seen as part of policy formulation, or as a reason for deciding to promote some projects or types of development over others. Resource-exploitation policies are focused on generating wealth, increasing added value, and ultimately, expand-

ing employment. Whether the increased wealth or employment opportunities benefit marginalised groups in rural areas is left largely
as a random effect of where the development takes place and what
sorts of skills or resources are needed by the people who take part in
the exploitation process.

The decline in state concern about directing improved life-chances
to the poorest in the society has been balanced, to some extent, by a
rising concern about protecting the natural environment. We suggested earlier that even when this concern is expressed through the
vocabulary of "sustainable development" it is unlikely to provide
much of a safeguard to the livelihoods of the rural poor who rely, often
within a pluri-active household survival strategy, on small-scale uses
of a range of natural resources. This is partly because of the empti-
ness of the concept itself, and its emphasis on securing the living
standards of future generations rather than on equalising those in
the present generation. It is also because "sustainable development",
as we saw with tourism, for example, is not something that can be
implemented and secured at the purely local level, leaving the rest of
the world to continue as before. It requires large-scale structural
changes in society, nationally and, increasingly, internationally. There
are, as already mentioned, obvious conflicts between the interest of
resource exploiters in not paying the environmental costs of their exploitation, and the interest of local people, rural or urban, in living in
a safe and unpolluted locality. More and more local rural groups in
Ireland, recognising that they cannot effectively control the resource
exploiter who comes in from outside, often with large resources of
capital and influence, are deciding not to allow them in at all.

This leads to the issue of the ownership, scale and form of production associated with natural resource exploitation in rural Ireland in
recent years. Following from the previous point, it is tempting to argue (and is often argued) that the forms of ownership and organisation of work most appropriate to rural development are those that are
small in scale, and non-capitalist in structure: familial or household
based, as individual units, or collectively mobilised through local co-
operatives. However, this position has been quite strongly criticised by
Ruddy and Varley (1991), as noted earlier, and also by Curtin and
Varley (1991) who see it as a populist ideology, which functions primarily to mask the real processes of change taking place in rural
Ireland — essentially, a trend towards ever larger and more capital-
intensive forms of production. Thus the apparently unstoppable advance of "productionism" in agriculture, with its accompanying mar-

ginalisation and demoralisation of a large section of poorer farmers, indicates the path that we can expect all forms of natural-resource exploitation to follow eventually.

The question of scale of production may in fact be ultimately less important than that of ownership and form. The evidence suggests that in rural Ireland, and probably throughout the whole society, the problem of unemployment today is not so much a problem of lack of suitable education or skills on the part of workers, but lack of demand for their labour by capital. An important argument in favour of familial and co-operative forms of production is that both of these are generally more responsible to the needs of family members or neighbours for work, than to the needs of capital for profit. But to the extent that this is true, both are operating counter to the most powerful economic tendencies of our times, and both would require extensive, sensitive, and probably permanent state support to survive.

However it is also important to note that household production may not always be ideal for promoting the objectives of an anti-poverty strategy for rural populations, for two reasons. First, the division of labour, rewards from labour, and access to work opportunities within families is still often organised along patriarchal lines, in which women are expected to supply their work to the household without being entitled to control the returns from it. The evidence from studies of agri-tourism suggests that this is not a major problem, but it is quite fragmentary and would need to be supported by further research. The three other forms of resource exploitation considered do not appear to allocate any specific role to women at all, even when organised through household production (for example, in aquaculture). Second, the organisation of work through households often takes for granted that households possess specific resources which are suited to the production in question — land, a boat, a house that is in reasonable physical condition, and so on. This can have the effect of excluding from involvement precisely those rural people who are in most need of access to work. The household or familial form of organisation of work then raises particular issues in relation to class and to gender, which would need to be very carefully monitored in any policy for its support. To the extent that work co-operatives are built on relations between households, they may also discriminate on gender or class lines unless similarly monitored.

References

Allen, R. and Jones, T. (1990): *Guests of the Nation — People of Ireland against the Multinationals*, London: Earthscan.

Bell, D. (1995): "Framing nature: first steps into the wilderness for a sociology of the landscape", *Irish Journal of Sociology*, 3: 1–22.

Bord Fáilte (1994): Developing Sustainable Tourism — Tourist Development Plan, 1994–99, Dublin: Bord Fáilte.

Bramwell, B. and Lane, B. (eds.) (1993): "Rural Tourism and Sustainable Rural Development", Proceedings of the Second International School on Rural Development, University College Galway, 28 June–9 July.

Brunt, B. (1988): *The Republic of Ireland*, London: Paul Chapman Publishing.

Brundtland Commission (World Commission on Environment and Development) (1987): *Our Common Future*, Oxford: Oxford University Press.

Byrne, A., Edmondson, R. and Fahy, K, (1993): "Rural tourism and cultural identity in the West of Ireland", in O'Connor, B. and Cronin, M. (eds.), *Tourism in Ireland — A Critical Analysis*, Cork: Cork University Press.

CERT — The State Training Agency (1993): Manpower Survey of the Hotel, Catering and Tourism Industry in Ireland.

Commission of the European Communities (1988): *The Future of Rural Society*, Luxembourg: EC Commission.

Cowen, B. (1993): "Mining and Exploration in Ireland", Policy Statement of the Minister for Transport, Energy and Communications in Dáil Éireann on 30 April.

Curtin, C. (1993): "Another Commons Tragedy? Shellfish Co-operatives in North-West Connemara", Paper to Circle for European Studies, Assisi, Cumbria, Italy, October.

Curtin, C. and Shields, D. (1988): "The Legal Process and the Control of Mining Development in the West of Ireland", in Tomlinson M., Varley, T. and McCullagh, C. (eds.), *Whose Law and Order?*, Belfast: Sociological Association of Ireland

Curtin, C. and Varley T. (1991): "Populism and Petit Capitalism in Rural Ireland", in Whatmore, S., Lowe, P. and Marsden, T. (eds.): *Rural Enterprise*. London: Fulton.

Deverre, C. (1995): "Social Implications of Agro-environmental Policy in France and Europe", *Sociologia Ruralis*, 35(2): 227–47.

Dhonau, N.B. (1992): Government Publication on Exploration and Mining, Dublin: Department of Transport, Energy and Communications.

Duggan, C. (1994): "Economic Diversity on Smallholdings: A Study of Pluriactivity in West Connemara", Unpublished PhD thesis, Trinity College, Dublin.

Dunnels, D. and Hitzman, M.W. (1992): *Mineral Exploration and Development in Ireland*, Dublin: Irish Association for Economic Geology.

Euradvice Ltd. (1992): Economic and Social Salvation in the West of Ireland — First Interim Report: *Ireland: Developing the West Together*.

Green 2000 Advisory Group (1993): "Executive Summary and Technical Papers", Report presented to the Taoiseach Mr Albert Reynolds, February, Dublin: Government Publications Office.

Hannan, D. and Commins, P. (1993): *Factors Affecting Land Availability for Afforestation*, Dublin: Economic and Social Research Institute.

Joseph Rowntree Foundation (1995): *Inquiry into Income and Wealth*, Vol. 1, York: Joseph Rowntree Foundation.

Kearney, B. and O'Connor, R. (1993): The Impact of Forestry on Rural Communities. Dublin: Economic and Social Research Institute.

Kearney, B. (1993): *Policy Challenges in Forestry*, Dublin: Economic and Social Research Institute.

Kelleher, C. (1986): "Forestry and Farmers", in *The Changing CAP and its Implications*, Proceedings of the 13th Annual Conference of the Economics and Rural Welfare Research Centre, AFT, Dublin: An Foras Talúntais.

Kousis, M. (1993): "Collective Resistance and Sustainable Development in Rural Greece: The Case of Geothermal Energy on the Island of Milos", *Sociologia Ruralis*, 33(1): 3–24.

Lane, B. (1992): "A Philosophy for Rural Tourism", in Feehan, J. (ed.), *Tourism on the Farm*, Environmental Institute, University College Dublin.

Marsden, T., Murdoch, J., Lowe, P., Munton, R. and Flynn, A. (1993): *Constructing the Countryside*, London: UCL Press.

Martell, L. (1994): *Ecology and Society — An Introduction*, Cambridge: Polity Press.

MINFO (1993): Exploration and Mining Division Information Service, Dublin: Department of Energy.

Mormont, M. (1987): "Rural Nature and Urban Natures", *Sociologia Ruralis*, 27(1): 3-20.

Murdoch, J. (1993): "Sustainable Rural Development — Towards a Research Agenda", *Geoforum*, 24(3): 225–41.

Murphy, R. (1994): *Rationality and Nature*, Boulder, CO: Westview Press.

O'Connor, B. (1993): "Myths and Mirrors: Tourist Images and National Identity", in O'Connor, B. and Cronin, M. (eds.), op. cit.

O'Connor, B. and Cronin, M. (eds.) (1993): *Tourism in Ireland — A Critical Analysis*, Cork: Cork University Press.

O'Connor, R., Whelan, B.J., Crutchfield, J.A., O'Sullivan, A.J. (1992): *Review of the Irish Aquaculture Sector and Recommendations for Its Development*, Economic and Social Research Institute, Paper no. 156,. Dublin: ESRI.

O'Dowd, L. (1990): *Gold Mining and the Irish Environment*, Bantry: Earthwatch, Ireland.

O'Hara, P. and Commins, P. (1991): "Starts and Stops in Rural Development: An Overview of Problems and Policies" in Reynolds, B. and Healy, S.J.

(eds.), *Rural Development Policy — What Future for Rural Ireland?*, Dublin: Conference of Major Religious Superiors.

O'Riordan, T. (1988): "The Politics of Sustainability", in Kerry Turner, R. (ed.), *Sustainable Environmental Management: Principles and Practice*, London: ESRC-Belhaven-Westview Press.

Quinn, J. and Keane, M.J. (1991): "Community Tourism in Rural Ireland", in Varley, T., Boylan, T.A., and Cuddy, M.P. (eds.), *Rural Crisis: Perspectives on Irish Rural Development*, Galway: Centre for Development Studies, University College, Galway.

Redclift, M. (1984): *Development and the Environmental Crisis*, London: Methuen.

Redclift, M. (1991): "The Multiple Dimensions of Sustainable Development", *Geography*, 76(1): 36–42.

Redclift, M. (1992): "The Meaning of Sustainable Development", *Geoforum*, 23(3): 395–403

Richardson, M., Sherman, J. and Gismondi, M. (1993): *Winning Back the Words*, Toronto: Garamond Press.

Robinson, P.C. (1991): "Tara: The Economic and Environmental Benefits, Local and National", in the 1991 Annual Review of the Association of Economic Geology, Dublin.

Ruddy, M. and Varley, T. (1991): "Sea Farming and Development in North Connemara", in Varley, T., Boylan, T.A., and Cuddy, M.P. (eds.): *Rural Crisis: Perspectives on Irish Rural Development*, Galway: Centre for Development Studies, University College, Galway.

Slater, E. (1995): "Contested Terrain: Differing Interpretations of Co. Wicklow's Landscape", *Irish Journal of Sociology*, 3: 23–55.

Tovey, H. (1993): "Environmentalism in Ireland: Two Versions of Development and Modernity", *International Sociology*, 8(4) (December): 413–30.

Tovey, H. (1994): "Rural Management, Public Discourses, and the Farmer as Environmental Actor", in Symes, D. and Jansen, A. (eds.): *Agricultural Restructuring and Rural Change in Europe*, Wageningen: Wageningen Agricultural University.

Treacy, N. (1993): Address by the Minister of State, Dept. of Transport, Energy and Communications, given at the Irish Mining and Exploration Group AGM, 2 June.

Urry, J. (1992): "The Tourist Gaze and the Environment", *Theory, Culture and Society*, 9: 1–26.

5: Rural Industrialisation and Rural Poverty

Tom Boylan

INTRODUCTION

The pursuit of regional industrial policies, which in the Irish context subsumes rural industrialisation, has been one of the principal mechanisms by which the State has influenced access to, and participation in, alternative non-farm employment. Ireland, in common with most developing countries in their post-independence attempts to achieve economic development, has pursued an active régime of policy intervention consistent with the dominant paradigm of development centred on the state provision of infrastructure and extensive state assistance to industrial development. Implicit in this strategy of development were a number of critical issues which impinged directly on the problem of poverty alleviation, but which did not receive either the attention of policy makers or the research priority that they warranted. These included such issues as the need for social and spatial targeting with respect to poverty, the mechanisms and criteria of accessibility and participation in the new economic activities generated by economic development by the most vulnerable social groups, and the provision of educational opportunities, both general and specific, in response to the needs of the most disadvantaged. While this list is more illustrative than comprehensive, and acknowledging that, in recent years, a more focused approach to a number of these issues has emerged, it is true, nevertheless that the systematic identification of critical aspects of the poverty problem, including its spatial distribution, is just emerging in the literature (Nolan, Whelan and Williams, 1994). Consequently, what is lacking is the comprehensive empirical base that would facilitate a more penetrating interrogation of a number of aspects of the poverty problem. This is particularly true with respect to the spatial dimension of the problem.

Consistent with the analytical objectives of this volume and keeping faith with the conceptual framework developed in Chapter 1, the focus in this chapter will be primarily on the dynamics of Irish state policy in the specific domain of regional and rural industrialisation. More specifically, it will be argued that state policy in this domain has moved through a number of well-defined phases, in the course of which increasing tensions and internal contradictions have arisen. These have been generated, it will be argued, by the increasing intensification of the globalisation process and the relentless internationalisation of capital, both financial and physical, in more recent decades. It is only against the background of these larger international developments that the changing configuration of domestic state policy in the area of regional and rural industrialisation can be analysed.

Given the constraints of space, the presentation strategy, while aspiring to provide as comprehensive an overview of the topic as is feasible, will be forced to invoke the use of selective illustration at particular junctures in the chapter. The structure of the chapter is as follows. The second section will examine the dynamics of the regional development policy debate up to the early 1980s, highlighting a number of major issues over the course of this period. The third section will examine the impact of rural industrialisation based on a number of existing illustrative studies, which, it must be noted, vary greatly in their scope and range of coverage. In the fourth section, the re-orientation of industrial policy from the mid-1980s is examined and a number of important implications are highlighted. The final section provides general conclusions arising from the chapter against the background of the central concerns informing the overall project.

REGIONAL INDUSTRIALISATION: THE POLICY CONTEXT

The purpose of this section is not to rehearse a comprehensive narrative of the evolution of regional industrial policy. This has been done on a number of occasions by different authors, (Ross, 1978; Johnson, 1981; Breathnach, 1985). The aim is to re-examine these developments in regional policy, viewed from the perspective of the implications for rural development. More specifically, a number of facets of this process will be highlighted, two of which are of particular significance. First, the conflict or tension that has existed at different periods between the requirements of national economic growth, on the one hand, and the needs of rural development on the other. At different periods this tension has been particularly pronounced, while in other periods elaborate attempts at compromise have been pursued. Secondly, this study will argue, using the West Planning Region (the counties of Galway and Mayo) to illustrate the argument, that even in the most elaborate phase of regional planning for the spatial dispersal of industrial employment, the outcome was considerably more modest than the stated aspirations would have anticipated. To the extent that poverty has a spatial dimension, as highlighted in Chapter 2 of this book, the relationship between the historical dynamics of industrial policy — more specifically the changing commitment to the spatial dispersal of industrial employment — and the spatial incidence of poverty takes on particular significance.

Emphasis on the purely spatial dimensions of rural poverty is inherently limited for obvious reasons. A fundamental distinction must
be borne in mind between spatial prosperity ("place prosperity") and
social group prosperity ("people prosperity"). Clearly, the average
standard of living for any particular area, as measured by the conventional criteria, such as per capita disposable income, can be
greatly improved while simultaneously exacerbating the gap between
the privileged and the disadvantaged social groups within that area.
This basic distinction would suggest that social, as distinct from spatial objectives, must be central to any analysis of poverty and social
exclusion. While accepting the compelling force of this distinction, the
emphasis here is on the spatial processes at work in the Irish context,
not in order to favour the spatial over the social, but to highlight a
number of issues consistent with the conceptual framework of this
overall study. More particularly, the shifts in state policy towards
spatial industrialisation since political independence reflects the internal policy discourse and the informative influences that have
shaped this discourse. At different times these influences have been
predominantly internal, but since the 1960s and with the re-
engagement of free trade, the influences have become increasingly
external. This is clearly evident since our membership of the European Union but, more recently, the influence of global restructuring
has greatly intensified its impact on all aspects of the Irish economy.
The potential of global restructuring to alter radically the configuration of international production through a new international division
of labour, and its corollary of a new spatial division of labour, is enormous. Ireland, as a small open economy whose industrial strategy
since the 1960s was based on providing a pivotal role to foreign direct
investment, is singularly vulnerable to these external influences.
Consequently, the need to decode the critical influences on the formation of public policy in the domain of spatial development, if not in
itself a sufficient reason in understanding the production and reproduction of rural poverty, is certainly a necessary one in that the
commitment or otherwise of the State to provide alternative employment opportunities in rural areas becomes crucial in identifying the
processes at work in the alleviation or creation of rural poverty.
Therefore, the logical sequence is the critical evaluation of the impact
of the spatial policies implemented — in this case, rural industrialisation — in achieving particular objectives for specific social groups

with respect to poverty and social exclusion. On this view neither the spatial nor the social dimensions are privileged, but a schematic sequential approach is identified which should facilitate discussion of the major themes of concern to this book. For this reason, this section will examine, albeit briefly, the changing constellation of factors which influenced spatial policy since political independence. Implementation of this policy over a particular period is illustrated by reference to the West Planning Region. A later section will return to the more recent considerations which are now exerting a powerful influence on policy formation in this area.

When Ireland became independent in 1922, it had a very fragile industrial base. This was evident in its low level of industrial employment: for example, in 1926 only 10 per cent of the workforce was engaged in industry (Breathnach, 1985). In terms of spatial distribution, the available industrial employment was very unevenly spread. During the term of office of the first government from 1922 to 1932 there were few explicit policy measures relating to regional or rural industrial employment. The principal preoccupation was with the development of the agricultural sector. This attention to agriculture was justified given the relative size of that sector in terms of employment and its importance as an export industry (O'Hagan, 1981). It was also justified given that the inherited industrial base was relatively underdeveloped and its development clearly was perceived as a longer-term objective.

With a change of government in 1932, a more active policy of national industrialisation was pursued, based on protectionism, import substitution and the exclusion of foreign investment (Meenan, 1970). This new strategy resulted in substantial development of the domestic industrial base, as domestic entrepreneurs availed of the captive domestic markets produced by extensive protection. Viewed from the perspective of the regional distribution of industry, this period did not see any major commitment to industrial dispersal. While it seemed that government policy favoured industrial dispersal in principle, and de Valera may well have been wedded to an ideology of ruralism, no formal state mechanism was implemented to attain a goal of industrial dispersal (Breathnach, 1985). This was to come later, in the early 1950s. As a result, the general pattern of industrial employment distribution was characterised by an unplanned and ad-hoc structure, with most of the new industrial growth taking place in the main urban centres. (O'Neill, 1971)

Viewed from the perspective of rural development, during the first 30 years of state policy no conscious policies of industrial location were followed with the objective of providing increased access to alternative employment opportunities outside agriculture in the less developed regions. The concern lay rather with the continued development of agriculture, the provision of a number of essential infrastructural facilities, such as the Shannon scheme, which were admittedly highly localised in their impact, along with the establishment of an industrial base primarily geared to supplying the domestic market (Boylan, 1984).

Against this background, the passing of the Undeveloped Areas Act, 1952 marked the beginning of an explicit spatial policy. It represented a conscious decision to assist the less-developed areas, which became known as the Designated Areas and included the counties of Kerry, Clare, Galway, Mayo, Roscommon, Sligo, Leitrim, Donegal, Cavan, Monaghan, Longford and parts of Cork and Limerick. The Act introduced a set of regionally differentiated grants and incentives in an attempt to rectify the extraordinarily durable problem of regional imbalance, reflected in the fact that the areas identified for preferential treatment in the 1952 Act were essentially the same as the Congested District Board areas of the late nineteenth century. The 1952 Act was followed in 1956 by the Industrial Grants Act, which extended the provision of grants to assist the location of industry to the rest of the country but with maximum grant level weighted in favour of the Designated Areas.

Further modifications were contained in legislation passed in 1959. These later pieces of legislation are conventionally interpreted as merely adding to the existing legislation to facilitate industrial development in general (NESC, 1982). An alternative interpretation, however, would view these later Acts as the beginning of a shift in emphasis, which gave an increasing priority to the needs of national economic development relative to the specific needs of particular regions and areas, particularly the more rural areas. This shift in emphasis gathered increasing momentum during the late 1950s and into the 1960s.

During the 1960s, a fundamental reversal of the national industrial strategy saw the end of protectionism and economic nationalism. These where replaced by a new strategy of export-oriented industrialisation, which was based mainly on foreign direct investment. The concerns of regional policy became more subservient to the needs of national economic development. This retrenchment in the policy commitment to industrial dispersal was evident throughout the 1960s, when the shift of emphasis was clearly on the maximisation of national economic growth. The official justification of this retreat from the policy of regional dispersal of industry was that it was a major constraint and potential obstacle to the achievement of rapid national industrial growth. The more generalised form of this argument was that, given the tendency to industrial agglomeration in the advanced capitalist economies, attempts to pursue a policy of industrial dispersal would inhibit, if not totally deter, such investment (Breathnach, 1985). This line of argument was clearly discernible in the seminal policy documents of Irish economic development, such as Whitaker's *Economic Development* in 1958 and later was argued cogently in the work of the influential advisory bodies such as the Committee on Industrial Organisation (CIO, 1963) and the National Industrial Economic Council (NIEC, 1965) during this period. When the Buchanan Report was published in the late 1960s (Buchanan, 1968), with its preferred option of a limited number of growth centres, in addition to containing the current international orthodoxy of the period, it merely reflected what was already a well-developed indigenous line of thought on that subject.

The political unacceptability of the Buchanan proposals highlighted the urgency of producing a compromise set of policies for the regional distribution of industrial employment. The task was bequeathed to the Industrial Development Authority (IDA) and the compromise was achieved in their Regional Industrial Plans 1973–77, which introduced the most detailed and articulated phase of regional industrial policy. The task which faced the IDA was both difficult and challenging. On the one hand, it had to translate into an operational set of policies what amounted to an extremely broadly stated set of goals contained in government statements of May 1969 and 1972 (NESC, 1975), while at the same time negotiating a modified version of the Buchanan proposals.

The underlying philosophy of the IDA's approach was based on two major premises:

(1) It accepted in general the basic line of argument contained in the Buchanan proposals concerning the need for selectivity in establishing a small number of large centres.

(2) It stressed the desirability and, more significantly from a policy point of view, the feasibility of achieving a greater dispersal of industry outside the selected large growth centres, and consciously planned for this development. This was largely seen as

being complementary to, rather than in conflict with, the Buchanan proposals.

The compromise approach proposed by the IDA was based on its capacity to influence successfully the location of new industry, both between regions and within individual regions. Within the proposed planning framework, each of the nine planning regions, which had been established following the Planning and Development Act, 1963, was allocated a target number of jobs in manufacturing which were to be created within the duration of the plan. In addition, each planning region was subdivided into "town groups" of neighbouring towns and villages, with each such group also being assigned a manufacturing job target over the period of the plan. This planning approach was essentially maintained for the IDA's second set of regional industrial plans, which covered the period 1978–82 (Breathnach, 1985).

This ambitious policy of industrial location, with its implications for rural industrialisation and regional accessibility, was no doubt motivated by the perceived pattern of industrial location during the 1960s, when the IDA operated a much more informal and less focused locational policy. Notwithstanding the argument against industrial dispersal which emerged during the 1960s, new industry, and particularly foreign industry, was not adverse to rural and small-town locations.

With the re-orientation of industrial strategy from the late 1950s and the central role given to foreign direct investment, the new policies of extensive grant provision and exemption from tax on profits from exports for foreign firms began to attract increasing numbers of these firms through the 1960s. By 1973, when Ireland joined the European Economic Community (EEC), foreign firms accounted for 27 per cent of total manufacturing employment (NESC, 1982). These firms accounted for two-thirds of all new grant-aided manufacturing plants established in the period 1960–73 (O'Farrell, 1975).

With respect to the locational distribution of new grant-aided manufacturing firms established between 1960 and 1973 and in particular the foreign firms, O'Farrell (1975, 1978, 1979, 1980) has analysed the topic in considerable detail. The most interesting result to emerge from O'Farrell's work was the fact that indigenous plants displayed a "marginally greater tendency to locate in the core (east) than foreign plants" (O'Farrell, 1980: 149). More specifically, 59.1 per cent of foreign plants located within the Designated Areas between 1960 and 1973, compared with 42.8 per cent of Irish ones. While these results can be critically interrogated and alternative explanations for this pattern of industrial location brought forward, the net effect was clear, in that the Designated Areas did benefit over this period and the basis was laid for further improvement in the period following the implementation of the Regional Industrial Plans from 1973 onwards.

Over the period of the Regional Industrial Plans (1973–82) substantial progress was achieved in the area of regional development. In a number of regions a new industrial base was established where previously little or no industry had existed, while in other regions older industries based on the traditional sectors were complemented by newer growth industries. These developments can be illustrated by an examination of the changing fortunes of a specific region, in this case the West Planning Region comprising counties Galway and Mayo, which will highlight the pattern of sectoral and spatial change over the period 1952–82. This period coincides, from a policy perspective, with the introduction of spatial differentiation, through the Undeveloped Areas Act, 1952, to the more ambitious spatial planning of the period 1973–82 with the Regional Industrial Plans.

At the beginning of this period in the early 1950s the West Region's economy was dominated by a pronounced sectoral imbalance as shown in Table 5.1 below.

Table 5.1: Employment Shares in Main Sectors of Economic Activity in the State and West Region, 1951–1971

Sector		1951	1961	1971
		%	%	%
Total	West Region	10.2	9.7	8.6
	The State	100.0	100.0	100.0
Agriculture	West Region	67.2	62.1	51.6
	The State	40.3	35.4	26.1
Industry	West Region	9.8	13.1	16.7
	The State	19.3	23.6	30.9
Services	West Region	23.0	24.8	31.1
	The State	40.4	41.0	43.9

Source: Census of Population 1951, 1961, 1971.

In 1951, agriculture accounted for just over 67 per cent of the region's total employment, compared with 40 per cent for the State. Industrial employment accounted for just under 10 per cent, while service-sector employment, mainly public-sector, accounted for almost 23 per cent. By 1971, the sectoral employment shares stood at 51.6 per cent in agriculture, 16.6 per cent in industry, and 31.1 per cent in services. Over this period, 1951–71, a certain pattern of industrial development within the region was also discernible. There was a shift, as reflected in the employment change, away from the older more traditional industries such as clothing and textiles, to the newer industries represented by chemicals, mechanical and electrical engineering. This trend was to become even more pronounced during the 1970s, which coincided with the implementation of the Regional Industrial Plans of the IDA. Taking the period 1973–83, the principal developments in industrial change can be summarised as follows, reflecting the pattern contained in Table 5.2 below.

Table 5.2: Average Annual Rate of Change in Industrial Employment, by Main Industrial Sector in West Region, 1973–1982

	Average Annual Rate of Change		
Industrial Sector	*1973–78*	*1978–82*	*1973–82*
Non-metallic Minerals	11.0	-10.2	1.0
Chemicals	37.4	4.9	21.8
Metals and Engineering	22.3	5.1	14.3
Food	1.3	3.4	2.2
Drink and Tobacco	0.4	-1.2	-0.3
Textiles	0.7	-7.3	-2.9
Clothing, Footwear and Leather	4.3	-4.6	0.3
Timber and Furniture	5.7	2.5	4.3
Paper and Printing	9.0	7.5	8.3
Miscellaneous	15.2	-6.3	5.1
Total	10.7	1.3	6.4

Source: IDA Employment Surveys (various years).

(1) There was rapid growth in employment in the chemical industry
     (21.8 per cent per annum), as well as in the metal and engineer-
     ing (including electronics) industry (14.3 per cent per annum).

(2) A more modest growth in employment was recorded in such in-
     dustries as paper and printing (8.3 per cent per annum); miscel-
     laneous (5.1 per cent per annum); and timber and furniture (4.3
     per cent per annum).

(3) Employment declined in the older industries such as textiles (-2.9
     per cent per annum); drink and tobacco (-0.3 per cent per annum);
     and there was stagnation of employment in the clothing, foot-
     wear and leather industries.

This was the general pattern of industrial development within the
West Region over the period.

   From the perspective of rural development, a critical aspect of this
development concerned the spatial distribution of this industrial employment change. Concentrating on the period 1973–82, which represented the period when public policy was most committed to the dispersal of industrial employment both inter-regionally and within regions, how did this employment distribute itself within the West Region over this period? There are two alternative ways of evaluating
this issue. The first is to take the performance of each town group
within the region over the planning period 1973–82 with respect to
industrial employment change. The town group was the planning
concept used by the IDA for intra-regional allocation of industrial
employment, and within each town group two sub-sets of towns and
villages can be distinguished: those explicitly identified and targeted
by the IDA, which we will refer to as the "listed" towns; and the remaining towns and villages, which we term the "unlisted" towns. The
performance of these town groups over the planning period can be
summarised as follows. Firstly, the dominance of the largest urban
centres within the region was very pronounced with respect to their
share of the region's industrial employment. Hence the town groups
centred on Galway city, Castlebar, and Ballina respectively dominated
their particular town groups. Secondly, the poor employment performance of the "unlisted" towns in each of the town groups was very
striking. The ability of the smaller rural towns to participate in economic growth, as reflected in their ability to acquire a share of the
region's industrial employment, was negligible or practically non-
existent if they were not explicitly selected by the development agen-

cies for specific development assistance. Finally, the poor performance of the town groups which possessed a poor urban structure was very evident. This was particularly reflected in the town-groups located in north-east Galway, south-east Mayo and east Mayo.

Alternatively, the pattern of intra-regional distribution of industrial employment can be examined by reference to the town-size distribution of manufacturing employment. This is summarised in Table 5.3.

Table 5.3: Manufacturing Employment by Town Size Category, 1973–82

Town Size Distribution	Number of Towns	1973	1978	1982
		%	%	%
0–200	7	1.3	1.1	2.4
201–750	20	5.7	8.8	7.2
751–1,500	11	10.0	10.5	12.0
1,501–3,000	1	2.8	2.5	2.3
3,001–6,000	3	21.2	12.1	13.9
6,001–15,000	3	21.0	24.5	24.0
15,000+	1	30.3	29.6	29.4
Gaeltacht Areas		7.8	11.0	8.0
Total		100.0	100.0	100.0

Note: Totals may exceed 100 per cent because of rounding.
Source: IDA Employment Surveys (various years).

Three aspects of the pattern of change, as summarised in Table 5.3, warrant brief comment:

(1) The seven largest towns in the region had over 72 per cent of manufacturing employment in 1973, and by 1982 they still, despite the attempts to disperse industrial employment, possessed over 68 per cent of this employment.

(2) The two smallest town-size categories (0–750) increased their share from 7 per cent in 1973 to 10 per cent in 1982.

(3) The medium town-size categories (751–3,000) increased their share of manufacturing employment from 12 per cent in 1973 to 14 per cent in 1982.

From this evidence it is clear that the changes in town-size share of manufacturing employment, notwithstanding the commitment to industrial dispersal over this period, were marginal rather than substantial. If, in addition, the decentralisation of public-service employment is taken into account as a component of employment dispersal, the largest urban centres within the region, such as Galway, Castlebar and Ballina, were the main beneficiaries, further compounding the intra-regional concentration of non-agricultural employment opportunities in the largest urban centres.

Since 1982, there has been continued restructuring of regional economies in Ireland, and the West Region was no exception to this process. The period between 1980 and 1987 witnessed the most pronounced period of contraction in manufacturing employment, when 46,251 jobs were lost in grant-aided enterprises (Walsh, 1995). By far the highest proportion of job losses occurred in the East Region, dominated by Dublin, which accounted for 57 per cent of the total job losses. This was followed by the South-West Region, which accounted for 14 per cent of the total job losses, with plant closures in Cork city accounting for a substantial proportion of this figure. This development gave rise to the perception of an increasing urban dimension to the employment problems, which was noted by a number of commentators (Drudy and McKeon, 1991). Ranked in descending order, the inter-regional distribution of industrial job losses over the period 1981–87 was as follows: East (56.5 per cent), South-West (13.9 per cent), Border (11.7 per cent), South-East (9.4 per cent), Midlands (4.7 per cent), West (2.0 per cent), Mid-West (1.8 per cent) (Walsh, 1995). The more recent period from 1988 to 1993 has seen an overall net expansion in industrial employment, with a new employment gain of just over 15,000 jobs in grant-aided industries. The inter-regional distribution of these net gains in industrial employment is uneven, with 22 per cent going to the East Region, while the Midlands and the North-West Regions picked up 2.3 and 2.5 per cent of the net gains respectively. The West Region gained 9.6 per cent of the net gain in industrial employment between 1988 and 1993. Clearly, the rapid and relentless restructuring that occurred during the 1980s not only exacerbated the problems of industrial development as a source of alternative employment in the weaker rural regions, but also highlighted the vulnerabilities of urban labour markets in the course of this process.

Of potentially greater significance, viewed from the perspective of social-class accessibility and more equitable gender participation, have been the continued changes in the sectoral composition within the industrial sector, which began during the 1970s and gathered increasing pace during the 1980s. The increased emphasis of industrial policy on the role of high-technology industry, which will be examined in a later section of this chapter, has given rise to what Walsh (1995: 26) has called "important regional contrasts between firms in relation to sectoral specialisation, technological capacity, productivity levels and commitments to research and development activity". A new typology of industrial establishments distinguishes between "high", "medium" and "low"-technology firms. The new preoccupation of policy-makers has emphasised the necessity of creating the regional capacities to attract and sustain their share of these high-technology industries. By 1990, the highest proportion of high-technology firms was located in the Mid-West Region, followed by the Dublin area (city and county), with the third highest proportion being in the West.

In the light of these developments, it is salutary to remind oneself that, when viewed from the perspective of the intra-regional distribution of industrial employment as a means of achieving spatial access to employment opportunities for the rural poor, the results have been rather modest as illustrated for the West Region. In addition, there was the issue of the evolving structure of the industrial change that occurred within the West Region, which highlighted the phenomenal growth of the electronic and chemical industries and raises the issue of accessibility based on the educational and skills requirement for these jobs. These latter issues remain poorly researched, particularly when viewed from the perspective of rural poverty and its alleviation through the provision of alternative employment opportunities. Against this background of changing policy régimes with respect to regional industrialisation, what was the impact of industrialisation in what were deemed to be specific rural locations?

THE IMPACT OF RURAL INDUSTRIALISATION

Studies of the local impact of rural industrialisation have been produced intermittently and have been extremely varied in the range of topics addressed. Rural poverty has rarely been the primary focus of these studies, except indirectly in that studies of the economic impact of rural industrialisation could be argued to be addressing rural poverty through long-term structural development of rural areas. The existing studies, the bulk of which are geographically focused on the Designated Areas or specific areas within it such as the Gaeltacht, shed more light on such aspects as the sociocultural problems, along with the demographic and economic impacts of rural industrialisation, rather than on rural poverty per se. In this regard, Breathnach (1985) has provided a useful survey of the principal studies undertaken with respect to the Designated Areas, at least up to the early 1980s, and the following paragraphs acknowledge the debt owed to his valuable work in providing a brief overview of these studies. The purpose is clearly not to rehearse Breathnach's review, but to convey the central thrust of a number of the existing studies and to include a number of additional studies that have been undertaken since the early 1980s. Indicative of the range of these studies is Breathnach's use of a three-way categorisation of these studies into what he terms the economic, demographic and socio-economic impacts of rural industrialisation (Breathnach, 1985: 186–92).

Demographically, the impact of industrialisation in the Designated Areas has arguably been extremely positive, either in reducing emigration or generating net immigration. The 1970s in particular, as is well documented, witnessed a historic turnaround in Ireland's demographic experience, with sustained net immigration being the dominant feature. The 11 western counties of the Designated Areas experienced a 10 per cent increase in population between 1971 and 1981. This was in contrast to declines of 9.5 per cent and 11.5 per cent in the inter-censal periods 1961–71 and 1951–61 respectively. However, in the decade following 1981, the economic recession re-established a pattern of net emigration from these regions, which was instrumental in invoking a response from the western bishops (Euradvice, 1994).

Among the existing studies of rural industrialisation, the study by Kane (1977), which examined a number of factories in the Gaeltacht, argued that these factories were not instrumental in preventing emigration in any significant way. At the time that the research for this study was undertaken in the late 1960s, the majority of the factory employees were young single females who perceived the factory as a transient source of employment, a useful preparatory ground before undertaking the final step of emigration. In their seminal study of Irish rural industrialisation, Lucey and Kaldor (1969) found that the majority of the workers surveyed, most of them male, indicated that they would have emigrated in the absence of the new industrial jobs being made available. Since most of these workers were married with families, the demographic effects of such emigration would have been even more dramatic on their local areas. An interesting characteristic of the workers surveyed in this study was the fact that about a third had relocated from other areas, most of them having returned from England. The Shannon area was the subject of a number of studies, namely those by Küpper (1969) and Hütterman (1978). The former study estimated that 29 per cent of male and 12 per cent of female workers were returned emigrants, while Hüttermans (1978) study of the same area showed that the take-up of jobs by returned emigrants had declined. Similar to the results in the Lucey and Kaldor (1969) study, in a survey of employees in a branch plant of a large synthetic fibre plant in rural North Mayo, O'Cinneide and Keane (1983) found that a third of the employees were returned emigrants from abroad. A study of two Gaeltacht areas by Breathnach (1984) found that over two-fifths and one-quarter of the indigenous respondents in the two locations respectively had lived outside Ireland. One interesting result emerging from these studies is that in the event of successful rural industrialisation projects being established, the concept of the local labour market must be greatly extended to accommodate the response of returning emigrants to avail of the new employment op-portunities.

A number of sociocultural dimensions of the impact of rural indus-trialisation have been identified and analysed in the existing studies. One such dimension, which had critical implications for the distribu-tion of income was the extensive participation by women in the indus-trial workforce, particularly over the 1970s. By 1981, there was a higher female participation in the industrial workforce in the West-ern regions than in the Eastern Regions. The studies by Kane (1977) and Harris (1983) commented on the persistence of the tradition, es-pecially in rural Ireland, of women retiring from the workforce after marriage. This would explain the predominant perception, also cap-tured in these studies, of participants who viewed their employment as transient rather than a career. Breathnach (1985) correctly attrib-utes to this pattern of female participation a number of negative con-sequences, which included the maintenance of a labour-force docility arising from a gender bias among trade unions controlled by men and pressure on female workers to maintain domestic duties, which was not conducive to attending meetings held outside work hours. Other factors analysed by Kane (1977) included the composition of the la-bour force employed in rural industrialisation projects. The attitude to a new industrial project taken up by a local community where this represented a novel departure depended, she argued, on the propor-tion of married men employed, in contrast to a project employing pre-dominantly single women. In addition, the problems of adaptation to new industrial work practices on the part of local employees, and the related problem of the management being able to adapt to local conditions, were examined in some detail by Kane (1977), while the issue of the linguistic subversion of the Gaeltacht areas as a result of rural industrialisation has been studied by Keane, Cawley and O'Cinneide (1983). These latter issues, while of interest in their own right, illustrate the varied range of topics addressed in rural industrialisation, though their relationship to rural poverty is minimal.

Of the various issues identified under the heading of sociocultural dimension, the factor which has undergone perhaps the most extensive change during the 1980s and into the 1990s has been the increased participation by women in the labour force in general, including the industrial labour force. It is also an area that has received increasing attention from researchers, extending from concern about the problem of the provision of information in official statistics on a gender basis as contained in the work of Blackwell (1987), Shortall (1991), and Byrne (1992, 1993) to work on explaining the growth of labour-force participation by women in Ireland over the past 20 years (NESC, 1991; Walsh; 1993; O'Connell and Sexton, 1994), to forecasting the occupational structures of women's employment to the end of the current decade (Canny et al., 1995; Punch 1995). From the perspective of this book, the more interesting work undertaken in Ireland with respect to gender concerns the links between the division of labour in occupational terms based on gender, the role and position of rural women in relation to industrialisation and the inequality in gender terms that rural women have encountered in the local development process. Perceptive insights into a number of these issues have been provided in the work of Harris (1983, 1984, 1989), Jackson and Barry (1989), O'Donovan and Curtin (1991), Owens (1992), and O'Connor (1995).

These studies differ in both the focus and range of topics covered, with some representing detailed studies of specific areas and time frames, while others represent more general discursive examination of the gender issues involved. What is lacking in the Irish context is the quantification of changing gender inequality on an inter-regional basis as analysed for the United Kingdom in Perrons (1995). Using an adaptation of the United Nations Human Development Index, Perrons constructs a composite index of gender inequality in employment, which she applied in a comparative framework of the European Union countries, and then at the national level where she applied it to the regions of the United Kingdom. Perrons' conclusions have interesting implications for Ireland in that she demonstrated that:

new forms of regional inequality have been developing over the last 20 years with the growth and spatial concentration of new high-tech industries and high level service jobs in a core of advanced areas in Europe (Perrons, 1995: 474).

Similar patterns have emerged in the United Kingdom with the south-east of England and adjacent regions emerging as the high-technology, high-level service centre of the United Kingdom. This spatial differentiation has been accompanied by growing inequalities in earnings and household income, driven by the relentless pursuit of the liberalisation of the market process during the Thatcher era. Perrons demonstrates and measures the gender dimension associated with the new forms of inequality in that the most advanced regions reflected the highest levels of gender inequality. In an Irish context, with the new emphasis on the role of high-technology industries and higher-level service jobs as the driving force of long-term economic development, the issues identified by Perrons in the domain of increasing gender inequality become particularly pertinent. The interaction between the spatial and social dimensions of rural industrialisation, which were discussed in the previous section and which will be returned to in the next section, become particularly significant in the area of gender equality in employment opportunities and occupational status.

The aspect of rural industrialisation that has arguably received the most attention has been the economic dimension. This attention has focused on a particular range of topics, and again rural poverty has not been an explicit concern of this research. The Lucey and Kaldor (1969) study was a detailed analysis at the micro-level of two industrial plants located in counties Sligo and Clare. The central focus of attention was the impact on the agricultural sector of providing industrial employment opportunities for workers primarily from agricultural backgrounds. A similar concern informed the study by Kane (1977). A result common to both studies was the capacity of the employees to retain their farming activities. The consequences of this alternative source of employment and income were on balance estimated by Lucey and Kaldor to be positive in their impact, in that there was little evidence of contractions in farming output for those participating, while many increased their output by reinvesting portions of their industrial incomes back into the farms. The implications for the household distribution of income in a locality for those participating in the rural industrialisation process were very considerable.

More formal studies of regional economic development, in the form of regional input-output modelling, were undertaken by Cuddy and Boylan (1983, 1984). The primary focus of these studies was to examine in some detail the anatomy of intra-regional economic structures and processes — in this case the West Planning Region was chosen for analysis. In addition, they highlighted the striking differences between the national and regional economies with respect to critical processes such as inter-industry linkages, the pattern of household expenditure, and the problem of profit repatriation. In 1980 imports from outside the region into the manufacturing sector in the West Region amounted to 61.4 per cent of manufacturing output, compared with a comparable figure of 25 per cent for the country as a whole. This highlights, among other things, the changing structure of new industry within the region, but more particularly it identified clearly the inability of the region's existing industry to capture the leakages, in the form of imported inputs, from these new industries. An ongoing preoccupation of industrial policy is the attempt to "capture" these leakages within the region, thereby creating value-added, employment and income. Similarly, the pattern of household or consumption expenditure is highlighted by these models. In 1980 the ratio of consumer imports to total consumption expenditure at the national level was 25.6 per cent, while in the West Region it was 53 per cent. Clearly, the challenge of capturing these leakages, in the form of import substitution at the regional level, is considerably greater at the regional level and, depending on the composition of products, may not even be possible. The problem of profit repatriation presents particular measurement problems, and at the regional level extreme caution must be exercised in any estimation of such outflows since they are essentially residual estimates (Boylan and Cuddy, 1987). Nevertheless it would appear that profits outflow as a percentage of output is much greater at the regional compared with the national level. Studies similar in type, though less formal in character and more limited in scope, have been undertaken by Lucey and Walker (1987). While these studies do not address the agenda of rural poverty, they nevertheless highlight critical issues pertaining to the process of intra-regional development by identifying major policy issues which clearly have important implications for rural poverty.

The studies reviewed in this section, which was meant to be illustrative rather than comprehensive in its coverage, represent an extremely wide range of concerns. Some of these are more germane to the central themes of this book than others. The overall impression remains that critical aspects of rural poverty are poorly understood and inadequately researched. Consequently, a number of gaps exist in the literature with respect to different aspects of rural poverty: its causes, consequences, persistence, and the effectiveness of measures of alleviation. Notwithstanding the array of issues addressed and the detailed work undertaken in the studies reviewed here, there remains the question of what is known about the extent and incidence of rural poverty and how rural industrialisation has impinged on this issue. The answer to the latter part of this question must remain largely unanswered since there are no schematic studies at the requisite spatial levels which directly address the central relationship between intra-regional industrial employment, social class participation, and the redistribution of income arising from this employment. Notwithstanding this knowledge gap, recent work has begun to shed some light on the first part of the question, particularly the spatial and social incidence of poverty. Of these two dimensions of poverty, considerably less was known about the spatial aspect, but the work of Nolan, Whelan and Williams (1994) has provided some valuable insights into this dimension of the problem.

While it is unnecessary to review all of the conclusions of this valuable study, it is instructive in the context of this chapter to highlight a number of the central conclusions of Nolan, Whelan and Williams (1994). The first concerns the spatial distribution of the risk of poverty, defined in their study as the proportion of households in any particular categorisation (in this case spatial categories) found to be in poverty. Based on the 1987 ESRI survey and using three different measures of poverty, the authors concluded that:

> [the] poverty rate or risk of poverty does vary substantially by area type with all three poverty measures. The highest rate is for households in small towns or villages, and the lowest is for those in Dublin, with the former about twice as high as the latter "Nolan, Whelan and Williams, 1994: 216).

The "small towns or villages" referred to are those under 3,000 in population and with reference to the examination in the previous section of the West Planning Region experience during what was argued to be the most active phase of dispersed rural industrialisation, these were precisely the locations that fared worst in gaining industrial employment opportunities.

These results highlight a critical inter-relationship between the mechanisms of rural industrialisation and detailed information on the participants in this process, an area that requires much more systematic study. The central results of the analysis by Nolan, Whelan and Williams (1994) clearly undermine the idea of poverty as being highly concentrated in a limited number of urban centres. As the authors point out, the pattern of the risk and incidence of poverty identified in their study:

> has major implications for our understanding of the nature of poverty and for policy design . . . whatever relevance such concepts as an urban underclass may have for particular sub-groups, the fact that most poor households are not in public housing in the cities means that such concepts are not central to the understanding of poverty in Ireland . . . the evidence suggests that "black-spots" with very high poverty rates can indeed be identified. . . . However, since most poor households are not to be found in such places, policies targeting specific locations, however effective, can be expected to reach only a minority (Nolan, Whelan and Williams, 1994: 218–19).

The second conclusion which warrants attention concerns the inter-regional comparison of poverty rates across the planning regions. While the authors point out that the 1987 ESRI survey does not provide a reliable basis for analysis at different spatial levels, particularly the county and sub-county level, it is possible to compare poverty rates at a regional level — in this case the planning-region level. The three regions which dominated the rankings for the highest poverty rates were the North-West and Donegal, North-East, and Midlands Regions respectively. Of interest here is the structural continuity of the regional incidence of poverty, since this regional pattern was similar to that found by Roche (1984), who used the 1973 and 1980 Household Budget Survey as the basis for his analysis.

Based on these important findings, which clearly indicate a pronounced spatial dimension to the problem and an identifiable spatial continuity with respect to its regional incidence, there may be a much more direct inter-relationship between the mechanisms of rural industrialisation and the incidence of rural poverty. This relationship will need more emphasis in the future than it has received in the past, particularly when combined with the social dimension as to who are the participants, and therefore the beneficiaries, of this process; the skill and educational requirements of this industrialisation; and the changing gender composition of its workforce. However, while these issues have emerged as an expanded agenda which rural industrialisation must address, the driving forces that began to shape the formation of industrial policy have undergone fundamental change during the course of the 1980s. These changes have been centrally driven by the concern of global restructuring, against which the Irish state could not immunise itself. The irony here is that just as new insights are beginning to be gained into the structure and spatial incidence of poverty in Ireland in response to which rural industrialisation may have a very significant role to play, public policy in this domain has been forced to reconsider its fundamental orientation in direct response to the pressure of external influences which characterise the rapidly integrating global economy. The re-orientation of industrial policy since the early 1980s is addressed in the next section in order to identify the major forces at work and the new responses that have emerged.

THE RE-ORIENTATION OF INDUSTRIAL POLICY

With the termination of the Regional Industrial Plans of the IDA in 1982, the most active period of articulation and implementation of spatially oriented industrial policy effectively ended. Since that date no similar-type plans have been produced. The 1980s were to emerge as a critical transitional phase in industrial policy thinking in general, with its corollary for regional and rural development. External factors, such as the global recession of the early 1980s and, later in the decade, the emergence of the Single European Market, acted as major catalysts in the re-orientation of industrial policy.

The re-appraisal of industrial policy was initiated in 1979 and was undertaken under the auspices of the National Economic and Social Council. It resulted in the publication of a number of reports specifically related to industrial development, which included a survey of the literature (NESC, 1981), the role of infrastructure (NESC, 1981); and an analysis of job losses in manufacturing (NESC, 1983). The central report was *A Review of Industrial Policy* (NESC, 1982), more commonly known as the "Telesis Report", along with the Council's own report entitled *Policies for Industrial Development: Conclusions and Recommendations* (NESC, 1982). While these reports constituted the basis for the re-orientation of industrial policy, they were not the only input into that debate. Considerable institutional energy was expended by the Industrial Development Authority by way of reaction to the "Telesis Report" during 1982 and 1983.

The protracted discussion over this period culminated in the publication of the Government's White Paper on *Industrial Policy* in

1984. This represented a pivotal document in the re-evaluation of the philosophy and strategic thrust of industrial policy, which had and continues to have profound implications for the spatial distribution of, and access to, non-farm employment opportunities in the Irish economy. While the White Paper did not envisage a radical re-alignment of the respective roles of the public and private sectors, it was underlain by a critical shift in emphasis with respect to the process of future industrial development. The stated objectives of the White Paper included the following:

(1) To create and maintain the maximum number of sustainable jobs, as many as possible of them high-skilled, in manufacturing and international service industries

(2) To maximise value-added by these sectors and to capture the wealth thus created for further investment and employment creation in the Irish economy

(3) To develop a strong and internationally competitive industrial sector in Ireland, made up of both Irish and foreign-owned industry

(4) To promote the more rapid development of our natural resource-based industries, particularly food and timber

(5) To promote the integration of foreign industry into the Irish economy through greater linkage with Irish industry and educational institutions

(6) To improve the rate of return on the Government's investment in the commercial state companies (White Paper, 1984: 5–6).

A number of significant implications followed from these objectives, two of which are of particular interest. Firstly, employment creation was no longer the principal objective of industrial policy as it was in the 1960s and 1970s. It was now to be one of a number of objectives all of which appeared to have equal status. Secondly, the new objectives envisaged a reduced role for industry in the creation of direct employment in the future. Corresponding to the shift of maximising the net domestic value-added, employment creation was to be generated elsewhere in the economy, primarily in the service sector, and consequently through a more indirect mechanism. A more succinct account of the central components of the new industrial strategy was provided by the chief executive of the IDA when he stated: "Output growth in industry would be the central focus rather than employment growth per se within firms" (White, 1983). He went on to stress, however, that the concentration on output growth would be selective. It would attempt, "to identify and develop the sectors where a particularly high volume of output growth can be achieved in electronics, computer software, natural resources (agribusiness, in particular) and specific segments of emerging technologies" (White, 1983).

The second component of the new strategy was to "capture within Ireland the wealth flowing from enhanced output and to deliberately convert it into the maximum number of jobs in the Irish economy" (White, 1983). An important aspect of the new strategy was the envisaged composition of the new employment arising from the growth in output in the high-technology industries. The new employment was expected to be primarily in the service sector, and within that sector, in the area of personal services. This scenario envisaged a considerable shift to a service-type economy as the main source of employment over the next 20 years.

With respect to regional policy, the White Paper reiterated the commitment, in very general terms, to the pursuit of regional development. It stated that, "regional development will continue to be an important factor in our industrial development policies" (White Paper, 1984: 47), but went on to announce what was to become the central theme of future regional industrial policy. It stated that:

> less emphasis will however be placed in future on job targets for individual town groups. The aim of policy is mobility and flexibility in the economy so industry must be placed where it can make greatest progress, rather than stick rigidly to job targets for particular town groups (*ibid*).

The theme of flexibility was taken up again under the heading of designation, where it was stated that in future the provision of higher grants would be only for, "clearly defined industrial sectors and limited periods" (*ibid*). The White Paper in effect outlined the architecture of a new emphasis and direction for industrial policy, with significant implications for regional and rural development. The principal components of the new strategic approach can be summarised as follows:

(1) A new emphasis on output growth and the maximisation of value-added primarily through the high-growth, high-technology industries

(2)   A relegation of direct employment creation per se, which was envisaged as taking place through a more indirect mechanism in future

(3)   A shift to a more service-sector dominated economy, primarily in the area of personal services

(4)   A severing of the direct connection between industrial and regional policy, with the emphasis on flexibility particularly with respect to the spatial distribution of industry.

Shortly after the publication of the White Paper, the Government directed the NESC to undertake a study of designation (NESC, 1985). This document developed the principles enunciated in the White Paper. The ostensible aim of the document was, "to consider the establishment of objective criteria for determining designation status", and considerable effort was devoted to identifying alternative criteria for purposes of designation. It would, however, be misleading to take the above stated aim as the central agenda of the document. The additional objective, if not the crucial one, was to argue the case for the re-introduction of a growth centre policy for future industrial location policy, driven by the new perceived locational requirements of the high-technology industries identified in the White Paper as the motivating force of future development. The document became, in effect, a re-run of the earlier 1960s arguments for growth centres during, which were examined in the second section of this chapter. The qualitative difference on this occasion was the need to provide a systematically derived set of criteria for purposes of spatial designation, in order to minimise the possibility of political lobbying on the part of those locations and regions which would fail to meet the requisite criteria for designation.

The crucial idea underlying this document was a basic distinction between a "needs" approach to spatial designation and a "potential" approach. The "needs" approach was associated with the *status quo* situation, in which the emphasis of regional policy as implemented to-date was interpreted as "the identification of the worst off areas within the economy for special assistance or designation on a *needs* basis". The "needs" approach was, however, seen as a major constraint in the new circumstances of intensified international competition and the requirements of a new industrial policy. The task then was to undermine the status-quo position and to replace it with criteria for spatial designation based on a "potential" approach. The "potential" approach, consistent with the principles of the White Paper, "would contribute to a maximisation of industrial growth in the economy", by requiring that:

> industry be actively encouraged to locate in the major population centres where viability and growth prospects would be higher and infrastructural development costs would be lower through the realisation of economies of scale. (NESC, 1985:2).

Here was a "new" rationale for the abandonment of the policy of industrial dispersal pursued during the 1970s, which had attempted to provide alternative industrial employment opportunities throughout the economy including the rural economy.

The critical issue was a basic conflict between equity considerations, which were linked to the "needs" approach, and efficiency considerations to which the "potential" approach was the new response. It was clear also that industrial-location policy to date was deemed to have placed too much emphasis on the equity considerations and "that it is appropriate that the efficiency factor be given increased emphasis". The informing principles of the proposed "potential" approach included spatial agglomeration based on cost and economies-of-scale arguments; selectivity with respect to projects, with an explicit bias towards high-technology operations; and a radical discrimination towards infrastructural expenditure to provide the facilitating spatial framework for "more quality oriented" — that is, high-technology — projects.

Following from these principles the conclusions drawn insisted that, "there were compelling reasons for adopting a more concentrated approach to industrial location". As in a previous rehearsal of these arguments, such considerations as the distribution of industry would be subservient to the need to maximise national industrial development. This conclusion was, in turn, buttressed by the argument that, "a more selective and quality oriented industrial policy can only succeed in the context of a high quality business environment which could only be provided in a few locations". While the NESC report was not prepared to provide detailed principles for selecting particular centres for future development, it was obvious from its guiding principles that only a very limited number of urban centres would meet the requirements of their "potential" approach. It was clearly stated that it would not be practicable to identify a "major centre in each county". The substantive issue was unambiguous. The essence of the proposals was, "that a larger share of resources would be focused on a smaller number of locations with the obvious implication that less would be available for the small towns and villages". In the new economic circumstances of the 1980s, characterised by continuing global recession, and a relentless drive towards liberalisation based on market-driven impulses and the consequent intensification of competition for high-technology international investments and their perceived locational requirements, the report concluded that the continued pursuit of industrial dispersal was untenable. This arose from the fact that, under a policy of industrial dispersal, expenditure on infrastructure was too thinly spread over too many locations and thereby militated against what the report termed "infrastructure excellence" in any particular location. The report, recognising the implication of its argument, concluded that it would be "very difficult to encourage footloose projects to locate in the underdeveloped areas". The implementation of the new policy régime elaborated in these two documents would have profound implications for the ability of the industrial sector to contribute directly to rural industrialisation, and thus to the alleviation of rural poverty. Clearly, the new policy régime would alter the structure and pattern of spatial accessibility through its impact on locational considerations, while the emphasis on high-technology projects raised issues of participation, given the skill requirements involved. The shift to reliance on the service sector raised a different set of issues with respect to its contribution to the rural economy.

The central thrust of the policy contents of the documents just examined anticipated, in an uncannily prescient manner, what was about to emerge as the major external development during the 1980s, namely the creation of the Single European Market. Arguably, the reorientation of industrial policy, as illustrated in the above documents, anticipated the ideological underpinnings of the Single European Market developments. It is important to recall that the critical consideration which informed the creation of the Single Market was the perceived urgency to liberalise the European economy, particularly the labour market, in order to meet the global competition emanating from the increasingly deregulated American economy and, even more pointedly, the spectacular success of the Japanese in penetrating and winning increasing shares of the European market. There is an easily identifiable compatibility between the principles underlying the need to facilitate domestically the new locational requirements of international companies and the larger, but eventually similar agenda which informed the thinking behind the Single European Market. The political debate surrounding the Single European Market was

increasingly couched in the vocabulary of social and economic cohesion, arising from which sizeable resources in the form of the Structural Funds were made available (Matthews, 1994). Notwithstanding
the political preoccupation with the Structural Funds, as instanced in
the general election of November 1992, or the various assessments of
the economic impact of these funds (Bradley and Fitzgerald, 1989;
Bradley et al., 1992), or that a second round of funds has been provided to cover the period 1994–99, they remain, in principle, a once-off
transfer of funds to facilitate our participation in an increasingly lib-
eralised European Economy.

The theme of liberalising the economy was central to the most recent contribution to industrial policy thinking, undertaken by the Industrial Policy Review Group (1992), more commonly referred to as
the "Culliton Report". In this report the emphasis was on reforming
what were considered to be the critical policies which impinged directly on industrial performance. These included taxation policy, infrastructural provision, and the role of education and training in supporting industrial development. The underlying philosophy was based
on providing the right policy environment which in turn should facilitate what should be essentially a market-led process. It is acknowledged that there remains a major problem with indigenous industry
and a number of proposals to deal with this sector were put forward.
One of these proposals, which to date has received most public attention, concerned the reorganisation of the public agencies concerned
with industrial development. The major proposal, implemented since
January 1994, was the division of the Industrial Development
Authority into two separate organisations. One of these, Forbairt, concentrates on the development of indigenous industry, while the other,
IDA (Ireland) is concerned exclusively with foreign industry. An um-
brella organisation, Forfás, co-ordinates the activities of these two
new organisations. Viewed from the perspective of the spatial organisation of industry, the Report has spectacularly little to say. The erosion of such considerations has continued relentlessly with this report, but it is consistent with the general principles of the re-
orientation of industrial policy, which, it was argued above, began in
1984 with the White Paper. The single reference to the "regional
structure" of industry is in the context of a proposal that if indigenous
industry is to develop to a stage where it can successfully compete in
the new competitive conditions, then a strategy of "industrial clusters" should be pursued. These clusters, in turn, should be identified
within "a limited number of promising niches and segments". The

choice of these market niches and industry segments should build on "existing successes and other sources of competitive advantage". The implications of this clustering strategy are treated in a single sentence where it is pointed out that there are "also implications for the regional structure of industrial development as geographical proximity of the component firms and proximity to educational and research programmes can be decisive for the success of a cluster". This represents a further endorsement of a highly selective spatial policy for future industrial development, resonant of the White Paper and compatible with the principles contained in the NESC Report on Designation. At the level of policy discussion, it is possible to decipher a powerful continuity in thinking from the early 1980s, representing a major reversal in the strategic orientation of regional industrial policy.

From the perspective of providing alternative employment opportunities within the rural economy and thereby contributing to the alleviation of rural poverty, this study of industrial policy thinking since the mid-1980s would suggest a much more indirect role for industry compared with the earlier period examined in the second section of this chapter. However, just as the process of abandoning regional policy was clearly evident by the early 1980s, by the mid-1980s new developments were emerging to fill the vacuum, albeit driven by external developments. These included the crisis in the Common Agricultural Policy, centred on the budgetary implications of its continued expansion; the uneven regional distribution of its benefits; and, belatedly, its impact, increasingly perceived to be negative, on the environment. The response at the European level was the recognition that alternative methods of support for farm incomes would have to be identified. The Commission's, *The Future of Rural Society*, which purported to provide the outline of a blueprint for the development of rural society, identified the need to activate and mobilise indigenous resources at the local level as the way forward, along with the search for new strategic approaches for achieving this aim.

These developments were given added and urgent impetus with the move to establish the Single European Market. The tensions posed by the need to liberalise the European economy, on the one hand, and the implications for the lesser developed regions, on the other, were quickly recognised and the issue of attempting to maintain a social and economic cohesion within the European Union became a major focus of European policy. Arising from this came the reformed Structural Funds embedded in a new menu of concepts which gave pride of place to the concept of integrated development

(Boylan, 1988). In addition to the centrality of integration as an organising concept, the reformed Structural Funds also included the principle of spatial selectivity, in that certain priority regions were identified, which for these purposes included the whole of Ireland. A radical shift in the method of funding was introduced, in that the financing of individual projects was abandoned in favour of multi-annual funding of operational programmes, and a new emphasis on the co-ordinated participation of various actors, public agencies, local communities and private entrepreneurs. This was in contrast to the previous arrangements where a single actor (public or private) could dominate developments. However, the attempts at a sub-national application of these principles as contained in the National Development Plan 1989–1993, involved an extraordinary display of tokenism on the part of the central authorities. This included devising a new set of regions, which had no rationale in theory or in practice except to divert potential criticism from Brussels, since these revised regions related to neither existing administrative nor organisational structures. In each region a Working Group, dominated by public servants who compiled the "regional plan", was established, along with an Advisory Group comprising local interest groups and elected representatives who essentially exerted little influence. In the event, no regionally based plans were published under the National Development Plan, 1989–93, though at a later stage "Sub-Regional Review Committees" were established to monitor the sub-national expenditure under the Structural Funds.

Notwithstanding the disappointing response to the heightened anticipation for major developments in local development contained in the National Development Plan 1989–93, there was a new set of informing principles emerging, which included integrated development, an emphasis on local or area-based developments, the need for partnership in development, the importance of a multi-dimensional framework to address developmental issues rather than a constricting single-sectoral approach, and the desirability of participation. These ideas, many of which emerged from development studies in Third World contexts and not always adequately acknowledged in the Anglo-European literature, came to dominate the academic literature and policy discourse of the developed countries by the later 1980s. In Ireland the first attempt to incorporate the concept of integrated development was the Pilot Areas Programme for Integrated Rural Development, which was administered by the Department of Agriculture and Food during 1988–90 (O'Malley, 1992). Other initiatives which incorporated different aspects or combinations of the new approach include the Area-Based Response to Long-term Unemployment, launched under the auspices of the Programme for Economic and Social Progress (1991). This involved the establishment of local companies termed "Partnerships", which reflected the strategy of partnership implemented at national level in the context of the National Development Programmes (Craig and McKeown, 1993). In 1990, the Government funded a special three-year programme, since extended, to assist the formation of a network of community development resource centres in areas of particular need in the country. Officially known as the Community Development Programme, it is supported by technical expertise from the Combat Poverty Agency and is aimed principally at providing advice and assistance to individuals and community groups, stimulating and facilitating the work of local groups and acting as a critical liaison mechanism between the statutory agencies and local groups. The creation of the County Enterprise Boards in 1992 represented a further step in facilitating access by local communities to funding for the development of their areas, and an attempt to achieve a greater degree of co-ordination of the State agencies at the county level. The two major developments, both funded by the European Union, which have attracted considerable attention are the LEADER Programme and the Forum project under the European Union's Third Poverty Programme (1989–94). It is not proposed to address these particular programmes, since they have been reviewed in NESC (1994).

All of the foregoing initiatives have emerged since the 1980s, mostly in response to policy developments emanating from the European Union. They are reactive in nature and consequently reflect an ad-hoc approach which lacks an overall coherence. However, they all share a new spatial focus, which is broadly an area-based approach. The NESC (1994) report attempts to provide a conceptual and operational coherence to these varied policy developments based on the principles of integration, both horizontal and vertical; multidimensionality, in that programmes rather than projects should dominate; a multi-annual planning horizon; and the principle of subsidiarity in administration. While it remains to be seen what response, if any, there will be to these proposals, a broader view of these developments raises more fundamental questions. The demise of the regional dimension, or what we may now call the "excluded middle", leaves us with the centralised state at one level and local development at another. The development process, properly understood, is a nationally negotiated process at different levels from the global economy to the most localised level. The main preoccupation of the State is to sustain national development within rapidly changing international circumstances, and as was argued in the second section of this chapter, internal domestic considerations such as regional or rural development will be made subservient to this aim. In the new international circumstances, whether a strategy based on area-based or local development is better placed than a regionally-based strategy of development remains a moot point. The shift to local development may alternatively be viewed as a compensating mechanism to fill the ideological vacuum created by the retreat of interventionist state policy in the area of regional and rural industrialisation. A critical test of the commitment to local development will focus on the political willingness to devolve real political powers, based on the principle of subsidiarity, to the local level. The emasculation of the regional structure of administration, such as it was, has removed any infrastructure for devolved administration of political functions at an alternative level. Thus the fragmentation of the spatial economy under an area-based strategy arguably could be viewed as a facilitating mechanism used by the State to implement a strategy of "flexibility", which is the motivating force of the neo-liberal underpinnings of the international economy. Pursuing this agenda would, however, be too much of a digression from the theme of this chapter.

CONCLUSIONS

The foregoing examination of the dynamics of industrial policy indicates a complex and rapidly changing agenda of issues. While a wide array of issues can be identified, it is not possible to provide an interrogation of such an extensive agenda. Rather, this section confines itself to a small number of issues which warrant further consideration, albeit briefly.

There has clearly re-emerged a heightened tension between the requirements of national economic growth and the needs of regional development. As in the past, this tension will manifest itself by representing a policy of regional dispersal of industry as a major constraint on maximising national growth. The shift from a "needs" approach to a "potential" approach examined in the previous section was a clear reflection of this re-orientation. The implications for spatial access to employment on the part of the rural population is obvious. Addressing rural poverty, however, requires a very specific and spatially focused strategy, which is clearly underlying the area-based development approach advocated in NESC (1994). In the absence of a policy commitment to industrial dispersal the potential of the area-based approach, at least viewed from the industrial component of this strategy, is vulnerable in a long-term perspective.

The momentum for spatial discrimination in the form of selected growth-centres is driven by the economic logic of the location requirements of high-technology foreign industry, which was the basis of the analysis of the White Paper, or the achievement of economies of scale for indigenous industry, which was the basis for the logic of "clustering" of the Culliton Report. The new locational requirements include, among others, such factors as:

(1) A high level of infrastructural resources, particularly telecommunications facilities

(2) Access to research and development facilities, such as those provided by universities or colleges of technology

(3) Access to a high level of services in general, ranging from banking and financial services relevant to the commercial activities of these high-tech firms to a wide variety of social and cultural services.

Clearly, these requirements are most likely to be met by a limited number of centres when translated into the Irish context. Consequently, the concentration of infrastructure, both physical and social, in the largest urban centres to facilitate high-technology operations or the process of clustering must occur at the expense of rural areas and their population.

A corollary to this envisaged long-term strategy for industrial development is the issue of occupational accessibility when viewed from the perspective of rural poverty. Against the background of the relentless development and application of new information technologies to industry, the agenda of educational achievement, skill levels, and occupational mobility become major issues for future policy consideration. If participation in the newly envisaged pattern of industrialisation looks increasingly problematic in the longer term, except for those with very specific skills derived from an extended educational investment on their part, the prospect of absorption in the service-economy must also be seriously questioned. If the envisaged future for industrial activity is likely to be highly concentrated, the conventional interpretation would have the derived service employment also highly concentrated. The issue to be raised is whether these service activities can be dispersed or are dominated by such factors as the size of urban centre and population density? If the greater proportion of envisaged service employment is to be in the provision of personal services — a much canvassed scenario by those drawing from the American experience in the 1980s — then they must be delivered at the point of consumption, given that the critical economic character- istic of personal services is that the point of production (or delivery) is in general the same as the point of consumption. The consequences of this are clearly against the spatial dispersal of this "new" service employment, which implies, arguably, a reinforcing mechanism for rural-urban migration in the absence of a coherent policy for the service sector to facilitate spatial and occupational accessibility.

While these considerations represent an illustrative cross-section of issues that can be identified arising from the topic addressed in this chapter, what of the implications for the overall concerns of this book? This examination has attempted to highlight the changing ba- sis of the State's negotiation of this domain of public policy. It has been argued that, particularly since re-engaging with the world econ- omy through trade liberalisation from the 1960s, particular tensions have emerged between spatial demands for participation in the eco- nomic growth process and the demands of that growth process itself. As has been discussed, the political negotiation of this issue has fluc- tuated between periods of explicit commitment to spatial equity or at least spatial distribution, to periods of retreat from such commitment. The latter strategic posture has dominated since the early 1980s and is legitimised by recourse to powerful external influences ranging from global restructuring to the liberalising demands of the Single European Market. Here the position of the Irish state has become one of facilitating what is clearly perceived to be the driving logic of re- structuring through market liberalisation. The dominant controlling ideas of long-term economic development include, among others, meeting the demands of international competitiveness and the ability to enhance the technological capacity of national economies. The pur- suit of these objectives has radical implications for the form and con- tent of the restructuring process, the long-term spatial and social re- configuration of the economy, the degree and status of Ireland's long- term integration in the European Union, and the very concept of peripherality itself. The consequences for poverty in general and rural poverty in particular are, in the absence of powerful counteractive policies, enormously far-reaching. While in this chapter constraints of space did not allow examination of this extensive agenda, the direc- tion in which the underlying policy disposition of the Irish state is moving is relatively clear, along with the forces that are motivating this change of direction, and the consequences of these changes. Set against an over-arching background of neo-liberalism as the guiding economic philosophy, the powerful forces now driving the underlying industrial changes — such as global restructuring, new information technologies, flexible specialisation, to name but a few — do not make for a benign environment to pursue a strategy of industrial location based on the needs of the rural poor.

References

Blackwell, J. (1987): "Gender and Statistics", in Curtin, C., Jackson, P. and O'Connor B. (eds.), *Gender in Irish Society*, Galway: Galway University Press.

Boylan, T.A. (1984): "The Drive to Industrialise", in Ryan, W.J.L. (ed.), *Irish Industry in the Eighties*, Dublin: Helicon Press.

Boylan, T.A. (1988), "Integrated Economic Development: A Critical Perspective", in Davis, J.P. and Van Der Kamp, H. (eds.), *Integrated Programmes, Resource Development and the Regions*, Dublin: Regional Studies Association.

Boylan, T.A. and Cuddy, M.P. (1987): "The Re-orientation of Industrial Policy: Regional Implications", in Boylan, T.A. and Drudy, P.J. (eds.), *Regional Policy and National Development*, Dublin: Regional Studies Association.

Bradley, J. and Fitzgerald, J. (1989): "The EC Structural Funds and Economic Growth", in *Medium-Term Review: 1989–1994*, Dublin: Economic and Social Research Institute.

Bradley, J., Fitzgerald, J., Kearney, I., Boyle, G., Breen, R., Shortall, S., Durkan, J., Reynolds-Reighan, A. and O'Malley, E. (1992): *The Role of the Structural Funds: Analysis of Consequences for Ireland in the Context of 1992*, Policy Research Series Paper No. 13, Dublin: Economic and Social Research Institute.

Byrne, A. (1992): "Statistics — What Do They Tell Us About Women?" *Women's Studies Centre — Review*, University College Galway, 1: 1–13.

Byrne, A. (1993): "Revealing Figures? Official Statistics and Rural Irish Women" in Smyth, A. (ed.), *Irish Women's Studies Reader*, Dublin: Attic Press.

Breathnach, P. (1984): *Community Perspectives for Development and Change in the Connemara Theas and Corca Dhuibhne Gaeltacht*, St Patrick's College Maynooth: Department of Geography.

Breathnach, P. (1985): "Rural Industrialization in the West of Ireland", in Healey, M.J. and Ilbery, B.W. (eds.), *The Industrialization of the Countryside*, Norwich: Geo Books.

Buchanan, C. and Partners (1968): *Regional Studies in Ireland*, Dublin: An Foras Forbartha.

Canny, A., Hughes, G. and Sexton, J.J. (1995): *Occupational Employment Forecasts 1988*, Dublin: FÁS/ESRI Manpower Forecasting Studies, Report No. 4.

Committee on Industrial Organization (CIO), (1963): *Fourth Interim Report: Industrial Grants*, Dublin: Stationary Office.

Craig, S. and McKeown, K. (1993): *Interim Report to the Central Review Committee on the Evaluation of Twelve Pilot Area-Based Partnerships in Ireland 1991–1992*. Dublin: Combat Poverty Agency.

Cuddy, M.P. and Boylan, T.A. (1983): *Integrated Regional Development Programmes: Test for Ireland*, Brussels: Commission of the European Community.

Cuddy, M.P. and Boylan, T.A. (1984): *Regional Input-Output Model for the West Region*, Brussels. Commission of the European Community.

Drudy, P.J., and McKeon, O. (1991): "Dublin Loses Out in the Drive for Jobs", *Irish Times*, 15 November.

Euradvice Ltd., *A Crusade for Survival — Final Report of Study of the West of Ireland*, Galway: Developing the West Together.

Harris, L. (1983): "Industrialization, Women and Working Class Politics in the West of Ireland", *Capital and Class*, 19: 110–17.

Harris, L. (1984): "Class, Community and Sexual Divisions," in Curtin, C., Kelly, M. O'Dowd, L. (eds.), *Culture and Ideology in Ireland*, Galway: Galway University Press.

Harris, L. (1989): "Women's Response to Multinationals in County Mayo", in Elson, D. and Pearson, R. (eds.), *Women's Employment and Multinationals in Europe*, London: Macmillan.

Hütterman, A. (1978): "Shannon 1976: The Industrial Estate and its Regional Implications, *Irish Geography*, 11: 179–83.

Industrial Policy Review Group (1992): *A Time for Change: Industrial Policy for the 1990s*, Dublin: Stationary Office.

Jackson, P. and Barry, U. "Women's Employment and Multinationals in the Republic of Ireland: The Creation of a New Female Labour Force", in Elson, D. and Pearson, R. (eds.), *Women's Employment and Multinationals in Europe*, London: Macmillan.

Johnson, J.J. (1981): "Republic of Ireland", in Clout, J.D. (ed.), *Regional Development in Western Europe*, New York: Wiley and Sons.

Kane, E. (1977): *The Last Place God Made: Traditional Economy and New Industry in Rural Ireland*, New Haven: Human Relations Area Files.

Keane, M.J., Cawley, M. and O'Cinneide, M.S. (1983): "Industrial Development in Gaeltacht Areas — The Work of Údarás na Gaeltachta", Paper presented to the 8th International Seminar on Marginal Regions, University College Galway.

Küpper, U.I. (1969): "Socio-Geographical Aspects of Industrial Growth at Shannon", *Irish Geography*, 6: 14–29.

Lucey, D.I.F. and Kaldor, D.R. (1969): *Rural Industrialisation: The Impact of Industrialisation on two Rural Communities in Western Ireland*, London: Geoffrey Chapman.

Lucey, D.I.F. and Walker, S. (1987): *New Jobs in Mayo — A Study of Recent Major Employment Developments*, Castlebar: Mayo County Development Team.

Matthews, A. (1994): *Managing the Structural Funds in Ireland*, Cork: Cork University Press.

Meenan, J. (1970): *The Irish Economy since 1922*, Liverpool: Liverpool University Press.

National Economic and Social Council (NESC) (1975): *Regional Policy in Ireland: A Review*, Report No. 4, Dublin: Stationery Office.

National Economic and Social Council (NESC) (1981): *Industrial Policy and Development: A Survey of Literature from the Early 1960s to the Present*, Report No. 56, Dublin: Stationery Office.

National Economic and Social Council (NESC) (1981): *The Importance of Infrastructure to Industrial Development in Ireland-Roads, Telecommunications and Water Supply*, Report No. 59, Dublin: Stationery Office.

NESC (1982): *A Review of Industrial Policy*, Report No. 64, Dublin: National Economic and Social Council.

NESC (1982): *Policies for Industrial Development: Conclusions and Recommendations*, Report No. 66, Dublin: National Economic and Social Council.

NESC (1983): *An Analysis of Job Losses in Irish Manufacturing Industry*, Report No. 67, Dublin: National Economic and Social Council.

NESC (1985): *Designation of Areas for Industrial Policy*, Report No. 81, Dublin: National Economic and Social Council.

NESC (1991): *Women's Participation in the Irish Labour Market*, Report No. 91, Dublin: National Economic and Social Council.

NESC (1994): *New Approaches to Rural Development*, Report No. 97, Dublin: National Economic and Social Council.

National Industrial Economic Council (NIEC) (1965): *Comment on the Report of the Committee on Development Centres and Industrial Estates*, Report No. 10, Dublin: Stationery Office.

Nolan, B., Whelan, C.T. and Williams, J. (1994): "Spatial Aspects of Poverty and Disadvantage", in Nolan, B. and Callan, T. (eds.), *Poverty and Policy in Ireland*, Dublin: Gill and Macmillan.

O'Connell, P.J. and Sexton, J.J. (1994): "Labour Market Developments in Ireland, 1971–1993", in Cantillon, S., Curtis, J. and Fitzgerald, J. (eds.), *Economic Perspectives for the Medium Term*, Dublin: Economic and Social Research Institute.

O'Connor, P. (1995): "Tourism and Development in Ballyhoura: Women's Business", *The Economic and Social Review*, 26(4): 369–401.

O'Donovan, O. and Curtin, C. (1991): "Industrial Development and Rural Women in Ireland", in Varley, T., Boylan, T.A. and Cuddy, M.P. (eds.), *Rural*

Crisis: Perspectives on Irish Rural Development, Galway: Centre for Development Studies.

O'Cinneide, M.S. and Keane, M.J. (1983): "Employment Growth and Population Changes in Rural Areas: An Example from the West of Ireland", *Irish Geography*, 16: 108–112.

O'Farrell, P.N. (1975): *Regional Industrial Development Trends in Ireland 1960–73*, Dublin: Industrial Development Authority.

O'Farrell, P.N. (1978): *An Analysis of New Industry Locations: The Irish Case*, *Progress in Planning*, 9(3): Oxford: Pergamon Press.

O'Farrell, P.N. (1979): "The Locational Pattern of New Manufacturing establishments: An Application of Discriminant Analysis", *Regional Studies*, 13: 39–59.

O'Farrell, P.N. (1980): "Multinational Enterprises and Regional Development: Irish Evidence", *Regional Studies*, 14: 141–50.

O'Hagan, J.W. (1981): *The Evolution of Manufacturing Industry in Ireland*, Dublin: Helicon Press.

O'Neill, H.B. (1971): *Spatial Planning in the Small Economy: A Case Study of Ireland*, New York: Praeger.

O'Malley, E. (1992): *The Pilot Programme for Integrated Rural Development 1988–90*, Broadsheet Series, No. 27, Dublin: Economic and Social Research Institute.

Owens, M. (1992): "Women in Rural Development: A Hit or Miss Affair", *Women's Studies Centre — Review*, University College Galway, 1: 15–19.

Perrons, D. (1995): "Gender Inequalities in Regional Development", *Regional Studies*, 29(5): 465–76.

Programme for Economic and Social Progress (1991): Dublin: Government Publications.

Punch, A. (1995): "Ireland Population and Labour Force beyond 2000", *Irish Banking Review*, Summer: 3–16.

Roche, J. (1984): *Poverty and Income Maintenance Policies in Ireland*, Dublin: Institute for Public Administration.

Ross, M. "Comprehensiveness in Regional Policy", in Dowling, B.R. and Durkan, J. (eds.), *Irish Economic Policy: A Review of Major Issues*, Dublin: Economic and Research Institute.

Shorthall, S. (1991): "The Dearth of Data on Irish Farm Wives: A Critical Review of the Literature", *The Economic and Social Review*, 22(4): 311–32.

Walsh, B.M. (1993): "Labour Force Participation and the Growth of Women's Employment, Ireland 1971–1991", *The Economic and Social Review*, 24(4): 369–400.

Walsh, James, A. (1995): *Regions in Ireland: A Statistical Profile*, Dublin: Regional Studies Association.

White, P.A. (1983): "Opportunity-Ireland", Paper Presented to the Dublin Chamber of Commerce, November.

White Paper on Industrial Policy (1984): Dublin: Government Publications.

6: Rural Poverty and Social Services Provision

Eamon O'Shea

INTRODUCTION

This chapter is concerned with the relationship between social services provision and rural poverty. Social services provision is analysed from the perspective of adequacy and effectiveness. The issue to be addressed is whether social services provision in rural areas, in its present form, serves to alleviate or to reinforce poverty and exclusion in rural areas. More generally, the question arises as to whether social policy for rural areas is so ineffective, perverse even, that instead of drawing people into society, providing them with the means whereby they can take up normal rights of citizenship, the opposite occurs and poor people end up further excluded from full participation in economic and social life?[1]

The analysis by economists of social services provision in rural areas inevitably (and usually quickly) turns into a discussion of the trade-off between efficiency and equity. Most economists accept the basic insight of Adam Smith that, under certain conditions, an economic system based on free or competitive markets will ensure that questions of allocation are answered in an optimal way. The same economists are likely to concede a role for government when market failure occurs or gross inequality exists, but would continue to argue for the primacy of efficiency in all areas of resource allocation. Le Grand (1991) has criticised orthodox neo-liberal economists for elevating efficiency to the status of a primary objective. He argues that efficiency is an objective which only acquires meaning with reference to other objectives such as equity or economic growth. The policy implication of this argument is that when considering decisions about the attainment of primary objectives, attention should be paid, not just to society's productive capacity to meet these objectives, but also to society's willingness to trade off the attainment of different objectives, such as greater equity or higher income.

The allocation and distribution of social services between rural and urban areas is rarely discussed in such terms in this country. Efficiency criteria are normally used to make final decisions on the allocation of scarce public resources. Social policy is, by and large, a

---

[1]   The chapter draws heavily on the FORUM project in north-west Connemara for quantitative information on exclusion in rural areas. Readers wanting to know about this project should read *The FORUM Project: Final Report* (1994), or consult the references Byrne (1991) and Harvey (1994). Comments received from Michael Keane, Mary Owens and referees are also gratefully acknowledged.

secondary policy objective, a residual to economic policy. Judgments on the wisdom and desirability of government intervention are too often made without reference to either the distributional consequence of different policies or the concept of social citizenship. It is largely taken for granted that social services provision in rural areas cannot be provided to the same level as in urban areas for reasons of cost associated with economies of scale arguments. When the number of people affected negatively by a particular policy is small and re-stricted to people living in peripheral areas, on the margins of society, the chances of distributional issues being taken into account are slight. That is another reason why spatial differences in social ser-vices provision have been accorded a low weighting in public policy decision-making.

The argument in this chapter is that equity in social services pro-vision should be accorded equal status with efficiency when decisions are being made concerning the allocation of scarce resources between rich and poor people and between urban and rural areas. Meeting basic needs is a necessary, but not a sufficient, condition for social citizenship. The welfare state must also guarantee the social rights of people, as well as nurturing feelings of civic belonging and commu-nity, if citizenship is to mean the same thing for all people. The shared citizenship concept is crucial to understanding much of what follows in this chapter. There is a package of rights, which includes access to basic social services, to which all people are entitled and with respect to which they are equal, wherever they choose to live, because they are members of the same society. If one accepts this approach, then combating social and spatial exclusion is a necessary part of the ex-tension of social citizenship in this country.

Following the introduction, the second section of the chapter con-tinues with a brief discussion on why social service provision in rural areas is different from provision in urban areas. Low population den-sity and dispersed clients/consumers in rural areas lead to low levels of demand for both market and non-market goods and services. As a consequence, economies-of-scale arguments are used to justify the absence of many social services in rural areas. The problem of access to social services for poor people living in rural areas is considered at length in the third section and is the main focus of the paper. The fourth section examines ways of improving social services provision in rural areas. The key to addressing the concerns of people living in rural areas is flexibility and innovation in the production and provi-sion of social services. For real changes to occur, however, there will have to be a radical reassessment of the relative weighting to be attached to efficiency and equity in the spatial allocation of social services. The next section provides an exposition of alternative theories of justice that can be used in considering equity in social provision. The final section of the paper draws together some of the main conclusions from the arguments and analysis that have gone before.

The social services considered in the paper are health care, education, housing and transport. While a case could be made for an extension of the discussion into other areas of social provision such as Garda stations, post offices and even income maintenance, the four areas mentioned above are conventionally seen as the "critical factors" in the literature on social services provision. Moreover, the conceptual argument and theoretical analysis used to support arguments for a more equitable spatial distribution of social services in health care, education, transport and housing could apply equally to other areas of social provision.

SCALE AND SOCIAL SERVICES PROVISION

What are the source and the consequence of differences in social services provision between rural and urban areas? Economies-of-scale arguments are most frequently invoked to explain spatial differences in social services provision. Almost all governments have justified centralisation of services on the basis of an economies-of-scale, efficiency-based, model of provision. Just as the market for private goods and services relies on strong levels of demand to support production, so also does social services provision rely on minimum-use thresholds, albeit not based on cash transactions, to sustain public provision. The problem in rural areas is that population density is low, with people dispersed over wide areas of territory. The result is that there are not enough people to sustain the levels of demand necessary to justify provision of services within local areas. Instead, social services tend to be concentrated in large towns and cities, where there are enough people to justify the cost of provision.

Once population decline sets in and changes occur in the age structure of the population, governments almost inevitably withdraw local social services in favour of more centralised provision. Cost and quality considerations tend to outweigh any other factors, such as the preferences and expectations of people living in rural areas, when decisions are being made about social services provision. Thus, for example, it was on this basis that the Fitzgerald Report (1968) on hospital location justified the following statement: "travel is part of the price that must be paid for higher standards of hospital treatment." The inference is that centralisation not only saves money but also leads to higher standards of provision and better-quality delivery. Similarly, the National Economic and Social Council (1978) asserts that: "modern health care simply cannot be made equally accessible to all localities." Cost considerations made it inevitable that people living in rural areas could not expect social services to be provided on the same basis as they were available to people in urban areas.

The economic reasoning behind the argument that service provision in rural areas is likely to cost more than similar services provided in urban areas is shown in Figure 6.1. The supply curves for the service are shown in terms of marginal costs, with the marginal cost of provision for rural areas (MC^R) lying above the cost curve for urban areas (MC^U). The marginal benefit curve reflects the level of demand for services in both regions. The optimal amount of service provision occurs at the intersection of the marginal cost and marginal benefit curves and is lower in rural areas than urban areas ($Q^R < Q^U$). Costs are also higher in rural areas than in urban areas ($C_R > C_U$). The lower output, higher cost result in rural areas reflects the economies-of-scale argument discussed above in relation to population density and usage patterns in rural areas.

Figure 6.1: Social Provision and Costs in Urban and Rural Areas

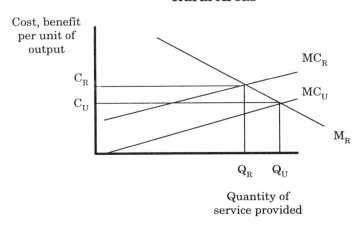

Source: Powe and Whitby (1993).

The problem with centralised provision of social services is that people living in the periphery may sometimes be offered poor and inadequate services, while people living close to services receive disproportionately higher levels of provision (Cawley and Stevens, 1987). Figure 6.2, based on Massam (1975), shows that with only one main centre of service provision (for example, a day hospital), people living in the periphery, far away from the centre, tend to have much lower levels of satisfaction than people living close to the centre of provision in the core. Access problems mean that people living in isolated areas must travel to the centre if they wish to avail of services. Huge costs may, therefore, be incurred just to reach the one centre where services are being provided. If, instead of just one major centre, five smaller centres of provision are provided across the region, the satisfaction levels of people living at the core and periphery eventually converge. The reason for this is that the distance problem has been solved and everyone has more or less equal access to the available provision.

Figure 6.2: Service Provision, Satisfaction and Access in Core and Peripheral Areas

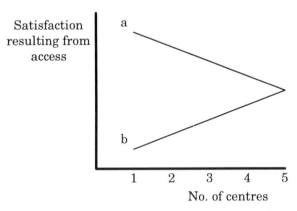

a = people living near the one major centre of provision
b = people living far away from the one major centre of provision

While Figure 6.2 is an overly-simplified representation of the access-satisfaction relationship, in that it ignores cost of provision, scale, quality and any consideration of the total number of people using services in the hinterland of each centre, it does serve to focus attention explicitly on the disadvantages that people face in living far away from public facilities, and the lower satisfaction levels resulting from spatial isolation. The argument is not that all local communities can, or should, have equal access to all types of social services. Rather, it is to make the point that scale arguments carry weight only to the extent that they deal with the relationship between cost and location. Equity arguments, based on notions of fairness and justice, must ultimately play a role in deciding on the allocation of scarce public resources to social services provision in rural areas. These issues will be examined later in the chapter when the philosophical basis for the pre-occupation with efficiency is explored in the context of an extended discussion of the relationship between efficiency, equity and values.

ACCESS PROBLEMS IN RURAL AREAS

Social services provision in this country is financed mainly by the exchequer. That being the case, the issue of social services provision in rural areas cannot be separated from the broader question of how prepared government is to act as catalyst for rural regeneration on a scale large enough to create the necessary and sufficient conditions for economic and social recovery in rural areas. This is not the place to discuss the broad issue of whether the Irish government recognises that it bears a major responsibility for promoting rural development in this country (Shorthall, 1994). What is important, however, is the absence of official recognition that social services provision is an important element in integrated programmes for rural development. Commins and Keane (1994) point out that the State's role in the deployment of its services cannot be separated from other policies that seek to generate local development and maintain rural population levels. Yet, access to social services continues to be a major problem in rural areas. The absence of a general policy commitment to rural development from government makes it difficult to be sanguine with respect to improving access to social services in rural areas. In this section, the particular problems of access and availability in four separate areas of social services provision are analysed. The areas considered are health care, education, transport and housing.

Health Care

Concern about the extent to which people living in rural areas are disadvantaged in terms of access to health-care services is not new. During the mid-1970s the National Economic and Social Council (NESC) (1976, 1977) voiced some disquiet about inequities and un-evenness in the geographical distribution of health-care facilities in Ireland. These concerns remain valid in the mid-1990s (O'Shea, 1993). Inadequacy of provision is, of course, not confined to rural ar-eas but is exacerbated by distance. For instance, community care provision for old people tends to be higher in the hinterland sur-rounding urban-based day hospitals than is the case generally across the country (Blackwell et al., 1992). Before expanding further on the differences in access between urban and rural areas, the more fun-damental problem of the general adequacy of health-care provision must be considered. The main emphasis throughout this section will be on community-care services, though some reference will also be made to hospital facilities. The reason for the emphasis on community care is the importance of provision in this area for the day-to-day lives of people living in rural areas.

General problems of access, irrespective of location, have been ex-acerbated in recent years by the curtailment of public expenditure on health-care services. Major cutbacks in public health-care expendi-ture occurred during the 1980s, resulting in expenditure falling from 8 per cent of GDP in 1980 to 6 per cent of GDP in 1988. The closure of institutional beds has created additional pressure on the community-care system. These pressures have, by and large, not been responded to by government in the form of additional resources for community services. For instance, there is some evidence that the public-health nurse service is underfunded (O'Shea, 1993). Access to home helps, paramedical services and meals-on-wheels is both limited and vari-able within and among health boards (O'Connor, 1987). Services, such as day-care centres and day hospitals, are poorly developed and are mainly confined to urban or large town settings. The absence of prog-ress on the transfer of resources to community care goes against the stated policy objectives in this area. However, lest one rely too much on the resources argument to explain the non-implementation of pol-icy, the point should be made that even when public resources for health care were plentiful in Ireland — during the period 1976–80 — real spending on community care increased at a slower rate than hospi-tal spending. The argument that policy implementation is always con-strained by a lack of resources is further undermined by the observation that some health boards have made more progress than others in effecting some of the crucial organisational changes in the care of the elderly as outlined in *The Years Ahead — A Policy for the Elderly* (1988) report produced by the Working Party on Services for the Elderly (Lundstrom and McKeown, 1994).

People living in remote rural areas face particular problems of access with respect to health-care services. Harvey (1994), in his evaluation of the lessons to be learned from the Third EU Poverty Programme in Ireland, reports from the Forum project in north-west Connemara that some people in that area forego health care because of the need to travel long distances to facilities. Byrne (1991) confirms the access problem in north-west Connemara. Respondents in her survey report much unhappiness with the poor ambulance facilities from remote areas to centrally-based hospital services. While satisfaction with medical treatment once received is high and certainly not a cause for concern, reports of some people having to pay £50 to £60 for a taxi service to bring family members to hospital confirm the existence of a problem of access in rural areas. Cawley and Stevens (1987) also report substantial costs incurred by rural-based patients in attending clinics in major centres of population, with people spending long periods of time travelling. The result, not surprisingly, is that many people fail to keep scheduled appointments because of high time costs.

Remoteness, isolation, bad housing and patchy community-care services combine to complicate placement decision-making for old people in some rural areas. So does unbalanced demography, exacerbated by high levels of emigration (Blackwell et al., 1992). A combination of some or all of these factors may lead to old people having to leave their home and be admitted to an institution, even though assessment of physical dependency may have deemed home care to be the most appropriate placement. Living at home, without much social contact, may not be a feasible option in a sparsely populated area. In these circumstances, an old person cannot be left alone, isolated physically and emotionally from normal social interaction. Efforts to reduce the number of old people in institutions are being hampered, at the margin, by inadequate attention to the spatial question. Evidence from Blackwell et al. (1992) confirms that spatial isolation, incorporating concern about the distance of old people from facilities and people, is a factor in the placement decision-making of some medical providers. This problem is exacerbated if the discharged old person is returning to live alone in their own house. Spatial access to services is clearly an important part of a coherent and comprehensive strategy for health-care provision in this country.

In support of this view, O'Shea and Corcoran (1990) argue that the local availability of general practitioner services induces in old people the belief that living at home remains a viable alternative, even if minor forms of illness were to occur in an uncertain future. One could add that easy access to general-practitioner care may also encourage preventive activities that slow down the onset of disability in old people in the first place. O'Shea and Corcoran also found that the availability of home-help services significantly increases the likelihood of old people remaining in their homes, even with relatively high levels of disability. Home helps provide many basic services that would otherwise be denied old people because of their incapacity and their subsequent inability to carry out activities of daily living. Home help is particularly beneficial if an old person does not have a network of family and friends to provide assistance with those activities. The overall provision of home-help service is, however, low across the country, with an average of 3.5 per cent of old people receiving some assistance (Lundstrom and McKeown, 1994). This is against the background of an estimated 17 per cent of old people having some form of disability and living at home (O'Connor et al., 1988). Moreover, and particularly relevant to our present discussion, the ratio of home helps per 1,000 elderly persons varies significantly across the country. The rate in the East is 30 home helps (full and part-time) per 1,000 elderly population — this is almost twice as high as the rate of home helps per 1,000 elderly population in the West, Midlands and South-West of the country (O'Shea, 1993).

Urban–rural differences emerge in the distribution of informal care provision for old people (O'Connor et al., 1988). At one extreme, dependent elderly people living in households headed by farmers are 25 per cent more likely than the average to be cared for at home. On the other hand, old people in professional/managerial households are 30 per cent less likely than the average to receive informal care; old people in other non-manual households are also 25 per cent less likely to be receiving care. The most recent national survey on carers suggests that three quarters of all carers are women (Blackwell et al., 1992). Carers spend an average of 47 hours per week providing care, with old people in the highest category of dependency receiving an average of 86 hours of care per week. Changes in family formation, an increase in the labour force participation rate of women, and the consequences of prolonged and ongoing emigration will, more than likely, reduce the pool of potential carers in rural areas in the future. This will weaken further the ability of old people living in rural areas to remain in their own homes should they become partially or seriously disabled as they grow older. O'Connor et al. (1988) have warned that the lack of statutory support services for carers is likely to result in the breakdown of the family caring system, sooner rather than later. Statutory support does not always imply public provision of care, but it does usually mean more public financing of community-care services, particularly in the areas of home help, care attendant schemes, home nursing, voluntary housing and informal community-support networks involving voluntary and community groups.

Access problems in rural areas are not confined to old people. Medical-card holders in rural areas tend to live much further away from their doctors than their urban counterparts. For instance, medical-card holders in the West are almost ten times more likely than the national average to be living more than five miles from their doctor. In some rural areas, there is effectively no choice of doctor. Distance from alternative providers is so great as to make the concept of choice meaningless in such cases. The result is that people unhappy with the delivery of general practitioner care, either process or outcome, have no choice but to continue with existing arrangements because of the absence of any alternatives. Distance from doctor is likely to be accentuated by the relative absence of private transport or telephones among the low-income section of the population. Harvey (1994) makes the point that, very often, problems of physical remoteness are compounded by the low rate of telephones in rural households. While the number of elderly households in rural areas without a phone has fallen dramatically in recent years, from 89 per cent in 1977 to 22 per cent in 1993, differences still persist between rural and urban areas (Fahey and Murray, 1994). In Ballyconeely, Co. Galway, 33 per cent of all residents do not have a phone, while 25 per cent of people living alone are without a phone (Byrne, 1991).

Dental services are also inadequate in rural areas. In some areas, a public service is available only for school children in the 5–12-year age group (Harvey, 1994). Even for this group, delivery of primary dental care is uneven throughout the country (Department of Health, 1994). Access is limited in rural areas because of a shortage of dentists relative to the number of people who are eligible for care. Areas which find it relatively easy to recruit dentists — for example, in the East of the country — are better able to meet the needs of public patients and provide a more comprehensive range of services. Orthodontic care for children in rural areas is particularly limited because of the unavailability of trained personnel. Services, where they are provided, are largely confined to urban areas and their immediate hinterlands. Evidence from the Forum anti-poverty project in Connemara confirms the inadequacy of dental care in peripheral regions of the country. The waiting list for dental treatment under the public scheme in this area is long — up to nine months. Access to private facilities is almost non-existent because of the distance people have to travel to avail of services.

Education

The whole debate about educational facilities in rural areas centres around issues of declining population and economies of scale leading to pressure for school consolidation and amalgamations. The crucial issue is whether large schools result in cheaper and better education and, if so, at what cost to the fabric of local communities? Even if the financial gains from economies of scale are significant, transport costs and the loss of community identity (so-called environmental costs), following the closure of local schools may be of such magnitude as to outweigh the gains from amalgamation. Evidence from outside Ireland suggests that while economies of scale do exist, they are likely to be offset by both transport and environmental factors, at least beyond a certain size of school (Keane, 1978). Recent survey-based research by Shucksmith et al. (1994) confirms the importance of local schools in the social and cultural life of rural communities in Scotland. Concern for the future of rural primary schools was strong in Scotland across all household types, even in households without children at primary school. The absence of research on the impact of school closures and amalgamations on rural communities in Ireland has not prevented both from occurring in this country. The worry is that school closures may interact with other factors to accelerate population decline in remote rural areas. More research is needed before any more definitive statements can be made with respect to the impact of local schools on community well-being in this country.

Rural communities may face special difficulties in relation to access to pre-school facilities. Pre-school facilities are more common in urban areas where high population density makes it more likely that participation rates will be high enough to guarantee the financial viability and profitability of these schools. Breen (1991) has identified the roots of early school-leaving in the pre-school environment of the student and in the complex relationship between school, family and community. Hannan and Boyle (1987) point out the need for a more developed public policy on pre-school provision, given its importance in providing the basis for a long school career. Pre-school facilities may also have a bearing on the choice sets available to some women with respect to their opportunities to participate in work, training and leisure. Byrne (1991) reports that very few parents in north-west Connemara send their children to pre-school. Cost and transport problems were frequently given as the reasons for not sending children to pre-school.

Once in primary school, children with learning difficulties are likely to need special remedial teaching to help them to overcome their learning problems. Resources for remedial teaching are, however, often absent in rural areas or, when available, are too thinly spread to have any real effect. In a comprehensive (90 per cent response rate) survey by the Irish National Teachers Organisation (INTO) (1993) of one-teacher rural schools, only 5 per cent of schools had access to a remedial teacher, while just 20 per cent had access to psychological services. Parents in north-west Connemara regard the weak provision of remedial facilities as being the single biggest gap in educational provision in the area (Harvey, 1994). Their concern is not difficult to understand given that almost one in three households in the area with children in the primary school system since 1980 has had at least one child having difficulty with reading, writing or other aspects of learning. Quite clearly, there is a need for a more formal public-policy response to the provision of remedial teaching resources. However, progress should not be measured solely on the basis of meeting area norms. The important point is that need rather than economies of scale should determine allocation procedures, with resources directed towards individuals and schools rather than areas.

The physical condition of a significant number of rural schools, in terms of both structure and amenities, is also poor. The National Economic and Social Council, reporting in 1978, commented that many small rural schools frequently lacked certain basic facilities, such as electricity and drinking water (NESC, 1978). While conditions have certainly improved since then, some rural schools continue to have problems as witnessed by occasional and well-publicised complaints by parents about the physical dereliction of their local schools. The INTO survey, referred to above, found that one-third of one-teacher schools suffer from significant dampness; 19 per cent do not have an adequate, safe heating system; over one-fifth suffer from vermin of various types; and, even more alarmingly, given their remoteness, over 50 per cent of schools did not have a telephone. In Byrne's (1991) baseline study of north-west Connemara about one-third of parents expressed dissatisfaction with their children's school for physical reasons: dampness, cold, lack of indoor toilets and inadequate recreational facilities were the main problems cited by the parents.

One of the problems of trying to effect an improvement in either buildings or amenities is that, very often, the local community is asked to supplement public resources from local funds for this purpose. Some areas are better able to raise additional monies than others. This is, of course, just one aspect of the more general inequality caused by the current policy of encouraging the "topping-up" of statutory provision, particularly in primary schools, through local contribution schemes involving the parents in local fund-raising activities. Some areas possess the earnings and income potential, with relatively easy access to private funds, to augment statutory spending on primary education — others do not.

It is now well documented that failure to obtain increasing levels of educational qualifications has serious negative effects on life-chances (Breen, 1991; NESC, 1993; Nolan and Callan, 1994). Unemployment in Ireland is heavily concentrated among those who have not completed second-level education (OECD, 1993). Those without qualifications face high probabilities of both current unemployment and future long-term unemployment, as well as the subsequent negative impact of that labour-market experience on future streams of income and wealth. Early school-leaving occurs in both urban and rural areas and differences in educational performance seem to be influenced more by class than by place. That said, it must be acknowledged that information on the relationship between place and education attainment is scarce and is an area where more research is needed. The information that is available comes from small-scale, locally-based, survey work. Harvey (1994), for instance, reports that early school-leaving is a significant problem in north-west Connemara. In contrast, Storey (1994) points to the relatively high proportion of people with higher education in remote areas of the South-West of the country, which are quite a geographical distance from the nearest third-level institutions in Cork city or Tralee. It is best not to read too much into micro-studies of the type referred to above. It is better to acknowledge what is known with some certainty from studies using more representative national data. What is known is that the poor, whether living in urban or rural areas, are predominantly poorly educated and are more likely to be long-term unemployed.

Failure to meet scale and viable population thresholds has also led to a very weak structure of adult education in some rural areas in Ireland. Adult education receives limited government support, leading one to question the overall commitment from official sources to the concept of lifelong learning. In considering the deep structural changes that have affected rural areas in the past 30 years or so, the absence of a commitment to life-long education and training in this country is even more puzzling. In an economy that has been transformed from a largely agricultural to a mainly industrial/service economy, the absence of a dynamic structure to mediate an understanding of that change for people living in rural communities is difficult to understand.

An opportunity was lost to provide people with the life-skills that might have allowed them to respond in a more flexible way to the economic and social changes that were occurring in their lives. Continuing education might have allowed people a better chance of surviving the changes, as well as having some influence on the direction of change. Adult and continuing education programmes can facilitate new ways of thinking about the organisation and structure of the economy and society, since they have the potential to affect both personal development and the capacity of an individual to engage in collective action for economic and social change (Lovett, 1989). By helping to foster social and community action, adult education can be an important countervailing force to the rapid economic and technological changes now occurring in modern societies. The fact that so many people left rural areas, or remained poor living in rural areas, is an indictment of official thinking on life-time education and training in this country Not only were policy-makers unwilling to make the connection between life-long education and the alleviation of poverty and inequality, but they could not even see the benefits accruing for efficiency and flexibility in the labour market and for growth in the economy. As Gelpi (1987) points out, technological innovation needs a favourable cultural and social framework within which to develop; adult education is an important part of the ongoing fertilisation process for that development.

It is only in recent years that the investment in human capital through adult and continuing education has been assigned the prominence it deserves in official thinking on strategies to promote growth and economic development. The recent White Paper on Education (Department of Education, 1995) refers to the need for life-long learning and the continuous retraining and updating of skills. In a similar vein, the Industrial Research and Development Advisory Committee of the European Union (1995) points to the importance of continuing education as a response to current technological, market and demographic trends in the European economy. The report of the Steering Committee on the Future Development of Higher Education (Higher Education Authority, 1995) recommends that continuing education should become part of the core mission of higher-education institutions. The Authority also recommends a more flexible response to the public funding of some adult-education courses in higher education institutions. It can only be hoped that the sentiments expressed recently in official documents will be translated into tangible progress with respect to the increased provision of adult-education programmes, based on the principles of solidarity, equality and respect between teachers and recipients of courses (Thompson, 1980).

Transport

The availability of transport as a means of access to both public and private services and facilities is a major issue for people living in rural communities. The centralisation of service provision means that transport plays an important role in the social integration of people living far away from major centres of provision. By corollary, the absence of public transport is, therefore, one of the major determinants of social exclusion in rural areas. There has been criticism that Ireland possesses no coherent transport policy (Barrett, 1991), particularly in the area of rural transport (National Council for the Aged, 1986). While it is true that both rail and bus transport receive generous social support from the exchequer, this has not prevented a significant erosion of public-transport networks in rural areas in recent years. Budgetary constraints have focused increasing attention on the commercial activities of state-supported public-transport companies, with the result that more and more unprofitable routes, hitherto surviving on the basis of a social services argument, have been terminated. The absence of public provision of bus services in rural areas leads to higher weekly expenditures on petrol and other vehicle expenses by rural car owners in comparison to their urban counterparts (Commins and Keane, 1994). Even greater hardship is experienced by the poorest sections of society — those who cannot afford to own a car have to rely on private arrangements or the generosity of others if they want to travel any distance at all.

The absence of an adequate public-transport system contributes to the social exclusion of poor people in rural areas. Transport difficulties were repeatedly raised by people in north-west Connemara as a serious obstacle to personal contact, access to health and social services, and economic and social development (Byrne, 1991). It is somewhat ironic that successive governments should place so much emphasis on investment in transport infrastructure as a policy response to Ireland's peripherality problem within the EU and yet be so neglectful of the significant transport inequalities that exist within the country between urban and rural areas. Inequalities in transport provision within the country affect both the morale of local people and the development opportunities of poorly serviced rural communities.

Even more ironic is the situation in some rural areas where elderly people, entitled to free transport on public bus and rail services, cannot avail of the facility because bus and rail services do not exist in their areas. Ireland has long had free public transport as a universal entitlement for all elderly people. This right is now so well established that it is almost taken for granted — even during recent periods of fiscal contraction, when all items of public expenditure came under close scrutiny, no one ever suggested doing anything to undermine this entitlement. However, if the public-transport system is weak or non-existent, it matters little that entitlement is universal. O'Mahony (1986) estimated that two-thirds of elderly people in Clifden rural district never used their travel pass, while 26 per cent used it only rarely. Public transport was not available in the area, or the services that did exist were not suitable for people's needs. In contrast, in Galway urban district, almost 50 per cent of elderly people used their pass at least once per week. Free travel for elderly people clearly benefits urban dwellers far more than those living in rural communities.

The absence of a comprehensive public-transport system means that private alternatives have to be used much more frequently in rural areas, especially for journeys to and from medical practitioners, hospital out-patient clinics, and even for social visits. The use of private transport can have serious cost implications for some old people. Even where public services exist, frequency may be low and confined to a couple of days in the week. Moreover, since many people in rural areas live miles from existing bus routes, public transport is not a realistic option for these people. The result is that poor people either pay for private transport or do not travel. As mentioned earlier, access to public transport and distance from facilities has been cited by Cawley and Stephens (1987) as playing a major role in determining access to out-patient facilities at Galway Regional Hospital. This is the most worrying aspect of the absence of a coherent and comprehensive strategy for public transport in rural areas.

Housing

Expenditure on social housing bore a major part of the cutbacks in public expenditure that occurred in this country at the end of the 1980s. Public spending on social housing continued to decline until 1993, when there was a significant expansion of the local-authority building programme to 3,500 units. While the cutbacks of the late 1980s are now being reversed, the number of people on local-authority housing lists has grown in recent years. Not surprisingly, given the concentration of the housing problem in urban areas, there has been a major emphasis on urban renewal programmes in recent policy-making, both for commercial development and for residential use. Rural housing policy has been somewhat neglected in recent years, though it must be acknowledged that there has been continuous progress in addressing rural housing problems over the past 30 years. In particular, there has been considerable improvement in the provision of water supply and sanitary facilities for rural areas during this time. Investment in these facilities has served to redress huge historical inequalities between urban and rural areas with respect to basic household sanitation.

For all the progress that has been made in this area, poor housing remains a feature of many rural communities. Comparative information on both the state of the urban and rural housing stock and the needs of both communities is scarce, however. For the most part, we have to rely on either small-scale local surveys or client-specific national surveys for reasonably up-to-date information. For instance, O'Mahony (1986) examined the housing conditions of old people living in three districts in Galway and found considerable variation amongst them. Overall, almost one-fifth of the houses examined needed major repair. The need for repair was, however, much higher in rural areas, as was the absence of normal sanitary facilities. Just under one-half of all respondents in Loughrea rural district and Clifden rural district did not have a flush toilet — the corresponding figure for respondents in Galway municipal borough was 2 per cent.

Concern about the poor quality of rural housing has also been expressed by Harvey (1994). His concern is based on survey data for north-west Connemara, which show that 7 per cent of households lack electricity, 12 per cent lack water, 17 per cent lack indoor toilets and 18 per cent lack a bath or shower (Byrne, 1991). The study by Fahey and Murray (1994) on the health and autonomy of the over 65s in Ireland highlights the vulnerable position of elderly single-person households in rural areas, with respect to household amenities. More than a quarter of this group had no bath/shower, while a fifth had no indoor toilet. The corresponding figures for single-person elderly households in urban areas are 7 per cent and 2 per cent respectively.

Government grant schemes for the purposes of renovation have proven to be an inadequate response to the very poor condition of some houses in rural areas. Some people continue to live in very poor housing. Information on similar types of schemes in Northern Ireland suggests that grant aid for the renovation of rural housing cannot hope to resolve all of the problems that require attention — a significant number of grant recipients (16 per cent) in the North felt that replacement grants should have been available to replace dwellings that were gone beyond the repair stage (McPeake and Murtagh, 1993). People do not want to live in squalor but they very often lack the financial means to do anything about their situation. The replacement of existing dwellings may be the only solution for these households. Such repair and building activity would also be a major boost to the developing social economy in rural areas.

IMPROVING SOCIAL SERVICES PROVISION IN RURAL AREAS

The problem with rural deprivation is not that it is radically different from urban deprivation but rather that it needs to be responded to in different ways (Moseley, 1980). For many poor people living in rural areas, the problem is that, far too often, social services are not available locally. This is especially true in relation to health-care services, where the twin problems of access and distance are particularly acute. While it is acknowledged that some health-care services such as high-technology acute-care hospitals will continue to be provided centrally, there is no reason why other health-care services cannot be based in local areas. The focus, therefore, should be on the production process and how innovative and flexible responses can be encouraged to deal with the twin problems of access and distance.

There is evidence that where this has happened, service delivery and accessibility problems have been improved. In recent years, the Eastern Health Board has implemented a mobile day-hospital service for old people living in rural areas in the region. Instead of having the task of organising transport for people to come to the service in Dublin, the Board now takes the service to the people. Initial, unpublished, reports suggest that the new service has proven to be very successful in overcoming the access problems of a relatively dispersed population of old people in the region in need of day hospital care.[2]

The Forum poverty project reacted to access problems in northwest Connemara by implementing locally-based flexible provision of community-care services, particularly for old people in the area. According to Harvey (1994), the results of the Forum initiative show that health services can be delivered locally and appropriately to a dispersed and depleted rural population in a relatively short period of time, at relatively low cost. The provision of an efficient and flexible ambulance service to bring people living in rural areas to central hospital facilities is also an important element of a strategy to overcome health-care disadvantage associated with living in rural areas. In general, solving the problem of exclusion associated with remoteness requires more emphasis on the supply side, rather than trying to deal with the access problem through the judicious manipulation of consumer behaviour.

Part of the problem of getting things done in rural areas is the absence of real power in local communities. Centralism in decision-making condemns peripheral areas to a subservient dependency role, not only in economic and social development, but also in relation to social-services provision, particularly in health care. The Department of Health and the large urban hospitals control the allocation and distribution of health-care resources, while the Department of Finance controls the money upon which the allocation and distribution ultimately depends. It is the responsibility of each health board to work out its own internal budget within the budgetary guidelines laid down by the Department of Health, although, even here, the latter has a major say, particularly if decisions are being made to effect major changes in service provision. This process leaves little opportunity for the members of health boards to have a major input into decision-making about the size, allocation and distribution of budgets. More often than not, the budget is presented to the Board as a *fait accompli*, as prepared by health-board officials within the financial constraints set by the Department (Fitzgerald, 1984). Although health boards have been given the task of representing the views of the public in the overall formulation of policy, the scope for exercising that

---

[2] Personal communication.

responsibility is limited, given that financial decisions are, by and large, taken elsewhere. This is not to suggest that health boards have no power or influence with respect to service provision. Intervention is, however, confined to expressing concerns about existing services provision and consequent reallocation at the margins.

O'Shea and Hughes (1994) have recently called attention to the variation in community-care provision among health boards, suggesting the need for explicit legislative criteria to bring about minimum levels of consistency in the implementation of agreed policy, particularly with respect to the transfer of resources from institutions to community care. Legislative criteria will not, however, solve all problems. The process of care also matters. Process is particularly important in the provision of services for old people. At a practical level, there is a need for greater co-ordination between statutory agencies, voluntary bodies and carers (Browne, 1992). This would allow information about actual and potential need to be generated locally, so that services might be planned and delivered in an orderly manner. Whatever structures for co-ordinating and defining local care are put in place, it makes sense to begin the process of care with a definition of need provided by people working closely with old people. This is far better than simply handing down centrally determined planning norms, very often derived from consideration of need and service provision in other countries (O'Shea, 1993).

While need is very important in planning social-services provision it is also important not to neglect the supply-side. In particular, some rural areas may find it difficult to attract suitably qualified health-care personnel to work in peripheral locations. Location decisions for health-care professionals are likely to be influenced, to some degree at least, by the earnings potential of a particular area. Rural areas cannot compete with urban areas in terms of generating similar levels of income for some health-care professionals. This is especially true for doctors and dentists. One way of addressing this issue is the introduction of sparsity-related incentive payments to encourage the provision of services in remote rural areas. Another approach would be the implementation of a scheme for the placement of medical graduates in rural areas on completion of their studies. This placement could be for a designated period of one or two years.

A more radical approach to addressing the problem of the availability of personnel in rural areas, particularly in the medical and dental fields, would be to train local substitute providers in the provision of basic care along the lines of the so-called "barefoot doctor" scheme in the Chinese health-care system. While the implementation of a local, low-technology and semi-skilled, community-based medical system would undoubtedly meet strong resistance from the professions and from the centralised bureaucracy, it might serve to alleviate access and transport problems, particularly in remote rural areas. Where services are considered essential, their availability should be guaranteed, irrespective of geographical location. Doing this may require a more innovative and flexible use of personnel than has been the norm in this country.

Resolving the problem of access to and availability of education services in rural areas is more straightforward, in that many of the educational disadvantages faced by poor people living in rural areas are also faced by their counterparts in urban areas. A key strategy to overcome disadvantages faced by poor people may be the provision of local education structures to co-ordinate and integrate service delivery in rural areas between the pre-school and primary sectors and between the latter and secondary levels. A local community-based structure would allow a coherent response to demographic changes occurring in an area, thereby providing an ideal forum for a collective and integrated response to changing needs.

Local education structures might also lead to an improvement in the targeting of resources to those pupils, families and schools that need them most. All the evidence suggests that resource allocation has to be very specific if it is to work in favour of the disadvantaged (Nolan and Callan, 1994). It is at the level of pre-school and remedial education that resources are most often lacking in rural areas, particularly for already disadvantaged children. This is an unacceptable situation given the high level of spending on third-level education in the country. Additional spending on disadvantaged children in the early years of schooling is much more likely to lead, albeit over a period, to a reduction in current inequalities in the Irish education system. In contrast, spending on third-level education merely reinforces, and in many cases exacerbates, class differences in our society.

Strategies to deal with educational inequalities in rural areas must also focus on adult education and training. Some people living in rural areas have been trained for obsolete or declining occupations. If they are to compete in the labour market, they may need training and education to give them the flexibility that they require to survive in modern labour markets. For some people, however, participation in state employment or training schemes can have a negative effect on psychological well-being (Hannan and O'Riain, 1993). Time spent on schemes tends to increase levels of personal stress for people who remained unemployed on completion of the scheme. Education for adults should, therefore, serve a wider function than simply training people for non-existent jobs. The definition of work should be extended to include much of what goes on in the social economy. People should be provided with a participation guarantee that goes beyond involvement in the market economy. Many adult people in rural communities do not possess even basic educational qualifications. Second-chance education would allow these people the opportunity to participate in the educational process on the same basis as younger people. Adult education often provides people with a new sense of confidence and self-worth, the very attributes that people living in poverty find difficult to maintain in difficult economic and financial circumstances. The general underfunding of adult education courses is aggravated in rural areas by problems of access.[3] This is not surprising and again points to the inter-connectedness of policies to alleviate exclusion in rural areas.

Even if one is sceptical about the relationship between continuing education and subsequent labour-market experience, the potential of second-chance education as a strategy to combat social exclusion should not be underestimated. As Shorthall (1994) reminds us, community is not a static entity and it is possible to encourage and develop its existence. Adult education, based on participative learning strategies, which build on people's own experiences, may be a key strategy in fostering community. In this case, what is being promoted is community, defined not in terms of place or blood, but in terms of intellect and the mind. It is clear from Chapter 8 of this book that community has now emerged as an important explanatory variable in the theory and practice of development in this country. Adult and continuing education for people in rural areas has a critical role to play in ensuring that the widest possible constituency share in the process and potential of community action and development.

One of the key areas where the rural poor suffer disadvantage is in relation to public transport. Remoteness and peripherality exacerbate the transport difficulties, and hence exclusion problems, faced by rural dwellers. The response of government to these problems has been weak and largely non-existent. There is no transport policy for remote rural areas in Ireland. Excessive centralisation and concerns

---

[3] The treasurer of AONTAS makes this very point in the supplement to *The Irish Times*, 6 September 1995.

about economies of scale and the cost of rural provision have combined to keep rural transport issues off the political agenda. The small numbers affected by government inaction in this area, at least when compared with the numbers affected by urban transport policy, means that there is very little pressure on the political system for action to be taken in relation to rural transport. Some communities have taken the initiative themselves in relation to the establishment of a viable community-based transport network for rural areas (Lightfoot, 1995). For instance, solving the transport problem quickly became an important element of the work of Forum in north-west Connemara. The project co-ordinated the establishment of four new transport routes in the area, largely based on privately-owned buses, supported by an agreement with the Department of Social Welfare that they would honour bus passes on these services. The community car scheme in the same area also improved matters for a small number of individuals who had great difficulty in accessing private and public facilities, including reaching existing bus routes. Similar social market-style transfer schemes have been tried in other areas, such as Glenamaddy and Tulsk, Co. Roscommon, with varying degrees of success.

Harvey (1994) is rightly critical of the absence of an integrated and innovative approach to rural transport policy in Ireland, given what is known about the benefits attained in other countries from the implementation of such a strategy. O'Mahony (1986) provides a comprehensive account of the various ways to improve mobility and access in rural areas, drawing on the experience of successful strategies in other countries. In England, there is a special Rural Transport Development Fund to encourage the provision of innovative transport services in sparsely populated rural areas. Legal and organisational barriers tend to be the most common obstacles to innovation, particularly in this country (Commins and Keane, 1994). The Danish experience of transport initiatives in rural areas also points to the constraints imposed by sector-rational economic behaviour, differences in the cultures of different organisations and the lack of knowledge about other organisations (Lightfoot, 1995). The absence of local transport networks in rural areas, for whatever reason, condemns many people, especially old people, to a premature disengagement from economic and social life. Given that the costs of implementing local transport networks may, on the evidence of the Forum project, be much less than previously expected, this is a serious indictment of our ability to resolve relatively simple problems of access in rural areas. This is an area where much could be done at little cost to the exchequer. The anomaly referred to earlier in our discussion on free travel for old people, whereby many old people living in rural areas cannot use their travel pass because there is no transport services on which they can exercise their right to travel, free or otherwise, also needs to be addressed. One practical way of dealing with this problem would be to issue travel vouchers to old people, redeemable on either public- or private-transport facilities. This would allow old people to travel on private transport in circumstances where public services do not exist or are only infrequently provided. This proposal would solve the access problem for rural elderly, by providing a more flexible response to the transport needs of those people. Confining free travel to public transport in rural areas has created an undesirable inequity between rural and urban dwellers and should not have been allowed to persist for so long. Congratulating ourselves that we are one of the few countries in the EU to have a free-travel scheme for old people is somewhat disingenuous, given the absence of a proper rural transport network on which old people can travel.

Our knowledge of the extent of inadequate housing in rural areas is limited. There is a need for a comprehensive survey of housing needs in both urban and rural areas. Limited evidence from locally-based surveys suggests that bad housing is a significant problem for some people living in rural areas. Solutions to housing problems need not always come directly from the Government. In recent years, the provision of housing by voluntary groups, supported by the exchequer, has been an important innovation in urban housing development in this country. The work of the Rural Housing Organisation has also been important in resettling former urban dwellers in new or refurbished rural housing. That said, the voluntary sector contributes less in Ireland than in many other countries to the housing of marginal groups such as people living in poverty and vulnerable old people. In order to encourage this sector to expand further, particularly in rural areas, more state funding may be required, not only for the maintenance and repair of buildings, but also for the purpose of construction.

Local Authority provision of social housing has taken off again in recent years, following a period when public investment in housing was very low. All the evidence suggests that the investment was timely and that a serious crisis in statutory provision has been averted. What needs to be recognised now is the sub-standard nature of existing privately-owned accommodation for a significant number of people living in rural areas. The strategy in response to such a problem will depend on the outcome of a needs-based survey, allied to an economic cost-benefit analysis of how best to deal with the problem, whether through replacement or renovation. Identifying the problem is the first step, however, and needs to be done immediately. Otherwise, urban housing problems, which are sometimes more concentrated and hence more visible, will continue to be the focus of much of the policy debate in this area. This is not to argue that urban housing problems are insignificant or not worthy of attention. Rather, it is to caution that rural housing problems should not be ignored simply because occurrences of homelessness or run-down facilities are more isolated and more scattered. The resulting problems for people and families affected by inadequate housing are just the same as in urban areas.

EFFICIENCY, EQUITY AND VALUES

Any move away from centralism and the geographic concentration of power and control of resources will require new thinking about the trade-off between efficiency and equity in resource-allocation decision-making. For the majority of economists in this country, efficiency is the primary criterion by which resource-allocation decision-making is judged. The interesting question to be addressed, however, is not whether efficiency is worthwhile — which, of course, it is — but whether, in some instances, concern with equity should take precedence. Trying to make a judgement on the relative weights to be assigned to efficiency and equity arguments in resource-allocation decision-making forces us to think about the values that underpin the choices we make about who gets what, and the subsequent implications of those choices for the lives of people and communities. Indeed, identifying the magnitude of the trade-off between efficiency and spatial equity may be the most important contribution that economists can make to the evaluation of spatial distribution problems. This final section is, therefore, an effort to reconcile the general thrust of this chapter with a set of philosophical foundations that may provide a basis for public policy-making different from the utilitarian, individualistic and efficiency-based approach favoured by neo-liberal economists.

The neo-classical paradigm associated with modern market economies is based on a utilitarian version of radical individualism. The assumption is that individuals seek to maximise their utility, rationally choosing the best means to serve their, usually given, ends. Individuals are autonomous units operating within market economies which can be shown to work best when no obstacles are placed in the way of individual decision-making. Utilitarianism is best described as an aggregative (as opposed to a distributive) principle. It states that social judgements should be based solely on the aggregation of individual utilities. Indeed, utilitarianism is prepared to contemplate endlessly sacrificing one person's good in order to maximise the overall good (Kymlicka, 1989). Far from conflict leading to chaos in the marketplace, the interaction of autonomous decision-making agents leads to maximum efficiency and well-being for everyone. Of course, some people gain and others lose in the free-play of market forces but that is the nature of the game. It is the expression and ultimately the satisfaction of individual preferences that provides the catalyst for growth and development in the economy. Equity and distribution are secondary objectives. When distributional questions are addressed, the discussion is frequently limited to technical arguments about the capacity of the exchequer to bear existing burdens or to withstand small marginal changes in social welfare and social services provision.

Sen (1992) has argued that the informational basis of utilitarianism is too narrow, as it focuses on just one characteristic (happiness) of a person's well-being. Happiness is a particularly limited metric in the context of interpersonal comparisons of well-being, since a person who has suffered severe deprivation may take great pleasure in small mercies (Sen, 1987). Sen has also criticised utilitarianism for not acknowledging the possibility that a person may value the promotion of certain causes or the occurrence of certain things even if these developments are not connected to a person's own well-being. Individuals may not always interact with other individuals solely in terms of the contribution that they might make to the realisation of their goals. Instead, individuality may exist only within community boundaries. People make decisions for all kinds of reasons and are influenced by their own values, as well as by the social, political and cultural climate within which they operate. Lewin (1991), for instance, shows that voters, politicians and bureaucrats are influenced not only by their own views about what is best for themselves but also by what they believe is best for the community as a whole.

This is not to deny that people are purposeful and have real choices in much of their economic and social decision-making. Rather, it is to make the point that people's choices are moulded by their social existence as well as by their cultural and institutional environment (Hodgson, 1988). The impact of community and socio-institutional imperatives on the actions of individuals transforms the market into a social process. The inclusion of an ethical dimension further modifies the market in a way that makes it almost unrecognisable from the legacy bequeathed by Adam Smith (1937), although Smith should not be blamed for contemporary interpretations of his work that are but partial reconstructions of his more general model of the interconnectedness between economic, social and political thought (Evensky, 1993). As Hutchinson (1976) points out, Adam Smith's conception of the scope and wide-ranging interdependencies of social and economic enquiry have rarely been followed by subsequent economists.

These types of criticism have led to the formulation of a number of different approaches to analysing the relationship between individual and social choices. Rawls (1972) developed a theory of justice, which he argued, took explicit account of individuals' social well-being. Because he tried to justify his theory by arguing that self-interested individuals would choose the particular principles of justice, his theory has received much attention from economists. He was concerned with people's separateness and with their moral equality. Hence his focus on the process or context in which decisions are made, as much as, if not more than, on the outcomes of this process (Mueller, 1989a; 1989b).

Rawls uses the device of the original position, and the ignorance of future events implied by decision-making, behind a veil of ignorance, to provide the framework for deciding on social principles. Individuals are asked to agree on a set of social rules without knowing what position they themselves will subsequently hold in that society. Since individuals cannot tell how they will fare in society, they are likely to choose a social structure that maximises the well-being of the worst off. The two principles chosen as the twin pillars of the just social contract are the "Equal Liberty" Principle and the "Difference Principle". The former is fundamental and states that "each person is to have an equal right to most extensive basic liberty compatible with a similar liberty to others". The Difference Principle is concerned that "social and economic inequalities are arranged so that they are both (a) reasonably expected to be to everyone's advantage, and (b) attached to positions and offices open to all". Taken together, these principles imply that all citizens must be guaranteed their basic primary goods before any trade-off in the distribution of other social goods can be considered. According to Rawls, the chief primary goods available to society are rights and liberties, power and opportunities, income and wealth, and self respect. The Rawlsian approach is broader than mere utility maximisation and has important implications for justice, fairness, liberty and citizenship. The approach has been used by both the Combat Poverty Agency and the Conference of Religious in Ireland, among others, to set out the requirements for developing and maintaining a society which allows for equal participation by all its members.

An alternative approach to thinking about questions of allocation, choice and distribution has been developed in recent years by Sen (1992), who argues that people's differences must be the starting point for any theory of equality. Sen is concerned with both the diversity in what people want to do, or achieve, or are, and the diversity across people in their ability to achieve or obtain what they want. He argues that people's freedom to do different things (and not just their ability to do the things that they actually do) is important for analysing welfare judgements. This is a useful way of thinking about social services provision in rural areas. It is the freedom to do different things which is inhibited by the weakness of social services provision in some rural areas. Social services provision does not, at the moment, allow fully for the different spatial circumstances of rural and urban recipients. People's differences are not the starting point for the distribution of services.

There are, of course, considerable differences across people in their ability to achieve or obtain what they want in life. Equalising resources is necessary to overcome these differences but it is clearly not sufficient. The capabilities of a person to achieve must also be addressed. Capabilities in this case refers to those characteristics of individuals beyond their immediate control. Failures that result from factors which are under the control of individuals should not be compensated against. At least, there is no moral imperative which leads one to the view that imbalances in capabilities which result from poor endogenous decision-making should be of interest to society. Only those capabilities beyond the control and sphere of influence of the individual deserve to be recognised and addressed.

The diversity of individuals leads Sen to conclude that all major ethical theories of social arrangement must share an endorsement of equality in terms of some focal variable. This view is also accepted by Cohen (1993) and Le Grand (1991). Cohen proposes equality of access to advantage. This is motivated by the idea that differential access is unjust, save where it reflects differences in genuine choice. In that respect, it is highly unlikely that people living in rural areas would not want better access to social services, like health care, education, housing and transport — in other words, that they would choose to have lower access to these services. This is very similar to the suggestion by Le Grand that a distribution is equitable if it is the outcome of informed individuals choosing over equal choice sets. The advantage of these theories is that by explicitly asking the question "equality of what?", they force people to confront what their views on equality are without getting into long debates over whether people are solely self-interested or not. Poor people living in rural areas do not have equal choice sets when it comes to social services, at least when compared to urban dwellers.

One of the problems that these egalitarian approaches face is to explain whether such theories would be widely accepted by a society. Although caution must be exercised about deducing moral values from empirical observations, the weight of evidence from party voting, experiments and social indicators suggests that the views of Le Grand and Cohen on fairness may not be universally shared (Hammond, 1991). The implications for other important values like freedom and efficiency may be simply too severe. The resource implications of equalising choice sets for poor people living in rural areas are also likely to act as a constraint on policy-makers. The equalisation of choice sets may require inequality of opportunity in the sense of positive discrimination. This costs money — much more money than governments have historically been willing to pay out. Nevertheless, as Le Grand (1991) points out, "a society with less inequality in choice sets will be one with less inequity." At the very least, thinking about the problem in this way is a much more satisfactory way of dealing with values than the current implicit approach of always relegating equity to a secondary position behind technical concerns about efficiency.

Dealing with the problem of social services provision in rural areas cannot, therefore, be confined simply to recommendations for additional resources to be provided in these areas. It is necessary to probe the commitment to rural life itself and, in particular, to examine the attitude to poverty and deprivation in rural areas. This is not an easy task, nor is it one that can be satisfied by the usual platitudes about the community aspect of rural living serving to alleviate the sense of alienation and exclusion felt by poor people living in rural areas. As Miller (1989) points out, if a community is to make a claim on our allegiance, it must represent a distinct way of life, something that makes it personal. When some people do not have the resources to participate in the normal patterns of living associated with rural life, any sense of shared community is weakened, to say the very least.

There is a tendency to underplay social division within rural areas, perhaps because it is often not as visible as in urban areas. In rural areas, however, hierarchy often replaces class divisions as the framework for social interaction, and a clear divide, as strong as social class boundaries in urban areas, is created between poor and non-poor people. While it is true that there are some social forces at work in rural areas which serve to mitigate social divisions and lead to a degree of interaction between poor and non-poor, particularly in respect of religious practice and participation in sport, divisions between rich and poor may still run deep. The result is that there may be differences of opinion within rural areas about strategies to alleviate poverty and, in particular, the extent to which social services can and should be used to combat poverty. We have become so used to hearing about the urban–rural divide with respect to resource allocation that we tend to forget that fundamental differences may also exist within rural communities about whose values should count most when it comes to establishing priority claims over public resources.

Finally, there is not enough discussion in this country about the type of society that we want, about whether we might ever realise a form of living that would reconcile freedom with solidarity, and efficiency with equity. It may not be possible to achieve such a balance, but if we continue to ignore these issues, or to confuse positive and normative judgements in resource-allocation decision-making, we will never know what can be achieved (Ignatieff, 1984). An unwillingness to think about the philosophical foundations of the welfare state, and the moral commitments that bind us together as a genuine community (Herzog, 1986), has contributed to a situation whereby poor people living in rural areas have been denied access to social services simply because of where they live. They suffer a double discrimination — by class and by place. The concept of social solidarity is meaningless while such inequalities persist. Ultimately, the full participation of poor people living in rural communities in economic and social life is conditional on more power and greater choice being available to them, thereby allowing them the normal freedoms and responsibilities associated with full citizenship.

CONCLUSION

This chapter has been concerned with the relationship between social services provision and rural poverty. Economies-of-scale arguments are most frequently invoked to explain spatial differences in social services provision. Scale arguments are often put forward as part of a wider efficiency rationale, which is commonly used to justify the rationalisation and curtailment of social services in rural areas. The disadvantages faced by people living in rural areas are real enough and have been documented above. In many cases, improvements could be made in the lives of the rural poor without much additional public expenditure on social services provision. For lasting changes to occur, however, there may have to be a radical reassessment of the relative weighting to be given to efficiency and equity in public policy-making. The enhancement of social citizenship and social solidarity requires that the distributional consequences of different policies be accorded a much higher priority. This can be achieved only by a willingness to reassess the philosophical foundations of the welfare state and the moral commitments that bind us together as a genuine virtuous community.

References

Barrett, S.D. (1991): *Transport Policy in Ireland in the 1990s*, Dublin: Gill and Macmillan.

Blackwell, J., O'Shea, E. Moane, G. and Murray, P. (1992): *Care Provision and Cost Measurement: Dependent Elderly at Home and in Geriatric Hospitals.* Dublin: Economic and Social Research Institute.

Breen, R. (1991): *Employment, Education and Training in the Youth Labour Market*, Dublin: Economic and Social Research Institute, General Research Series, Paper No. 152.

Browne, M. (1992): *Co-Ordinating Services for the Elderly at Local Level: Swimming Against the Tide — A Report on Two Pilot Projects*, Dublin: National Council for the Elderly.

Byrne, A. (1991): *North-West Connemara: A Baseline Study of Poverty*, Galway: Corrib Printers Ltd.

Cawley, M.E. and Stevens, F.M. (1987): "Non-attendance at Out-Patient Clinics at the Regional Hospital, Galway, Ireland", *Social Science and Medicine*, 25(1): 1189–96.

Cohen, G.A. (1993): "Equality of What? On Welfare, Goods, and Capabilities", in Nussbaum, M. and Sen, A. (eds.), *The Quality of Life,* Oxford: Clarendon Press.

Commins, P. and Keane, M.J. (1994): *New Approaches to Rural Development.* Dublin: National Economic and Social Council.

Department of Education (1995): *White Paper on Education.* Dublin: Stationery Office.

Department of Health (1994): *The Dental Health Action Plan.* Dublin: Department of Health.

Evensky, J. (1993): "Ethics and the Invisible Hand", *Journal of Economic Perspectives,* 7(2) Spring: 197-205.

Fahey, T. and Murray, P. (1994): *Health and Autonomy Among the Over 65s in Ireland,* Dublin: National Council for the Elderly, Report No. 39.

Fitzgerald, E. (1984): "Decision-Making: The Experience of a Health Board Member", in The Council for Social Welfare (ed.), *Future Directions in Health Policy,* Dublin: The Council for Social Welfare.

Fitzgerald Report (1968): *Consultative Council on the General Hospital Services, Outline of the Future Hospital System.* Prl. 154, Stationery Office, 1968.

Forum (1994): *The Forum Project: Final Report.* Connemara: Forum: A Rural Development Partnership in N.W. Connemara.

Gelpi, E. (1987): "Education, Production, Development and Technological Innovation", in Leirman, W. and Kulick, J. (eds.), *Adult Education and the Challenge of the 1990s.* London: Croom Helm.

Hammond, P.J. (1991): "Interpersonal Comparisons of Utility: Why and How They Are and Should Be Made?", In Elster, J. and Roemer, J.E. (eds.) *Interpersonal Comparisons of Well-Being,* Cambridge: Cambridge University Press.

Hannan, D. and Boyle, M. (1987): *Schooling Decisions: The Origins and Consequences of Selection and Streaming in Irish Post-Primary Schools.* Dublin: Economic and Social Research Institute.

Hannan, D. and O'Riain, S. (1993): *Pathways to Adulthood in Ireland.* Dublin: Economic and Social Research Institute, Paper No. 161, General Research Series.

Harvey, B. (1994): *Combating Exclusion: Lessons from the Third EU Poverty Programme in Ireland 1989-1994.* Dublin: Combat Poverty Agency, DTEDG, Forum, PAUL Partnership, Research and Development Unit.

Herzog, D. (1986): "Some Questions for Republicans", *Political Theory,* 14, 3: 473-493.

Higher Education Authority (1995): *Report of the Steering Committee on the Future Development of Higher Education,* Dublin: Higher Education Authority.

Hodgson, G.M. (1988): *Economics and Institutions,* Cambridge: The Polity Press.

Hutchinson, T.W. (1976): "Adam Smith and the Wealth of Nations", *Journal of Law and Economics,* 19(3).

Ignatieff, M. (1984): *The Needs of Strangers,* London: The Hogarth Press.

Industrial Research and Development Advisory Committee of the European Union (IRDAC) (1995): *Quality and Relevance — The Challenges of European Education*, Brussels: IRDAC.

INTO (1993) *One-Teacher Schools: Countrywide Survey*. Dublin: Irish National Teachers Organisation.

Keane, M.J. (1978): "Economics and the Size of Rural Schools", *Canadian Journal of Agricultural Economics*, 26(3): 47–52.

Kymlicka, W. (1989): *Liberalism, Community and Culture*. Oxford: Clarendon Press.

Le Grand, J. (1991): *Equity and Choice: An Essay in Economics and Applied Philosophy*, London: Harper Collins Academic.

Lewin, L. (1991): *Self-Interest and Public Interest in Western Politics*. Oxford: Oxford University Press.

Lightfoot, G. (1995): *North-West Connemara Community Transport Study: Final Report*, Forum, Galway: Taylor Lightfoot Transport Consultants.

Lovett, T. (1989): "Adult Education and the Working Class" in O'Sullivan, D. (ed.), *Social Commitment and the Working Class*, Cork: Cork University Press.

Lundstrom, F. and McKeown, K. (1994): *Home Help Services for Elderly People in Ireland*, Dublin: National Council for the Elderly, Report No. 36.

McPeake, J. and Murtagh, B. (1993): "The Rural Housing Problem in Northern Ireland", in Murray, M. and Greer, J. (eds.), *Rural Development in Ireland*, Aldershot: Avebury.

Massam, B. (1975): *Location and Space in Social Administration*, London: Edward Arnold (Publishers) Ltd.

Miller, D. (1989): *Market, State and Community*, Oxford: Clarendon Press.

Moseley, M. (1980: "Is Rural Deprivation Really Rural?" *The Planner*, 66(4): 97.

Mueller, D.C. (1989a): "Individualism, Contractarianism, and Morality", *Social Justice Research*, 3,(1): 1–19.

Mueller, D.C. (1989b): *Public Choice II. A Revised Edition of Public Choice*, Cambridge: Cambridge University Press.

National Council for the Aged (1986): *The Elderly in the Community: Transport and Access to Services in Rural Areas*, Dublin: National Council for the Elderly.

NESC (1976): *Rural Areas: Social Planning Problems*, Dublin: National Economic and Social Council.

NESC (1977): *Some Major Issues in Health Policy*, Dublin: National Economic and Social Council.

NESC (1978): *Rural Areas: Change and Development*, Dublin: National Economic and Social Council.

NESC (1993): *A Strategy for Competitiveness, Growth and Employment*, Dublin: National Economic and Social Council.

Nolan, B. and Callan, T. (1994): *Poverty and Policy in Ireland*. Dublin: Gill and Macmillan.

O'Connor, J., Ruddle, H., O'Gallagher, M. and Murphy, E. (1988): *Caring for the Elderly. Part II. The Caring Process: A Study of Carers in the Home.* Dublin: National Council for Elderly, Report No. 19.

O'Connor, S. (1987): *Community Care Services: An Overview*, Dublin: National Economic and Social Council.

O'Mahony, A. (1986): *The Elderly in the Community: Transport and Access to Services in Rural Areas*, Dublin: National Council for the Aged, Report No. 15.

O'Shea, E. and Corcoran, R. (1990): "Balance of Care Considerations for Elderly Persons: Dependency, Placement and Opportunity Costs", *Applied Economics*, 22: 1167-1180.

O'Shea, E. (1993:) *The Impact of Social and Economic Policies on Older People in Ireland*, Dublin, National Council for the Elderly.

O'Shea, E. and Hughes, J. (1994): *The Economics and Financing of Long-Term Care of the Elderly in Ireland*, Dublin: National Council for the Elderly.

O'Sullivan, D. (1989): "Adult and Continuing Education in the Irish Republic: A Research Synthesis", *International Journal of Lifelong Education*, 8(3): 211-234.

OECD (1993): *Education at a Glance*. Paris: Organization for Economic Co-operation and Development.

Powe, N. and Whitby, M. (1993): *Is There an Optimum Configuration of Settlement Sizes?* ESRC (The British Economic and Social Research Council) Countryside Change Initiative. Working Paper 41.

Rawls, J. (1972): *A Theory of Justice*, Oxford: Oxford University Press.

Sen, A. (1987): *On Ethics and Economics*, Oxford: Blackwell.

Sen, A. (1992): *Inequality Reexamined*, Oxford: Clarendon Press.

Shorthall, S. (1994): "The Irish Rural Development Paradigm — An Explanatory Analysis," *Economic and Social Review*, 25(3): 233–60.

Shucksmith, M., Chapman, P., Clarke, G.M. et al. (1993): *Disadvantage in Rural Scotland: How it is Experienced and How it Can Be Tackled, Summary Report*. Aberdeen: Rural Forum Scotland.

Smith, A. (1937): *The Wealth of Nations*, New York: The Modern Library.

Storey, D. (1994): "The Special Distribution of Education and Health and Welfare Facilities in Rural Ireland," *Administration*, 42(3): 246–68.

Thompson, J.L. (1980): "Adult Education and the Disadvantaged", in Thompson, J.L. (ed.) *Adult Education for a Change*. London: Hutchinson and Co.

Whelan, C. (ed.) (1994): *Values and Social Change in Ireland*, Dublin: Gill and Macmillan.

Years Ahead, The. A Policy for the Elderly (1988): Report of the Working Party on Services for the Elderly, Dublin: Stationery Office.

7: Back to the Future? Communities and Rural Poverty

Chris Curtin

INTRODUCTION

A major theme in recent social commentary and analysis is that we
are living in an age of momentous change and radical transformation.
Critical dimensions of this change are deemed to include the restructuring of work and economic life, the rapid dissemination of scientific
knowledge, technology and new cultural forms and the re-ordering of
political structures. The worldwide scale and impact of these changes
is such as to reduce greatly the space and time barriers that previously separated societies and cultures and to open up the prospect of
a world without borders with a rapid flow of images, ideas, goods and
people. In this global, post-modern world, where people's aspirations
and actions are, it is often suggested, less and less determined by
their immediate environment, it is remarkable that there has also
emerged in development discourses and debates, a growing interest in
the role of communities.

In the context of the Irish Republic at least, the urge towards
community is not, of course, new. For example, Muintir na Tire was
making the case for community-based self-help strategies in the
1930s. What is novel, however, is the "official" recognition of community by the State, support for community groups by a variety of state
agencies, and the emergence of a policy environment in which
"partnership" and "participation" have become key concepts and development projects have increasingly focused on sharing responsibility and resources and the building of formal organisational structures
of co-operation between state agencies and local communities. Examples of this state-driven "partnership" approach include the Department of Agriculture and Food's Pilot Programme for Integrated
Rural Development, the PESP area-based response to long-term unemployment, the LEADER Programme and the Third EC Programme
to Combat Poverty.

It is not altogether clear why community has now emerged as an
"official" actor in development initiatives and programmes. Perhaps
instead of one factor, several factors are involved. These include the
failure of existing development models to deliver jobs, and the resultant state inadequacy in fulfilling its employment creation role — an
inadequacy which threatens to provoke a crisis of legitimation, particularly in the most disadvantaged rural and urban areas (Curtin
and Varley, 1995). The general restructuring of rural economies in
European Union countries has been given a decisive impetus by the
reorganisation of the Common Agricultural Policy. Since rural development policies historically have been anchored to the expansion of

agricultural production, there is clearly an urgent need for new policies and strategies which offer the prospect of an effective response to rural deprivation in the new conditions of restricted agricultural production.

The re-emergence of community has also to be considered in the context of the economic and cultural changes that have swept through the capitalist world since the early 1980s. These changes have involved the cutting back of welfare expenditure, the privatisation of public assets, and the transfer of what were previously state-provided services, to the market and the voluntary sector. The concern with community can also be located in the framework of new social movements which place an emphasis on alternative values and life styles and the defence of civil society against the challenge of the technocratic state (Scott, 1990). Fowler (1991) for example, observes that the growing interest in community is one of the most significant developments in contemporary political thinking in the United States. On a more pragmatic level, the funding being made available through European Union programmes has also acted as a spur to both locally based groups and state agencies. In this context, community groups are, often in desperation, increasingly demanding more involvement in the decisions that they deem critical to their future, and more resources for "their area". Or they are seeking to reverse what they regard as unfavourable public-policy decisions on such issues as physical infrastructure, education or policing.

If a single explanation for the elevation of community in development discourse cannot be established, neither is it easy to find agreement or clarity on what exactly constitutes community and what precise benefits follow from pursuing community-based development. This is hardly surprising given that community has always been a contested concept and a bewildering variety of definitions abound in social science literature (Plant, 1980).

In the left-populist perspective, community is best understood as expanding participatory democracy, providing for more direct forms of government, decentralised decision-making and even political and economic equality.

> Viewed in this way community provides the basis for empowerment and small-group decision making which respects each person, ensures his or her essential equality and strives to achieve a deep and intensive relationship among its participants (Fowler. 1991: 43).

Community, from this perspective, offers the prospect of popular power, based on "grass roots" experience of the most oppressed groups. Community, however, is also much in favour in the conservative political tradition. Here, however, the emphasis is on the notion of community as common good, on public-spirited individuals with respect for the rights of others, on authority and order and on reducing civil society's dependence on the State. Community is also held up by other groups as offering the best prospect for reorganising society along more humane, co-operative lines. Thus, while some feminists may declare community to be reactionary and inegalitarian (Okin, 1989), other feminists favour community if it is socialist and egalitarian, if it offers an alternative to the family, or if it manifests itself as solidarity among women. Finally, community may be viewed in highly pragmatic terms — as a means to an end — that is as a strategy or as part of a strategy for mobilising all local actors to solve socio-economic problems.

The concern with, and favourable views of, community crosses conventional political lines, from left to right and from radical to traditional. This is so perhaps because, as Cohen (1987) argues, community is a symbolic construct capable of invoking for all its supporters, the positive notion of communality and sharing, but also presenting the possibility of being subjected, in each case, to particular meanings. To complicate matters further, advocates of community rarely provide explicit accounts of their "version" of community. This creates considerable confusion, particularly so perhaps for rural areas whose inhabitants are often assumed to have a "natural" inclination towards communal co-operation. Given this particular difficulty, the first concern in this chapter will therefore be to discuss, based on a reading of the ethnographic literature, the social structural features of rural communities that are most likely to influence their interest in or capacity for collective action. Next, the versions of community that have characterised rural community development initiatives and programmes will be examined, along with the manner and extent to which considerations of poverty are present. Since rural poverty has several dimensions, the chapter then moves to a consideration of the economic, social and political outcomes of a variety of community development programmes. In the final section, an attempt is made to evaluate the strengths and weaknesses of community development as a strategy to combat rural poverty, trace the factors that most influence success and failure, and speculate on the future prospects of this approach to tackling rural disadvantage.

RURAL COMMUNITIES

It has been suggested — mainly in frustrated responses to the myriad and bewildering variations in the use of the concept of community — that there is no such thing as community, but rather that "community has many meanings, it involves different sets of experiences for different people, and for the same people at different times in their lives" (Crow and Allan, 1994: 183). It is often assumed, and indeed sometimes stated, that rural communities have special "positive" features that draw on notions of sameness, a shared sense of space, isolation from external influences, self-sufficiency and the positive images associated in particular with small family farms. This form of "rural romanticism" is an interesting phenomenon in its own right. However, it tends to draw attention away from the complexity of rural social structures and from both inter- and intra-rural community diversity. And this diversity proves to be critically important for explaining the different organisational forms that community development takes and the variable capacity of rural areas to generate collective and sustainable initiatives.

Community is clearly about shared identity, solidarity and interests. Communities are not, however, "natural", but are actively constructed and developed in response to specific circumstances and conditions. This is true as much for urban as it is for rural communities (Bulmer, 1986). The critical issue then becomes: under what circumstances and conditions are communities constructed? Of significance here would appear to be settlement patterns — longevity and physical proximity — people's age, occupation and gender, values and perspective on obligations towards others and the dominant societal beliefs on individualistic, as against communal, solutions to solving critical problems.

While official statistics and surveys provide valuable information on the social structure and changing socio-economic conditions of rural areas, they do not deal with the many nuances of change that affect individuals and groups in carrying out their everyday tasks and how the various aspects of local social relationships are interconnected. Social scientists, using the methods of ethnography go a long way towards filling in the gaps in our knowledge of local social experience because "of their interest not only in what people say but in what they actually do, when faced with the pressures and joys of day-to-day, month-to-month and year-to-year living" (Curtin and Wilson, 1989: viii). There is a long tradition of ethnographic research in Ireland. Much of this work has been concentrated on rural areas and

perhaps unduly concentrated on peripheral and island communities
in the West of Ireland. Although most ethnographic studies have not
been undertaken with the express purpose of elucidating the socio-
economic and cultural features of rural areas that most influence
their inhabitants' willingness to create community and their capacity
to engage in collective action, they do nonetheless provide valuable
information on these issues.

Ireland's best-known ethnographic study, Arensberg and Kimball's
Family and Community in Ireland (1940, 1968), profiled the social
world of small farmers, in Co. Clare in the 1930s. The study has been
controversial because of the questions raised by some commentators
about its undue emphasis on harmony and continuity in local social
relations and on the economic independence from market forces of
farm households. The book's title summarises what the authors consider to be the critical dimensions to local social life: the emphasis on
family and emergence of community as a necessary extension of familial functions. Local social relations were firmly grounded on notions of kinship and neighbourliness. Arensberg and Kimball write
that "in a country region such as Lough all the families are united by
duplicated bonds of marriage and descent, and disloyalty to the kinship group was felt as a 'deadly crime' against the group." Kinship
and neighbourhood groups fulfilled critical social security and economic support functions by performing, through co-operative arrangements, essential tasks which were beyond the individual household's capacity. These ranged from the provision of emergency aid in a
crisis to inter-household labour exchanges and more communal activities associated with such tasks as hay-making and turf-cutting.

The forms of communal behaviour, described in considerable detail
by Arensberg and Kimball, are the sort of actions often referred to as
indicating the "natural" tendency for co-operation and community in
rural settings. It is necessary, however, to note several contextual aspects of these "expressions of community". They were, at that time,
necessary to the survival of small farm households, and co-operation
had a clear self-interest dimension. Both a powerful sense of obliga-
tion to co-operate and definite sanctions (exclusion from local networks) to punish the non-co-operators were present. Formal communal organisations were entirely absent, and the norm of reciprocity
was in operation — co-operative acts were engaged in on the basis
that they would be reciprocated. Failure to obey this norm could ultimately be sanctioned by exclusion from communal activities. Also,
some households lacked the resources necessary to participate in

these communal exchanges. Thus, of the 24 households in Lough — one of the areas studied by Arensberg and Kimball — five did not form any part of these relationships. Of these, two were the homes of relative newcomers and three were bachelor households (Varley, 1981).

Distinctions between farm households based on the amount of property owned were not a feature of these Clare communities — the only "large" farm in the Lough area did not participate in co-operative exchanges and relied instead on hired labour. Divisions along generational lines, however, were quite strong. The old, we are told, "live long because they have power, much to live for and represent the community before priest, school master, merchant, cattleman and government official" (*ibid.*: 171). These elders, who met in a local designated house on a regular basis to review communal events and affairs, could be the subject of young peoples hatred and resentment. The young, Arensberg and Kimball write, "recognise themselves as forming a distinctive group with interests and sentiments of its own, opposed in the scheme of rural life to the elders".

Cohen (1987) has drawn attention to the importance of ritual and symbol in distinguishing who is inside and who is outside community, and to the flexible and changing nature of communal boundaries. Arensberg and Kimball perceptively observe that the rural community is not easily defined in geographical terms and that small farmers' social relationships extend over a wide range of territorial divisions from the townland outwards. For the small farm household there are many allegiances — "the small farmer was willing to back the men of Lough against the men of the neighbouring town land; to back those of the mountain region against those of the valley lands; those of his parish against the rest; those of the countryside against the towns of Lisdoonvarna and Ennistymon; those of North Clare against other sections of the county; those of Clare against all other counties" (Arrensberg and Kimball, 1968: 274).

In the rural communities studied as part of the Limerick Rural Survey (Newman, 1964), the splintering of local social relationships along age lines is again strongly evident. Resentment of delayed inheritance and patriarchal authority was frequently voiced by young males. The strained relationship between farmers and farm labourers was also much in evidence in these localities. Farmers were having increasing difficulty in recruiting live-in servants and had strongly opposed recent legislation which introduced standard hours and wages for labourers. Sharp status distinctions existed between employer and employee as was evident in the practice of separate eating arrangements.

Cresswell's (1969) study of a south Galway parish in the 1960s provides further insight into the complexity of communal boundaries. He shows that the parish could unite behind its sportsmen when they were in opposition to other parish teams. On other occasions, however, divisions between the village and outlying areas or between the northern and southern or eastern and western parts of the parish could manifest themselves and sometimes result in open hostility. The impact of depopulation on local social relations and community survival was also explored by Cresswell. In his assessment, population loss had reached a level where it threatened the functioning of critical social and economic networks. Rural communities were, in his view, in a state of transition towards some new form of social organisation. For Brody (1973), Scheper-Hughes (1979) and Messenger (1969), however, rural communities had moved into a stage of terminal decline. The central theme of Hugh Brody's study, *Inishkillane*, is communal demoralisation. His account is of:

> the transformation of rural Ireland's traditional farm communities from an integrated working system to their present demoralised and contracted vestiges. In the rural communities, the people are demoralised, they feel outside their social system and have no faith in its continuing. They are lonely and withdrawn and have lost their belief in the social advantage or moral worth of their small community (Brody, 1973: 7).

Communal breakdown is attributed by Brody to the demise of the small-farm economy, the growing dependence on emigrant remittances and to feelings of relative deprivation induced by increased contacts with the outside world. Inter-household and other forms of communal co-operation had all but disappeared and "mutual aid has made way for an ethic of independence" (*ibid.*: 36).

In this changed environment, co-operation is feared because it may bring more advantage to the other participants. Brody cites two incidents to support his argument. In one, local farmers failed to agree to a county council request to improve a lane which gave their farms access to the main road because it was felt that it would be of more advantage to some than to others. In the second case, a parish priest attempted to improve farmers' incomes in a west Cork parish through a pig-breeding scheme. While government officials were prepared to build a pig-fattening station in the nearby town, farmers' agreement to the scheme was not forthcoming. One explanation for the farmers' failure collectively to support the scheme put forward by Brody was the suspicion that not everyone would make an equal contribution although all would be gaining equal benefit. He quotes one farmer as saying "they (the other farmers) would not do the job properly, but would still be getting the benefit" (Brody, 1973: 151).

Generational division is a theme which is very much in evidence in Inishkillane. Patriarchal authority has, according to Brody, been undermined by the economic and cultural decline of small-scale farming. Fathers are often treated by their sons as figures of fun, and "daughters in farm families are as separated from their fathers today as they always have been" (*ibid.*: 126). For the older males — married and unmarried — the bar is at the centre of community life. This is the group most committed to remaining on the land. In the summer season, these men are joined in the bar by the tourists The shop, by contrast, is at the centre of social life for women, and younger people in the community — those who are least committed to farm work and least committed to remaining in the countryside. Their outlook is most informed by events in and values of the outside world.

The theme of communal decline and demoralisation is again strongly present in Scheper-Hughes's (1979) study of a Kerry parish. Her conclusion was that rural Ireland was dying and that people had been terminally afflicted with the disease of despair and anomie. A similar concern is present in Messenger's *Inishbeg* (1968), which also emphasises the harsh interpersonal nature of local social relationships and the prominence, envy, jealousy and distrust. However, perhaps a somewhat more balanced view of the impact of change on rural areas is to be found in Hannan's (1970) Roscommon study. In his view, the change in farm technology, in communications and transport systems, in the household economy and frequency of contact with external groups and agencies had produced a complex picture of social organisation. While many people continued to experience loyalty to their immediate localities, wider networks of relationships and new group loyalties were also being established. Individualistic achievement values had come to rival more "traditional communal values". One of Hannan's informants illustrates the changing attitudes and new values of young farmers in particular:

> In the old days your friends and neighbours were given to you and you had no choice about it. Now I can't stick my first cousins and my neighbours are real stick-in-the-muds. So I'd much rather go out with somebody I like for a drink. And it's much better to co-operate with somebody who thinks the same as you (Hannan, 1970: 186).

Hannan's work shows that economic, social and recreational life in rural areas had become less spatially restricted. Curtin's (1978) study of south Mayo indicates that farmers had a much wider range of social contacts than their wives. While the business of the farm increasingly brought the male farmer outside the more local environment, farmers' wives were much more confined to the household. Yet, generational differences between farm women were also important: younger women with access to motor cars participated in a much wider social network. Rural industrialisation created in many instances more jobs for women than men. With this factory work came some degree of financial independence and, as Harris (1984: 154) argues, "an erosion of patriarchal relations within both the domestic and public spheres".

While sporting events and competitions provide the most frequent and common opportunities for the expression of community, they are surprisingly not much discussed in the ethnographic literature. The Catholic church has played a critical role in defining community boundaries along parish lines. Brody (1973: 178) suggests that "around the church the communities gather in solidarity", while Curtin (1978) observes that the station mass, held on a rotational basis in local households, was the only occasion when all members of a neighbourhood shared a common space together. Taylor's (1989) research on the mission in a south-west Donegal parish indicates that while the mission may be interpreted as evidence of the Catholic church's penetration of Irish rural culture, it can also be construed as "a local event and its meaning for those in the community are derived from its place in their own fields of religious experience" (Taylor, 1989: 3).

The volume of ethnographic research on rural Ireland has declined considerably in recent years. As the physical isolation of communities has been increasingly undermined, our understanding of social change is diminished by the absence of studies on such issues as insider/outsider distinctions, the role of "new-comers" and "strangers" and the varying consciousness of community membership. The ethnographic research that is available, however, highlights the complexity of social relations, and the divisions and material circumstances which critically influence each individual's experience of community and shows that "community has many meanings: it involves different sets of experience for different groups of people, and indeed for the same people at different times in their lives (Crow and Allan, 1994: 183).

REPRESENTING COMMUNITY

Given the complexity of rural social structures and the diversity of local social relationships, it can now be asked how community development organisations have sought to represent community, and whether and in what manner they have addressed questions of poverty in their organisational structures. In a somewhat crude manner it is possible to distinguish two dominant models of community development. In one, sometimes referred to as the consensus model, the emphasis is on all the people within a particular area working together and taking actions to improve the "whole" community. Although disparities of income and access to other resources may be recognised, the underlying assumption is that similarity of interests are powerful enough to form the basis for building consensus. The emphasis in this approach is on widespread voluntary participation and extensive community involvement.

For over 50 years, Muintir na Tire was Ireland's premier community development organisation. First established in 1931 as an agricultural producers' co-operative, after meeting with little success, it had by 1937 shifted its focus to the parish. Strongly influenced by the debates on vocationalism, Catholic social teaching, nationalism (Ó Cearbhaill and Varley, 1991) and the example of a number of European social movements — the Belgian Boeronbond in particular — it sought to counter what it regarded as the divisive influences of class and party politics by establishing all-embracing parish councils. Each parish was understood to comprise sections — farmers, labourers, professionals and business people, women and young people — each of which was expected to select representatives that would form and direct the parish council. Muintir operated very much on the consensus model of community development. Officially eschewing state support — because it might stifle voluntary initiative — the emphasis was placed on the "whole community" working together through a programme of self-help projects. The fundamental aim was to build up community institutions and strengthen community relationships. Thus while the existence of different social groups is clearly recognised, it was assumed that complementary interests existed and a programme of local projects could be undertaken which would have both appeal and advantages for all, including the poorest and most disadvantaged.

For reasons that included declining membership, rapid social and economic change and a concern for a more democratic form of representation (Ó Cearbhaill and Varley, 1991), Muintir decided in 1970 to replace parish councils with community councils. The concern with the "whole" community continued, however, and the parish continued to be the critical point of departure. The community council comprised elected representatives, nominated representatives of other local voluntary organisations and co-opted individuals. Community councils were expected to engage in a wide variety of short, medium and long-term projects, which related to each area's social, cultural, economic, educational and recreational needs (Muintir na Tire, n.d.: 4–5). Official distrust of the State had now given way to the idea of partnership. This "partnership" approach was also extended to public representatives, but political-party branches were typically excluded from the community-representation process.

The Muintir ideal of consensus-based community development was severely tested by local disparities in income and access to resources. From the Limerick Rural Survey, it can be seen that while rural workers had equal rights of representation on the parish council, most influence was wielded by those of higher social standing. Local workers suggested to the ethnographer in this study — McNabb — that the farmers wanted nobody "to have a say but themselves" and that this "is not a parish hall, it's a farmers' hall". While McNabb notes that this might be a somewhat exaggerated claim, his observations were that positions at hall meetings were structured according to social status, age and sex:

> In the front two rows of seats were to be found middle-aged people of professional or business class and farmers of high standing. These people were the spokesmen and answered for the whole community. While they were present it was difficult to get other members of the audience to participate in discussion. In the next few rows were to be found other adult members of the farming class; the men and women were usually segregated. Behind them again were seated women of the working class. At the back of the hall were to be found young people most of them segregated according to sex. In the last few rows, or standing at the back of the hall, were the male workers (Muintir na Tire, n.d.: 208).

McNabb also kept a record of the lectures on rural problems given in the west Limerick region and not once were the problems of the rural worker the subject of a lecture. Eipper (1986) also reports that the control of parish councils was very much in the hands of representatives of local propertied classes and Devereux's (1987) research shows that leadership positions were dominated by farmers, priests and teachers. While Muintir's leading advocate, Canon Hayes, declared that "Muintir na Tire is not concerned with political parties present or future again in practice, it proved difficult to realise this ideal as is evidenced by Bax's (1976) study. Muintir's aspirations to be representative of the whole community was, according to Bax, challenged by other voluntary groups. The GAA had dominated the area's recreational life, but the arrival of a pro-Muintir priest initiated a period of intense rivalry between the two organisations — a rivalry which, in turn, was imbedded in local political affiliations.

The stress placed by Muintir on representativeness in its community council phase was based on high value placed on the democratic mandate and legitimacy that the community council was expected to confer. Priority was given to the elected membership, rules and procedures for elections were established, but flexibility was allowed to individual community councils in voting procedures. However, of the 15 West of Ireland community councils studied by Ó Cearbhaill and Varley (1986), one had never held elections and four had abandoned elections in favour of recruitment at public meetings. In the other nine, the majority experience was of the same members being returned again and again, resulting in fatigue and eventual unwillingness to serve. As part of the same research programme, Ó Cearbhaill and Varley's survey of 100 founder members of 25 community councils shows that the vast majority were males, married, in the 30–60 age group and clustered in a relatively small number of middle-income occupations. A similar profile is present in Ó Cearbhaill and O'Cinneide's (1983) study of Killala Community Council.

The consensus-oriented, "whole"-community-together approach to tackling rural disadvantage and deprivation has also been adopted by the Gaeltacht community-development co-operatives (Breathnach, 1986), numerous stand-alone development associations, the Integrated Rural Development Programme and the Leader Programme. It is also advocated by the National Development Plan 1994–1999, which identifies communities as having an important role in developing "innovative projects for training, enterprise and local development".

The second model of community development — the conflict model — has similarities to the consensus model in that it also favours the approach of bringing people together to discuss their problems and organise collectively in search of solutions. Its focus, however, is more directly on the poor and disadvantaged and "empowering" those who are outside the power structure. This perspective on community development is most in evidence in the Poverty Programmes, the PESP Local Area Companies and the Community Development Projects

funded by the Department of Social Welfare. In the first poverty programme, the overall aim of the rural projects was to revive "dying
communities on the basis of wide and direct participation". The work
of the project teams commenced with a community profile, in which
they analysed the economic and social problems of the area. The team
then identified key local leaders and worked with them in drawing up
a self-help plan of action based on "felt needs". Each of the projects
identified disadvantaged groups with whom they would work and assist. In Connemara, for example, these included small-boat fishermen,
small farmers, mussel farmers and householders who were seeking
electricity and water supplies. This project also worked with two area-
based organisations, Connemara West, a community-based development company, and Ballyconneely Community Council. The report of
the Review Team on Poverty One notes that this project team, which
managed to combine support for these area-based organisations, was
also directing most of its resources "towards the most deprived sections of the community". Interestingly, the project team stopped
working with the farmers' mart group when it became apparent that
it was an issue of benefit mainly to large farmers (Review Team,
1980: 100). Given the controversy that surrounded the First Poverty's
Programme's "radical" structuralist view of the causes of poverty, it is
also interesting to note that this local team largely directed its efforts
towards enabling groups to work through, rather than against, the
system. A similar approach to community development appears to
have been adopted by the rural projects in West Cork and West Donegal — combining a local development brief with a particular emphasis
on assisting the poor and most disadvantaged and the development of
co-operatively-based activities. In these projects, however, creating
awareness of the structural foundations of poverty brought the project teams into direct confrontation with local power-holders including the Catholic church and prominent business people.

In the Second European Poverty Programme the three rural projects (in North Connemara, Inishowen and Louisburg) were managed
by a local development association. In each case the project's target
population was given as the "local population" with special groups —
the elderly, small farmers, and youth — being identified for special
attention. In this first evaluation report of this programme, the
evaluator (O'Cinneide, 1987) expressed concern that in these projects
not enough concern was being displayed for the participation of the
poor. The rural projects were unfavourably compared to the urban
projects in their interest in supporting target groups of the most dis-

advantaged. This theme is also very much present in the review of social policy issues arising from the Second Poverty Programme (Cullen, 1989), which states that "none of the three rural projects currently has a stated strategy for separately mobilising those members of their communities who are most poor and disadvantaged" (op. cit.: 23). One Irish rural project — Forum in north-west Connemara — participated in the Poverty 3 Programme. Forum supported area-based community organisations such as community councils and development associations, special interest community-based groups including women, young people and the elderly and co-operative initiatives to develop tourism and shellfish aquaculture. Forum's efforts to involve the "community sector" in the management of the project were hampered by the absence of representative councils or associations in many areas. In response to this difficulty, in nine geographical areas in north-west Connemara, representatives were elected at public meetings to form five working groups associated with the project's target groups. Each working group then selected a member to serve on Forum's Board of Directors. While this process greatly facilitated community involvement in the project, community representatives were still left with the dilemma of not having any agreed procedures for reporting back to "their communities" and for aggregating local demands and concerns.

The PESP area-based partnerships — four of the 12 companies were located in rural areas — comprise community, state agency and social-partner representatives. An evaluation of the pilot initiative (Craig and McKeown, 1994) suggests that this partnership model allows "communities" a say in determining that services are provided in a manner appropriate to particular local needs. Several of the companies are supporting community-development groups and initiatives through the provision of education and training programmes and ongoing assistance from professional community-development workers. However, this report also states that "partnerships differ on what constitutes "community" and "community representation" (op. cit.: 75–6) and that the rural partnerships' focus on area-based initiatives in tourism, enterprise and heritage may not result in the expected benefits for the poor and most disadvantaged.

DOES COMMUNITY DEVELOPMENT MAKE A DIFFERENCE TO THE RURAL POOR?

The difficulty with answering this question is, as has been seen, that there are differing views about what constitutes "community", what the primary aims of community development should be and how communities should engage in the development process. Nonetheless, how communities have succeeded, and the degree of their success, in tackling rural poverty through economic, social and "political" programmes and projects has to be addressed.

What is sometimes referred to as community economic development has taken several forms, but three in particular can be identified, namely:

(1) Communities have sought to establish and manage enterprises themselves.

(2) Communities have sought, usually in negotiation or partnership with state agencies, to bring jobs into their areas.

(3) Communities have, again typically in conjunction with state agencies, sought through such means as the provision of workspace and training and educational supports, to promote indigenous enterprise.

In their 1984 survey, Ó Cearbhaill and Varley (1986) show that only 21 per cent of Muintir na Tire community councils in Counties Galway, Mayo and Roscommon were engaged in economic projects. Community councils' weak role in economic development has been attributed to their financial weakness, lack of professional expertise, legal difficulties, delays associated with securing community consensus, and inadequate and inconsistent support from state agencies (Commins, 1985) However, there are some good examples of community organisations successfully managing economic projects. For example, Connemara West has constructed and profitably operated a self-catering holiday cottage scheme, and the Gaeltacht community-development co-operatives generated 206 full-time jobs (Breathnach, 1986). However, Keane and O'Cinneide's (1987: 33) survey of community enterprise groups in the Mid West Region indicates that "many of the jobs created were marginal in character with respect to rate of wages, holiday pay, and general employment conditions".

A feature of the Poverty Programmes has been their emphasis on supporting community ownership and management of local natural resources. These programmes have assisted the formation of craft, fish farming, credit, tourism and agricultural co-operatives. Advocates of co-operatives argue that not only can they mobilise and effectively exploit under-utilised natural and human resources, but they can also ensure that resulting benefits are distributed on an equitable basis.

Critics of co-operatives are, however, highly sceptical of these claims. Some are prepared to accept a limited role for co-operatively controlled economic activity — for example, where it can exploit resources that would be "off limits" to private entrepreneurs. More hostile critics argue that the effective exploitation of local resources is best guaranteed when left in the hands of private individuals. It is also interesting to note that some of the most successful community-owned businesses have been privatised in recent years (Curtin and Varley, 1992). There are, however examples of successful and continuous expansion of business activity along collective lines. Killary Shellfish Co-operative in north-west Connemara was established in the mid-1970s with support initially from the First and later from the Third Poverty Programme. While the increase in production (mainly mussels) has been less than members had hoped, it has nonetheless been significant. Critical dimensions of this "success" have been the continued commitment of the membership to the co-operative ideal, and the consistent support that has been available through the Poverty Programmes and the Fisheries Development Board (BIM).

Rural community groups have a long tradition of attempting to solve economic problems and create jobs by "bringing in" industries (Curtin and Varley, 1986). Perhaps the most successful example is that of the Killala Community Council, which attracted the Asahi Synthetic Fibre factory to Killala with more than 400 jobs. This form of proactive recruiting of industry can involve community groups in the provision of land, the construction of industrial sites (usually in conjunction with state agencies), and even the recruitment and "management" of labour. It also induces fierce competition between communities for what are often poorly paid jobs. While this approach may bring much needed employment in the short term, it rarely provides much by way of longer-term sustainable development. Also, many of the industries that are prepared to move to rural areas may bring with them the prospect of pollution or environmental damage and may be opposed, at least by sections of, the proposed host community.

Changing national and international circumstances have greatly reduced the numbers of firms seeking to locate in rural areas. Community groups have increasingly, usually in partnership with state agencies, or as part of rural development programmes such as LEADER, encouraged the establishment of locally controlled enterprises. This approach involves the provision of education and training, managerial and marketing supports and, most crucially, grant aid, and offers the prospect at least of broad-based participation and involvement by disadvantaged groups. However, even the best efforts to encourage the establishment enterprises may be undermined by the lack of minimal start-up capital (Barrett and Curtin, 1991). An innovative attempt to overcome this difficulty has been revolving loan schemes established by the rural PESP Companies in Waterford and Mayo.

Programmes such as LEADER, the PESP Area-Based Companies and Integrated Rural Development are perhaps most accurately defined as local-development programmes. Communities have played a varied role in LEADER 1. In a small number of companies a community group has been the organisation that has taken the lead in applying for and managing the programme. In most, community organisations have been partners alongside statutory and private agencies. Most of LEADER grant aid has been directed towards private individuals rather than community-owned enterprises — that is, towards enterprise development in the community rather than towards community-owned enterprise. In the Integrated Rural Development Programme, less than 10 per cent of projects were classified as "community development". The vast majority were concerned with promoting economic activity and enterprise generation. However, over half the projects were promoted by local community groups or development associations (O'Malley, 1993: 250). As already mentioned, the PESP Local Area Companies organised a number of innovative education and training initiatives, and the Area Allowance Enterprise Scheme had a very positive impact on the capacity of unemployed people to establish enterprises. An evaluation of this programme argues, however, that community involvement was hampered by the limited resources for community development and for community-driven training, employment and enterprise projects (Craig and McKeown, 1994).

Rural community groups have had a long tradition in the provision of social and recreational services. One of the projects most favoured by Muintir na Tire Parish Councils was the provision of parish halls. The study by Ó Cearbhaill and Varley (1986) of 15 community councils showed that most were concerned with the provision of social infrastructure (31 per cent) or the supply of recreation, education, or sporting facilities (28 per cent). Community groups have also played an important role in developing new services such as water or electricity (McDyer, 1986) or in improving existing services (Varley et al., 1990).

Working on their own, or as part of development programme, community groups have assumed, in some areas, a critically important role in the care of sections of the rural population with special needs — in particular the elderly, people with literacy problems and people with physical and mental handicaps. Community care for the elderly in Glenamaddy Co. Galway and by community groups supported by the Forum project in Connemara represent some of the best examples of this type of community development. Community groups have also become increasingly interested in the provision and quality of all forms of education in their areas. This has resulted in the provision of community-based pre-schools, innovative initiatives in remedial education (Curtin, 1994) and in the second-level curriculum (Craig and McKeown, 1994) and expansion in the provision and take-up of adult-education classes (Cullen, 1994, Curtin, 1994).

Communities' involvement in the provision of social care historically has been on a voluntary basis. Until the 1965 Health Act, which introduced grant aid for voluntary groups, services were provided without state aid. Provision was also voluntary in the sense that community groups could decide whether to be involved or not. This created a situation of uneven provision — excellent services in some areas and a complete absence of similar services in others. The experience of the Poverty Programmes and the Rural Community Development Projects indicates that the assistance of paid workers in co-ordinating and delivering services is essential if the value of community involvement is to be maximised. Where this condition is met, as in the case of the Forum Project in north-west Connemara, substantial progress can be made in the provision of innovative and effective community-based services for children, adolescents and the elderly.

All community-development initiatives involve, at least at a rhetorical level, some commitment to the redistribution of power. They differ in the degree of prominence they give to this aspiration and the strategies that are deemed necessary to its achievement. But empowerment is a concept that bears most relation to the conflict model of community development. This model, which is particularly associated with Alinsky (1971), suggests that the poor and downtrodden should form self-help organisations and seek power through direct action and confrontation with the powerful. In Ireland, this model first came to prominence in the First Combat Poverty Programme. The National Committee on Pilot Schemes to Combat Poverty agreed on the need for greater equality in the distribution of resources and power in Irish society, and one of the aims of the pilot schemes at community level was to provide for the greater participation of the poor. The National Committee's view, as indicated in its Final Report, was that the pilot projects had brought about definite changes in the "amount of relative power which groups have acquired as a result of being enabled to organise themselves" (Final Report, n.d.: 216). Particular examples of empowerment mentioned by the Committee were the National Salmon and Inshore Fishermen's Association and the Land League. This report also draws attention to interesting differences in the rural projects approach to facilitating empowerment and participation. While the Beara Project worked at a deliberate distance from power structures, the Connemara and West Donegal projects worked with and were supported by local bodies.

In the Second and Third Poverty Programmes, community groups were encouraged to tackle poverty in partnership with state agencies. However, notions of empowerment and participation continue to be strongly associated with community development. The Combat Poverty Agency (CPA) views community development as the mechanism for linking the development of social rights and local responses to disadvantage and states that "from a social rights perspective local people need to be empowered and resourced to become involved in the political process, in the development of their own localities and in influencing and contributing to public service provision" (CPA, 1991, 21). The Area Development Management Company, which manages the Global grant for local social and economic development and the Department of Social Welfare's community development funded projects, also includes empowerment as a critical feature of community development. However, empowerment is to be achieved through a strategy that involves sharing power in formal partnership structures and by participation of "communities and groups experiencing the most disadvantage" in constructing and implementing integrated area action plans.

Nevertheless, however it is construed, the participation of the poorest sections of communities presents particular difficulties. This was recognised by the Review Group of the First Poverty Programme, which noted that all the projects "found eventually that they worked largely with people who had sufficient resources to enable them to become involved in group work and who were not living from crisis to crisis as the poorest appeared to be" (Report of Review Group, 1980: 43). Cullen's (1989) review of the work of nine projects in the Second Poverty Programme indicates that the participation of the poor was encouraged by such measures as establishing resource centres, holding public meetings, publishing newsletters and community magazines, community radio, and building confidence and self-esteem through personal development and training initiatives. The success or otherwise of these ventures in actually achieving increased participation is not, however, evident from this study. Forum, the rural project in Poverty 3, in its final report noted that while the overall level of local participation was high, it had considerable difficulties in ensuring that the poorest were actively involved in its management structures (Curtin, 1994: 98). The participation of community groups in the PESP Area-Based Partnerships has been hindered by the costs of participating, the inadequate resources available to support community development, and the "lack of a constituency to which community directors can relate back the issues raised at partnership level" (Craig and McKeown, 1994: 31). Remedial measures undertaken by the Rural Companies in this programme include training and educational provision, the appointment of community-development workers and personal-development courses.

While the concern with empowerment may have grown out of the radical conflict tradition in community development, most of its current advocates suggest that it can now be best achieved through negotiated partnerships with state agencies. But community groups have not entirely abandoned the conflict approach, and, identifying the State as the problem, have protested against state inaction or have sought to defend "their areas" against industrial closures, public-service cutbacks, and decisions to locate environmentally threatening activities in particular localities. In this context, rural community organisations have successfully resisted hospital closure in Roscommon and polluting industries in Cork (Curtin and Varley, 1995). Some of these protests and campaigns can have a unifying influence on communities. For example, the Roscommon Hospital Campaign brought together a powerful coalition of over 50 community organisations from different parts of the county, succeeded in returning the Dáil Deputy who negotiated the "Foxe Deal", and celebrated the opening of a new in-patient psychiatric unit at the county hospital in February 1992. In Cork, opposition to Merrell Dow united local farmers and resulted, in a successful appeal against the planning permission to build the industrial complex (Peace, 1993). However, other issues, such as the location of Interpretive Centres have proven to be highly divisive to local community relationships.

CONCLUSION

The notion that community groups should have a role in tackling problems of rural poverty and disadvantage is neither novel or peculiar to Ireland. Community development was fashionable in the 1950s when it was sponsored by the United States and the United Nations as the solution to the problems of rural areas in over 60 states in Asia, Africa, and Latin America (Holdcroft, 1982). In Ireland, as noted earlier, self-help was favoured as the way forward for rural communities from the 1930s onwards by Muintir na Tire. What makes the current phase of community development different, however, is the extent to which it has been driven by state agencies, usually in the framework of "partnership" programmes. State agencies and government departments have, in the Irish Republic, as in other liberal-democratic régimes, sought to manage the policy process through the establishment of corporatist arrangements or policy networks (Smith, 1993) involving the key organised groups in society. Such groups — Trade Unions, Business Organisations, Farmers' Associations etc. — usually represent well-defined interests, are organised at national as well as regional and local levels and are represented on a day-to-day basis in the policy making process by paid officials. By sharp contrast, as many studies reviewed in this chapter make clear, there is no agreement on what exactly communities are, how they should be organised or how they should be represented in the policy-making process.

In attempting to account for the emergence of community as an "official" actor in the policy process, this chapter referred, among other factors, to the notion that this may be part of wider policy agenda of moving away from direct state to private-sector provision. This would suggest, in line with state autonomy theory (Stockpol, 1985) that it is state interests as much as "bottom-up" demands that has "elevated" community in the policy agenda. Several state agencies have developed community-based programmes that appear to reflect both different perspectives on communities, and beliefs as to how to solve problems such as rural poverty. This diversity certainly increases the possibility of community groups influencing the formation of policy, as their "support" may be critical to particular state agencies. The implications that follow, however, may be the exclusion of groups which are not part of a community–state-agency coalition and the removal of protest and conflict from the policy agenda. Playing according to the rules of this new game may mean that empowerment of the poor is now to be achieved not through protest and conflict with power-holders, but through consensus-based partnerships. Of course the possibility continues to exist for community groups and organisations, which believe that the state itself plays an important role in sustaining rural poverty and disadvantage, to engage in protests and confrontation. This is most likely to happen either when community groups oppose a government decision or when concern emerges about the decline of an area or region — a decline which is associated with state action or inaction.

Community groups' efforts to come to tackle the economic dimensions of rural poverty have included the establishment and management of enterprises, campaigns to "bring in" industries and programmes of support — workspace, training and educational schemes, grant aid and soft loans for promoting local economic initiatives. Evaluations of communities' role in enterprise and job creation have, at best, been cautious and usually conclude by pointing to the limitations of this strategy. At the same time, there are examples of the valuable role played by community organisations — usually where they have received consistent state support — in developing natural resources in a sustainable manner and in encouraging the involvement of the least privileged. Most recently, the LEADER Programme has provided grant aid to an impressive range of local enterprises, and the PESP Local Area Companies have been engaged in innovative educational and training initiatives. Many community groups have, for some considerable time, demonstrated a strong capacity to deliver a wide range of social and recreational services and supports and to involve individuals who are most excluded from the more formal decision-making processes.

Community groups vary greatly in their capacity to undertake development initiatives — community organisations have a considerable presence in some rural areas, are almost entirely absent in others, and are everywhere hampered by all the difficulties associated with voluntary organisations. All the available historical and comparative evidence indicates that community development is not a substitute for broader government economic and social policies and interventions and that community development is most effective when set in the context of an integrated development strategy which recognises the connections between the social, cultural, economic, political and environmental aspects of development and the importance of planning and co-ordination (Frazier, 1991).

The emergence of community-based initiatives and their success or otherwise in having an impact on rural poverty are influenced by both local and external factors. Critical and variable local factors include the degree of heterogeneity in the population, informal social networks, the distribution of power, a culture of community service, and commitment to the notion of a common good. Favourable local circumstances provide the basis for communities to emerge but the active involvement of people is essential for communities to be created and recreated. While advocates of community development emphasise the importance of widespread participation, ultimately much depends on local leaders. People differ in their willingness initially to engage in collective action. Granovetter (1978) referred to this as the individual's collective-action threshold: that is, the number of other people — leaders — who must be participating in collective action before a decision is taken to participate. Even small differences in the distribution of thresholds in the population may make a substantial difference to any community group's collective-action capacity. Leaders also contribute much-needed resources for collective action — sometimes money, but more usually time and, above all, organisational skills. The ethnographic literature reviewed in an earlier section reveals the social diversity and differentiation that characterises rural communities and indicates how factors such as occupation, income, gender and age can have a critical bearing on how community development is organised and how resources and benefits are distributed. Yet the evidence is inconclusive as to whether community efforts to alleviate rural poverty should be focused on most disadvantaged or whether the gains to the poor are ultimately greater when emphasis is placed on involving the "whole" community and increasing the resource base and opportunities for all. However enthusiastic and energetic community groups may be, their lack of authority to mobilise resources, other than that which can be obtained on a voluntary basis, places severe limitations on their activities. It is in this context that the state, often in conjunction with European Union programmes plays a critical role in supporting, financially and otherwise community-development initiatives.

All community-development programmes share one characteristic in common — their temporary nature. Thus, for most community groups long-term planning is next to impossible, professional staff can rarely be employed for more than a few years and community organisations are dangerously exposed once programmes have been wound up. The policy environment which surrounds community groups' efforts to tackle rural poverty is both complex and contradictory. At one level, the critical symbols of many rural communities — schools, post offices and Garda stations — are being closed or are under the threat of closure. At another level, communities are being encouraged to play a much more active role in their own survival and in the provision of social care.

Communities have in the past played, and can in the future continue to play, an important if limited role in tackling rural poverty. They cannot, however substitute for government provision and can only function effectively in an environment of consistent and ongoing support and funding. Perhaps one of the most disappointing aspects of the support framework for community development is the inability to learn lessons from the myriad of pilot programmes that have come and gone since the 1970s. In the immediate future it seems likely that the interest in community development in rural and urban areas is likely to continue and even to expand further. There is, however, a danger that without explicit and realistic expectations of what this approach can deliver in tackling poverty and disadvantage, the results will be disappointing, and even the contribution of communities discredited. In the end, much may depend on estimating what it is that government agencies do best and what they must continue to do, and also on recognising the limitations of state intervention and the importance of policies that allow for the dynamics of different local situations, that permit diversity and maintain the discretion of rural people, and that appreciate local perceptions of the outside world, how local interpretations of events are constructed, and the significance of local knowledge.

References

Alinsky, S. (1971): *Rules for Radicals. A Practical Primer for Realistic Radicals*, New York: Random House.

Arensberg, C. and Kimball, D. (1968): *Family and Community in Ireland*, 2nd Ed. Cambridge, MA: Harvard University Press.

Barrett, T. and Curtin, C. (1991): "Training for Self Employment: A Study of the LINC Start-Your-Own-Business Programme" in Varley, T., Boylan, T. and Cuddy, M. (eds.), *Rural Crisis: Perspectives on Irish Rural Development*, Galway: Centre for Development Studies.

Barrington, T. (1991): "Local Government in Ireland" in Batley, R. and Stoker, G. (eds.), *Local Government in Europe*, London: Macmillan.

Bax, M. (1976): *Harpstrings and Confessions: Machine Style Politics in the Irish Republic,* Assen: Van Gorcum.

Breathnach, P. (1986): "Structural and Functional Problems of Community Development Co-operatives in the Irish Gaeltacht" in Ó Cearbhaill, D.

(ed.), *New Approaches to the Development of Marginal Areas*, Galway: Marginal Regions Association.

Bulmer, M. (1986): *Neighbours: The Work of Philip Abrams*, Cambridge: Cambridge University Press.

Cohen, A. (1985): *The Symbolic Construction of Community*, London: Tavistock.

Cohen, A. (1987): *Whalsay: Symbol, Segment and Boundary in a Shetland Island Community*, Manchester: Manchester University Press.

Commins, P. (1985): "Rural Community Development: Approaches and Issues", *Social Studies*, 8,: 165–78.

Craig, S. and McKeown, K. (1994): *Progress Through Partnership*, Dublin: Combat Poverty Agency.

Cresswell, R. (1969): *Une Communauté Rurale de l'Irlande*, Paris: Institut d'Ethnologie Musée de l'Homme.

Crow, G. and Allan, G. (1994): *Community Life. An Introduction to Local Social Relations*, London: Harvester Wheatsheaf.

Cullen, B. (1989): *Poverty, Community and Development*, Dublin: Combat Poverty Agency.

Cullen, B. (1994): *A Programme in the Making: A Review of the Community Development Programme*, Dublin: Combat Poverty Agency.

Curtin, C. and Varley, T. (1995): "The State and Community Action in Ireland" in Clancy, P., Drudy, S., Lynch, K. and O'Dowd, L. (eds) *Irish Society: Sociological Perspectives*, Dublin: Institute of Public Administration.

Curtin, C. and Wilson, T. (1989): *Ireland From Below*, Galway: Galway University Press.

Curtin, C. (1978): "Family and Land in the West of Ireland", Unpublished PhD Thesis, Hull University.

Curtin, C. (1994): *The Forum Project: Final Report*, Letterfrack: Forum.

Curtin, C. and Varley, T. (1986): "Bringing Industry to a West of Ireland Town", *Sociologia Ruralis*, 26: 170ñ85.

Curtin, C. and Varley, T. (1991): "Populism and Petty Capitalism in Rural Ireland" in Whatmore, S., Lowe, P. and Marsden, T. (eds.), *Rural Enterprise: Shifting Perspectives on Small-Scale Production,* London: David Fulton Publishers.

Curtin, C. and Varley, T. (1992): "Co-operation in Rural Ireland An Approach in Terminal Crisis?" in O'Cinneide, M. and Cuddy, M., *Perspectives on Rural Development in Advanced Economics* (eds.), Galway: Centre for Development Studies, Social Sciences Research Centre, University College Galway.

Devereux, E. (1988): "Muintir na Tire: The Theory and Practice of Community Development, 1931–1988", Unpublished MA Thesis, University College Galway.

Eipper, C. (1986): *The Holy Trinity. A Community Study of Church, State and Business in Ireland,* Aldershot: Gower.

Foradvice Ltd. (1994): *A Crusade for Survival: Final Report of the Study of the West of Ireland*, Galway: Developing the West Together.

Fowler, R. (1991): *The Dance with Community*, Kansas: University Press of Kansas.

Frazer, H. (1991): "Integrated Approaches to Development" in Vanrees, W. (ed.), *A Survey of Community Development in Europe*, The Hague and London: Community Development Foundation.

Granovetter, M. (1978): "Threshold Models of Collective Behaviour", *American Journal of Sociology*, 88: 1420–43.

Hannan, D. (1970): "Kinship, Neighbourhood and Social Change in Irish Rural Communities", *Economic and Social Review*, 1: 163–88.

Harris, L. (1984): "Class, Community and Sexual Divisions in North Mayo" in Curtin, C., Kelly, M. and O'Dowd, L. (eds.), *Culture and Ideology in Ireland*, Galway: Galway University Press.

Holdcroft, L. (1982): "The Rise and Fall of Community Development in Developing Countries, 1950–1965" in Jones, J. and Rolls, M. (eds.), *Progress in Rural Extension and Community Development*, Chichester: John Wiley.

McDyer, J. (1984): *Fr. McDyer of Glencolumckille: An Autobiography*, Dingle: Brandon.

Messenter, J.C. (1969): *Inis Beag: Isle of Ireland*, New York: Holt, Rinehart and Winston.

Muintir na Tire (n.d.): *Community Development and the Representative Community Council*, Tipperary: Muintir na Tire Publications.

National Committee on Pilot Schemes to Combat Poverty (n.d.): *Final Report on Pilot Schemes to Combat Poverty, 1974–1980*.

Newman, J. (1964): *The Limerick Rural Survey*, Tipperary. Muintir na Tire Publications.

Ó Cearbhaill, D. and O'Cinneide, M. (1983): *Community Development in the Killala Area*, Galway: Social Science Research Centre, University College, Galway.

Ó Cearbhaill, D. and Varley, A. (1986): "A Longitudinal Study of Twenty-five West of Ireland Community Councils" in Ó Cearbhaill, D. (ed.), *New Approaches to the Development of Marginal Regions. The Organisation and Development of Local Initiative*, Vol. 2, Galway: Eighth International Seminar on Marginal Regions in association with University College Galway.

Ó Cearbhaill, D. and Varley, T. (1991): "Muintir na Tire and the Crisis of Community Development in Ireland" in Leroy, M. (ed.), *Regional Development Around the North Atlantic Rim*, Vol. 1, Nova Scotia International Society for the Study of Marginal Regions.

O'Cinneide, M. and Keane, M. (1987): *Community Self-Help, Economic Initiatives and Development Agency Responses in the Mid-West Region of Ireland*, Research Report No. 1, Social Science Research Centre, University College Galway.

O'Cinneide, S. (1987): *Ireland: First Report of the Programme Evaluation Team*, Bath: Joint Committee for the Second Programme to Combat Poverty.

O'Malley, E. (1993): "The Pilot Programme for Integrated Development 1998–1990", in Murray, M. and Greer, J. (eds.), *Rural Development in Ireland*, Aldershot: Avebury.

Okin, S. (1989): *Justice, Gender and the Family*, New York: Basic Books.

Peace, A. (1993): "Environmental Protest, Bureaucratic Closure: The Politics of Discourse in Rural Ireland" in Milton, K. (ed.), *Environmentalism: The View from Anthropology*, London: Routledge.

Plant, R. (1980): Political Philosophy and Social Welfare, London: Routledge and Kegan Paul.

Report of the Review Group (1980): Review of the Activities of the National Committee on Pilot Schemes to Combat Poverty.

Scheper-Hughes, N. (1979): *Saints, Scholars and Schizophrenics: Mental Illness in Rural Ireland*, Berkeley and Los Angeles: University of California Press.

Scott, A. (1990): *Ideology and the New Social Movements*, London: Unwin Hyman.

Stockpol, T. (1985): "Bringing the State Back In: Strategies of Analysis in Current Research" in Evans, P., Rieschemeyer, D. and Stockpol, T. (eds.), *Bringing the State Back In*, Cambridge: Cambridge University Press.

Smith, M. (1993): *Pressure, Power and Policy*, London: Harvester Wheatsheaf.

Taylor, L. (1989): "The River Would Run Red with Blood: Community and Common Property in an Irish Fishing Community" in McKay, B. and Acheson, J. (eds.), *The Question of the Commons*, Tuscon: University of Arizona.

Varley, T. (1981): "Functionalism, Ideology and Concrete Practices in Arensberg and Kimball's *Family and Community in Ireland*", Paper presented to the Eighth Annual Conference of the Irish Sociological Association, Limerick.

Varley, T., Curtin, C. and O'Donoghue, K. (1990): "Theory and Practice of Community Development in Two West of Ireland Community Councils" in Wright, S. and Buller, H., *Rural Development Problems and Practices*, Aldershot: Avebury.

8: Local and Regional Administrative Structures and Rural Poverty

Carmel Coyle

INTRODUCTION

Changes taking place in the economic and political spheres are giving rise to fundamental shifts in the relations between supra-national, national and sub-national levels of government. Two trends in particular characterise developments in the period since the early 1970s: a reduction in the rate of growth of public spending and a re-organisation of state institutions, for the most part in the direction of decentralisation. The majority of European states have undertaken a major amalgamation and consolidation of sub-national administration involving substantial transfers of powers and functions from central to regional and local governments. This process began in the Scandinavian countries in the late 1960s and early 1970s, reaching France only in the 1980s and is still ongoing in a number of countries such as Spain, Greece, Portugal and the former Eastern Bloc countries. In some cases this was the outcome of a genuine desire to enhance local democracy. In others it was undertaken for ideological reasons (France) or in response to political aspirations (Belgium and Spain). In almost all cases, however, it was seen to be the most efficient way of delivering services.

Notwithstanding this expansion, sub-national governments have been adversely affected by the fiscal rectitude policies of governments throughout Europe. Local governments' options for raising revenue are generally constrained in so far as they are normally required to operate within the framework of monetary and taxation policies determined by central government. This limits the scope for local authorities to pursue redistributive policies (Peterson, 1981). Paradoxically, this period of stagnant or declining revenue has seen new demands placed on local and regional administrations. In an attempt to respond to rapid economic change and the accompanying social tensions, it has fallen to local and regional governments to assume a new entrepreneurial role as agents of local economic development. One of the insights to emerge from the global economic crisis of the past years is that the traditional reliance on large-scale, central-government-initiated development strategies has failed to stem local economic decline. Moreover, this approach has debilitated the capacities of local communities to confront the problems of economic recession through the adoption of indigenous, flexible and innovative responses. This has resulted in entire local and regional communities succumbing to what Stohr (1990) has termed "societal immune deficiency syndrome" as a result of the "virus" of global economic restructuring.

Public expenditure cut-backs and the resultant reduction in services has given rise to new and vibrant self-help movements at the local level. The burgeoning of issue politics, and the growing politicisation of community groups mean that local administrations are now being confronted by a more sophisticated public and new forms of political activism. This new style of local politics is occurring in a period when more emphasis is being placed on socially responsible and environmentally friendly development, reflecting the emergence of a more subtle strategy for the economic and social order. There is a widespread desire to replace centralised and bureaucratic forms of organisations with more flexible, devolved and consumer-responsive bodies.

> One of the principle observations made by Western political science over the last two decades is that policy-making is increasingly made up of negotiating spaces within which state-actor dominated vertical hierarchies are the exception rather than the rule (Smith, 1995: 46).

Rather, there is an increasing emphasis on the concept of a partnership between the state, state agencies, the private sector and voluntary groups in economic and social governance At the national level in Ireland we have seen the development of negotiated economic and social policy between the state and the "social partners". At the local level, area-based partnerships of public, private and voluntary agencies are now widely accepted as a core policy instrument for promoting local and rural development and for tackling long-term unemployment and social exclusion.

This chapter seeks to examine the role of local and regional administration in Ireland in this new partnership structure and the extent to which the conditions exist within such structures for addressing the problem of rural poverty. The first section charts the development — or perhaps more appropriately, the *demise* — of local and regional administration, and outlines the current structures and prospective changes. The second section examines the development of the European Union's Regional Policy and how it has increasingly promoted the involvement of local and regional actors in local economic development. However, the opportunities for "bottom-up" involvement are ultimately determined by the nature of centre–local relations at the national level. In the third section, the extent to which the combination of a narrow functional remit and a conservative reactive style of management have seriously limited the role of local government in Ireland in tackling rural poverty is analysed. The concluding section seeks to identify the most appropriate institutional arrangements for tackling the problem of rural poverty.

LOCAL AND REGIONAL GOVERNMENT
IN IRELAND

Historical Background

Local government in Ireland has no constitutional basis. Rather, local
authorities have their origins in, and derive their powers from, Acts of
the Oireachtas (Parliament). The present system is still based largely
on the Local Government (Ireland) Act, 1898 enacted by the British
administration. This Act transferred to elected county councils the
administrative functions which were hitherto carried out by Grand
Juries. The latter consisted of wealthy landowners who assisted the
Crown judges on their twice-yearly assizes. The Grand Juries were
authorised to propose public works, oversee the maintenance of
public buildings and pay the salaries of county officers. The 1898
Act thus ended the dominant role of the ascendancy class in local
politics in Ireland and put local government on a representative
basis.[1]

Structure

The administrative division of Ireland established by the 1898 Act
essentially remains today with the *county* being the basic unit of local
administration. Until recently there were 27 county councils — one
for each of the twenty-six counties that comprise the Republic of Ireland, but two for Co. Tipperary. In January 1994, Dublin County
Council was re-organised into three new administrative counties to
reflect the huge growth in population in the Dublin region over the
past few years. This brings to 29 the number of *county councils* now
in existence. There are also *county borough corporations* in the five
largest cities with the same powers as the county councils. These 34
local authorities comprise the core of the local administrative system
in terms of powers, functions and finance.

No comprehensive system of local government operates at the sub-
county level. Within the county boundaries a number of towns have
their own directly elected councils, whether in the form of *borough
councils* (in five large towns), *urban district councils* (in 49 urban
areas) or *town commissioners* (in 26 towns). The *rural district coun-*

---

[1]   For a detailed account of the historical development of local government
      in Ireland, see Roche (1982).

cils which had been established under the 1898 Act were abolished in 1925 and their functions — mainly road maintenance and sanitary matters — were transferred to the county councils (Roche, 1982: 52). The sub-county tier of local government is now considered to be seriously outdated in terms of the functional remit of the units, their boundary demarcations and the absence of a uniform system throughout the country. In January 1995 the Government established a *Local Government Reorganisation Committee* to make recommendations for a modernised system of local government in towns, including those which have no separate local council at present.

Table 8.1: Comparative European Local Government Systems

	1	2	3	4	5	6	7	8
Country	*Pop. 1988*	*Area sq. km*	*GDP* 1989*	*Land / Region*	*County / Kreis*	*Commune / Municipality*	*Total No. of Units*	*Rank*
Austria	7.6	83.9	66	9	—	2,304	2,313	7
Belgium	9.9	30.5	67	3	9	589	601	10
Denmark	5.1	43.1	71	—	14	275	289	16
Finland	4.9	338.0	73	—	—	461	461	13
France	55.9	549.0	71	26	95	36,757	36,878	1
Germany	61.4	248.6	75	11	328	8,413	8,752	2
Britain	57.0	244.8	70	—	63	457	520	11
Greece	10.0	132.0	35	13	51	5,999	6,063	5
Ireland	3.5	70.3	43	8	34	80	122	18
Italy	57.4	301.2	68	20	95	c8,000	8,115	3
Luxem.	0.4	2.6	81	—	—	126	126	17
Netherl.	14.8	40.8	67	—	12	714	726	9
Norway	4.2	324.2	87	—	19	454	473	12
Portugal	10.3	92.4	36	—	—	305	305	15
Spain	39.0	504.8	49	17	50	8,038	8.094	4
Switz.	6.7	41.3	86	26	c208	c3,400	3.634	6
Turkey	54.0	780.6	21	67	—	1.800	1,867	8

*   Index relative to US$100
Source: Barrington: 1991a: 55; Irish figures adjusted by author to take account of recent re-organisation.

The comparative data above demonstrate how badly off Irish citizens are relative to their fellow Europeans in terms of the numbers of local authorities, even when factors such as size and population are taken into account. Our position at the bottom of the league table with 122 units is even more problematic when one considers the fact that the 80 municipalities cover only 15 per cent of the population, represent only about half of the small towns of comparable size in the country and collectively only account for around 6 per cent of the total expenditure of Irish local authorities, thereby reducing them to "not so much a tier as a ledge" (Barrington 1991b: 152).

The establishment of eight statutory *regional authorities* in 1994 marked a watershed in the development of sub-national government in Ireland. For the first time in almost a century a new set of statutory representative institutions, based wholly within the local government system, has been created. Until then there were no elected provincial or regional authorities between central government and the local authorities. Membership of the regional authorities consists of local councillors nominated by the constituent local authorities in the regions. The main role of the regional authorities is to co-ordinate the provision of public services in their regions. To facilitate co-ordination, a broadly-based operational committee, comprising local authority managers and the chief executives of various public bodies, will advise and assist each regional authority. The authorities also have responsibility for monitoring and advising on the implementation at regional level of the various Operational Programmes under the EU Structural and Cohesion Funds. For this purpose, the operational committees will be augmented with representatives of the social partners, including voluntary and community groups.

Functions

When contrasted with other European countries, the range of functions performed by Irish local authorities is very limited and mainly concerned with the physical environment, which broadly comprises two spheres, namely:

(1) Planning and Development

(2) Environmental Management and Control.

They effectively have no involvement in the major policy areas like education, agriculture, social welfare, police, public transport and public utilities such as gas and electricity. The absence of any direct links to the key government departments and state agencies highlights the fundamental inadequacy of local government in Ireland — it is seen as the sole preserve of one minister and one department — namely, the Department of the Environment. Relations between local authorities and central government are regulated through the Department of the Environment, which exercises financial, administrative and technical controls over their affairs.

Finance

The narrow range of functions performed by local authorities in Ireland is reflected in their level of spending. In 1994 current expenditure by the local authorities (IR£1,154 million) represented around 10 per cent of total non-capital public expenditure. Local authorities have three main sources of revenue to finance current expenditure: namely, central government grants; rates on commercial property; charges for the supply of goods and services. In 1994 these sources accounted for 39 per cent, 35 per cent and 26 per cent of revenue, respectively (Department of the Environment, 1995). The decision to abolish domestic rates in 1977 and the subsequent constitutional challenge which resulted in the abolition of rates on agricultural property, has been widely criticised as a major blow to the autonomy of local government.

The absence of financial autonomy within the local authorities severely curtails their scope for independent action since the bulk of their funding is in the form of block grants from the Department of the Environment, earmarked for specific projects. Irish local authorities are not permitted to apply directly to Brussels for the main EU Structural Funds. In June 1995, as promised in the Programme for Government, a firm of management consultants was commissioned to undertake a study of local government finance as a preliminary to the publication of a White Paper on the subject.

Management System

During the 1930s a management system was put in place in Irish local authorities modelled on the example of city management in American cities. Under this system, the functions of local authorities are classified as "reserved" and "executive". Reserved functions cover major policy issues, finance, legislation and the nomination of elected representatives to public bodies. These are the sole domain of elected representatives. Anything that is not specified as a "reserved" function is deemed to be an "executive" function and falls within the competence of the manager, a public servant appointed on merit by the independent Local Appointments Commission. In practice, however, as permanent, professional, salaried officials, the managers and their staffs are in a strong position *vis-à-vis* the unpaid, part-time, perhaps transient elected councillors, and play a key role in initiating policy and in advising the council. While the management system has generally worked well in terms of administrative efficiency, it has been criticised as being undemocratic because it vests substantial authority and power in the hands of non-elected officials.[2]

Reform

Ireland is almost unique among its European neighbours in not having implemented any major reform of local government in the post-war years. Instead, as new services were demanded of central government, the trend has inexorably been to create new single-function executive agencies at national or regional level outside the local authority structure, rather than to up-grade the capacity of the local authorities and devolve new responsibilities to them. The past 25 years saw the publication of numerous reports on local government reform by successive governments, political parties, academic institutions and social/interest groups, none of which were implemented. The most recent report from the *Advisory Expert Committee on Local Government Reform* (1991) appears to be enjoying more success than its predecessors, and a number of the proposals have already been implemented, such as the establishment of the new regional authorities discussed above. In the current programme for government there is a commitment to implementing "a phased programme of devolution and a widening of the role of local government" (*A Government of Renewal*, 1994: para. 70).

---

[2]   For a more detailed account of the management system, see Collins (1987).

Impact of EU Membership

The absence of a vibrant system of local and regional government has left Ireland ill-prepared to take advantage of new opportunities opening up for sub-national involvement within the European Union. Until very recently, local authorities in Ireland had no direct contact with EU institutions and all EU funding, and information on EU policies that impacted on their operations, was channelled to the authorities via the Department of the Environment. The Department is relatively peripheral to EU negotiations except in areas for which it has specific responsibility, notably environmental protection. Other government departments play a more pivotal role in policy formulation, but local authorities have no access to these except indirectly via the Department of the Environment. Central government has taken a very cautious approach to the opening up of direct links between Brussels and the local authorities. In the early days of EU membership, such direct contacts were effectively prohibited. This position has gradually softened to a situation where today, while such contacts are not actively encouraged, neither are they systematically obstructed. In the past couple of years the local authorities have established their own Brussels-based EU consultants and the majority of local authorities now have an officer with special responsibility for EU affairs.

With Ireland's accession to the European Communities in 1973, the focus shifted from internal regional disparities to disparities between Ireland and the other Member States as the government sought — successfully — to have the whole country classified as a single underdeveloped region, in order to benefit from maximum EU funding. Since then, the Irish government has been pressing for a comprehensive Community regional policy from its own increasingly centralised position within Ireland. The effect of having the Irish Republic designated as a single underdeveloped region is that the Irish government *is* the regional authority for the purposes of EU Structural Funds, and so only a single national development plan is required. The government established a consultative mechanism at sub-regional level to facilitate input from public and private interests at the local level, including the local authorities and the voluntary sector, into the preparation of the National Development Plans for 1989–93 and 1994–9. In each case, however, the plans submitted to Brussels were based on national sectoral programmes rather than integrated sub-regional ones. The inclusion of chapters on *Local Development* (Chapter 7) and *Community Initiatives* (Chapter 10) in the 1994–9

Plan are welcome additions over the earlier one. In their analysis of the *National Development Plan 1994–1999*, the *Community Workers Co-operative* acknowledged the incorporation of some of the concerns of the voluntary and community sector, notably the direct targeting of social exclusion and the greater involvement of the voluntary and community sector in terms of more direct access to funding and a role in monitoring a number of the Operational Programmes (Community workers Co-operative, 1993: 5).

This shift in emphasis, however slight, is the outcome of pressures brought to bear by local groups and the European Commission on the Irish government for a greater degree of sub-national involvement in local and regional development. As stated earlier, the recently established regional authorities are now responsible for monitoring the implementation of the Structural Fund Programmes with the advice and assistance of, inter alia, representatives of the voluntary and community sectors.

THE EUROPEAN UNION AND SUB-NATIONAL GOVERNMENT

European integration has traditionally been seen as a process of gradual change from inter-governmentalism to supra-nationalism. The focus of attention has been primarily on the balance of power between the Member States and the European Union's institutions. The underlying assumption was that integration would take place at the level of the nation-state and that national governments were the prime movers in determining the pace of integration. The extension of the European Union's competence into policy areas such as education and culture — traditionally the domain of local government — has given rise to demands from sub-national governments, notably the German Länder, for more involvement in the decision-making process. The outcome of these demands has been the inclusion of two new elements in the Treaty on European Union: namely, the application of the principle of subsidiarity and the establishment of a Committee of the Regions. The principle of subsidiarity, which calls for the decentralisation of decision-making to the lowest effective and efficient levels of administration, is enshrined in the Treaty as one of the basic principles of the new Union:

> In areas which do not fall within its exclusive competence, the Community shall take action, in accordance with the principle of subsidi-

arity, only if and in so far as the objectives of the proposed action cannot be sufficiently achieved by the Member States and can, therefore, by reason of the scale or effects of the proposed action, be better achieved by the Community (Treaty on European Union: Art. 3b).

Under Article 198 of the Treaty on European Union, a new Committee of the Regions, comprising representatives of the regional and local authorities of the Member States, shall be consulted on matters concerning economic and social cohesion and where specific regional interests are involved. This is an important development for local and regional authorities since the Treaty of Rome does not recognise them as having a formal role in Community negotiations.

The pushing efforts of sub-national governments for a greater involvement in policy formulation have been reinforced and complemented by the pulling efforts of the Commission and the European Parliament. The European Union's Regional Policy seeks to promote the economic convergence of the core and periphery economies of the Union. When it was established in 1975, the European Regional Development Fund (ERDF) essentially provided financial support for the regional developments policies of the national governments in the Member States. Their impact was limited by the small scale of the funds and the national quota arrangements, which meant that both rich and poor countries received financial allocations. Reforms introduced in 1979 and 1984 modified the national quota arrangements and gave the Commission a greater say in the allocation of the funds. The enactment of the Single European Act (SEA) in 1985, however, and the acknowledgement that the impact of the single market was likely to exacerbate the problem of economic divergence, led to increased demands from the less-developed regions for substantial financial transfers from the richer regions of the Community. Although Article 2 of the Treaty of Rome refers to the aim of achieving a "harmonious expansion" of the economic activities of the Member States, the EU's role in actively promoting economic and social cohesion was only given formal recognition with the enactment of the SEA in 1985, which gave the Community's Regional Policy explicit Treaty status (Art. 130).

The political pressure from the less-developed Member States for meaningful measures to promote economic and social cohesion resulted in major reforms of the financial instruments of three of the EU's policy areas, namely, the European Regional Development Fund (ERDF), the European Social Fund (ESF) and the Guidance Section of the European Agricultural Guidance and Guarantee Fund (EAGF) —

collectively referred to as the *Structural Funds*. The reforms of the Structural Funds introduced in 1988 were based on four principles, namely:

(1) **Concentration**: The level of funding was doubled in real terms between 1989 and 1993 and resources were concentrated on five specified objectives, namely:

- *Objective 1:* The less-developed regions

- *Objective 2:* Areas of industrial decline

- *Objective 3:* Long-term unemployment

- *Objective 4:* Integrating young people into the workforce

- *Objective 5:* Development of rural areas.

Furthermore, over 75 per cent of the Structural Funds were allocated to Objective-1 regions.

(2) **Additionality**: An "additionality" requirement was introduced to ensured that EU funding would be in addition to, and not simply in lieu of, funds provided by national governments.

(3) **Programmes**: There was a move away from funding individual projects in favour of integrated programmes for clearly defined geographical areas, with Member States being required to submit regional development plans to Brussels for Community support.

(4) **Partnership**: The partnership principle encompasses both a vertical network of actors (at EU, national and regional levels) to prepare regional development plans and also a horizontal network (local government, the private sector and community groups) with responsibility for transforming intentions into actions. At both levels, partnership is promoted by the fact that the programmes are never financed entirely by the Commission but are rather co-financed by the partners (Smith, 1995: 52).

The Structural Funds are the most important financial instruments available to Member States to combat economic and social exclusion. The less-developed Objective-1 regions, which receive the vast bulk of the funds, are largely rural in character as measured by the proportion of total employment engaged in farming or agriculture-based activities and the low density of population. Rural areas in the Objective-1 regions are doubly disadvantaged in that they constitute a substantial portion of the less-developed regions of the Community and do not, therefore, benefit from being in the hinterland of a prosperous metropolitan area. In 1993 some slight modifications were made to the Structural Funds for the 1994–9 period, including an extension of the areas designated as "Objective-1" regions; the merging of Objectives 3 and 4; and the introduction of a new Objective 4 to facilitate the adaptation of workers to industrial changes.

The bulk of the Structural Funds (around 90 per cent) is distributed through Community Support Frameworks negotiated with the Member States on the basis of their regional development plans. In 1989, however, the Commission introduced a new range of programmes, accounting for around 9 per cent of the Structural Funds and collectively known as *Community Initiatives*, with the long-term aim of supporting regions ill-equipped for the Single Market. Under the Community Initiatives, the Commission may invite submissions for funding from regional and local authorities and community development groups in respect of measures of significant interest to the Community and which are not covered by the development plans of the Member States. These initiatives are distinguished by their support for the development of transnational, cross-border and interregional co-operation and for their emphasis on innovative projects and "bottom-up" implementation. They give local communities direct access to alternative sources of funding and new channels through which to influence policy. Over the period 1989–93 Ireland received 250 million ECUs under various Community Initiative Programmes and is set to receive funding of the order of 490 million ECUs during the 1994–99 tranche.

Following the publication of a Green Paper on Community Initiatives (European Commission, 1993) and the subsequent consideration of submissions from the Member States, a number of changes were introduced to the programme for the 1994–9 period. As a result, there are now 14 Community Initiatives in total, grouped around seven main priorities, namely:

(1) Cross-border and inter-regional co-operation and transnational networks for transport and energy — *INTERREG / REGEN*

(2) Rural Development — *LEADER*

(3) Most remote regions, that is, French, Spanish and Portuguese overseas territories — *REGIS*

(4) Employment and the development of human resources — *NOW* (women), *HORIZON* (handicapped and disadvantaged), *YOUTH-START* (youth)

(5) Adaptation of workers to industrial change — *ADAPT* (industrial change), *RECHAR* (coal-mining), *RESIDIR* (steel), *KONVER* (defence), *RETEX* (textiles) and *SME* (small and medium-sized enterprises)

(6) Revitalisation of urban areas — *URBAN*

(7) Development of the fishing industry — *PESCA*

(European Commission, 1994).

As well as facilitating greater local autonomy, the rationale behind the Commission's requirement for more bottom-up involvement in local development stems from the small size of the Brussels bureaucracy which makes the policing of its policies very difficult. Working in partnership with local and regional agents gives the Commission access to better-quality information on the actual operation of the programmes on the ground, and greater capacity to adapt those programmes to local circumstances.

It must be borne in mind that the EU as a political institution has internationalising interests of its own. The core objectives of the Community are economic and political integration. By encouraging greater involvement of sub-national actors and cross-border links, the Commission is seeking to break down the nationalistic elements in EU policies. Goldsmith (1993: 690) has described the Commission's approach as a strategy of incorporation similar to that adopted by national governments seeking to bind sectional interests to them.

At the end of the day, however, domestic politics are still national and it is the countries with the most developed systems of local and regional government who will benefit most from the new opportunities opening up for sub-national involvement at the EU level. National governments will not permit Brussels to decide on the internal distribution of power in the Member States. Christiansen (1992: 11) distinguishes between the material demands of the regions for transfers of resources, which are directed at Brussels, and the structural demands to participate in Community decision-making, which are dependent on the nature of centre-regional-local relations.

A recent comparative study of the implementation of EU rural development programmes in Britain, France and Spain clearly demonstrates this point (Smith, 1995). Like the situation in Ireland, the British approach to implementing EU structural support has been marked by the concerted efforts made to leave elected local authorities on the sidelines (Smith, 1995: 52).

> Against a backdrop of increased centralisation and run-down in national finance for local action groups, in some instances LEADER has helped keep alive discursive links between the efficiency of public action by non-state bodies and the ideals of local democracy. Nevertheless, in the absence of visible political leaders at district or infra-district level, it would be absurd to overstate the global significance of this change (*ibid.*: 59–60).

Despite the recent decentralisation programme in France, the advent of Operational Programmes has produced a picture which is not so different from the British one. "Operational Programmes have tended to become sources for reinstating the authority of state actors both in Paris and at local levels" (*ibid.*: 52). The inter-ministerial *Délégation a l'Aménagement du Territoire et a l'Action Regional* (*DATAR*), which is responsible for regional development, was opposed to the introduction of the LEADER Programme and took strong exception to the idea that the Commission was to form partnerships directly with local areas, thus circumventing their authority.

> Couching their dismay in terms of concern over the capacity of local actors to administer subsidies in a sufficiently rigorous fashion, the DATAR mounted an ultimately successful campaign to impede the release of funding to local action groups, generally slow everything down and then recapture control through the establishment of an intermediate body. . . . [T]hose wedded to top-down approaches to rural development (notably prefects) have gradually been reintegrated into the networks of actors concerned (*ibid.*: 58–9).

DATAR unsuccessfully attempted to thwart the renewal of the LEADER programme (LEADER II) (*ibid.*: 58). However, in regions such as Brittany and Limousin, where there is a strong tradition of local autonomy, genuine partnership between elected local councils, state agencies and local economic actors had emerged (*ibid.*: 55).

By contrast, in Spain, which has seen the emergence of a federal-type administrative structure over the period since the late 1970s, EU structural policies seems to have been transplanted onto ground that is more fertile for greater openness and participation in the running of these programmes (*ibid.*: 56). Spanish officials have seized upon possibilities offered by the channelling of EU funding in order to bolster their attempts to reconstruct a conception of central government in a sense alongside, rather than above, the Autonomous Communities (*ibid.*). Enthusiasm for LEADER at central government level was apparently never in question: ". . . the administrative channels necessary to put LEADER into operation were rapidly created, funding released and local action groups allowed to get under way" (*ibid.*: 59).

LOCAL AND REGIONAL ADMINISTRATIVE STRUCTURES AND RURAL POVERTY

The narrow functional remit of the local authorities in Ireland, and their limited financial resources, have seriously constrained their scope for tackling the problem of rural poverty. Their response has also been hindered by a certain inertia on the part of the authorities themselves, particularly their failure to act as partners and facilitators for a range of local voluntary and community initiatives. This section looks at the effects of these shortcomings and also examines the opportunities and potential for a more effective role for the local authorities in the future.

Provision of Public Services

Irish local authorities are excluded from any involvement in the provision of those basic public services which constitute the fabric of social life, such as schools, hospitals, social welfare, public transport, police stations, post offices and public utilities such as electricity and gas — services which generally come within the broad ambit of local authorities in most developed countries. In many countries the local authorities will not necessarily provide these services directly, but will almost always be involved in arranging their provision or in providing them in partnership with private firms, co-operatives or neighbourhood councils. In Ireland, however, the narrow range of services for which the local authorities are responsible seriously limits their relevance to the daily lives of citizens. This is especially true for people living in rural areas and who do not benefit from those basic services which are provided by the local authorities and which are taken for granted by urban dwellers, such as street lighting and cleaning, refuse collection and, often, water supply and sewage schemes. Remoteness from urban centres also reduces the access of rural communities to recreational amenities provided by the local authorities — such as libraries, parks, art galleries and swimming pools — which serve to enhance the quality of life.

The provision of public housing is one of the main areas where local authorities can affect the quality of life of low-income earners. While the encouragement of home ownership has been the dominant feature of Irish housing policy, there has also been a tradition of local authorities providing public housing for low-income households. More-over, this is one of the few areas where the local authorities venture into the field of social welfare and redistribution in so far as they operate a differential rent scheme for tenants of different income levels in similar-type accommodation.

The *Lord Mayors' Commission on Housing* was set up in 1992 to examines the housing policy of Dublin Corporation, but the analysis contained in the Commission's Report (Dublin Corporation, 1993) could be generally applied to all local authorities. In the Commission's view, the traditional local authority role in meeting the objectives of social housing policy is not cost-effective. According to the Report:

- The construction cost of the average local authority dwelling is higher than that of the average speculatively built private dwelling.

- Local authority housing is susceptible to "sales schemes" imposed by central government at enormous discount on the market value and the replacement cost of the property.

- The concentration of socially deprived low-income households in large local authority estates has exacerbated existing social problems and has given rise to higher social costs than would have arisen if low-income households had been more widely dispersed.

- The local authority tenure system is characterised by a lack of incentive to good performance on the part of both the tenant and the landlord.

(Keegan, 1993: 279).

A major new housing policy document launched in 1991, *A Plan For Social Housing* (Department of the Environment, 1991), introduced some new approaches to social housing needs and some significant changes in the traditional role played by local authorities in this area. While local authorities will continue to be engaged in the construction and provision of dwellings, they will also have a new promotional and facilitating role aimed at improving and speeding up access to housing. New initiatives include provision for shared ownership, voluntary and co-operative housing and tenant involvement in estate management (McDonagh, 1993). The Housing (Miscellaneous Provisions) Act, 1992 provides the legislative framework for implementing the provisions of the plan. All local authorities are now required to have a written statement of policy on the management and control of local authority housing. Local authorities are also required to make provision for tenant consultation and participation in the management of housing estates. Some reservations have been expressed about the fact that support for the concept of tenant involvement in estate management is primarily motivated by the cost-effectiveness of this approach (McDonagh, 1993: 245). It has also been pointed out that unless this initiative is part of a wider programme of community development, tenant participation will be just a token gesture and on the landlord's terms (Blackman, 1993).

Local authorities have a statutory duty to determine the accommodation needs of traveller families in their administrative areas and to develop programmes for the provision of appropriate accommodation, including permanent and temporary halting sites. This has been one of the most contentious roles for the local authorities in recent years. On the one hand, the rights of the travelling community to accommodation or halting sites with certain basic facilities, such as running water and toilets, is now widely accepted. On the other hand, however, there is still a very high level of public opposition to halting sites and to the allocation of local authority houses to traveller families. Existing facilities fall far short of an acceptable standard, both in terms of the level of services available on halting sites and also the absence of appropriate mechanism for facilitating an input by the travelling community in determining accommodation requirements. The recently published *Report of the Task Force on the Travelling Community* (1995) emphasised the importance of local authorities engaging in meaningful dialogue and consultation with the travelling community in relation to the latter's housing and other social needs. While the Task Force was of the view that the local authorities should retain their existing obligations in relation to the provision of traveller accommodation, it recommended that this arrangement should be supplemented by the establishment of a statutory *Traveller Accommodation Agency* at national level (*ibid.*: para 3.1.2). This recommendation was not supported by the Department of the Environment representative on the Task Force who felt that the creation of such an agency would "delay the provision of urgently needed accommodation for traveller people by creating uncertainty in the responsibility and role of local authorities and by providing a further focus for opposition to halting site locations" (*ibid.*: 117). He was, moreover, of the view that "The establishment of a further statutory body in the Local Government sector is not compatible with a programme of devolution and a widening of the role of Local Government" (*ibid.*).

Structure

The absence of a comprehensive system of local government at the sub-county level is another factor which makes local government in Ireland peripheral to the daily lives of most citizens. People living in rural areas, in particular, do not live close to local authority offices, which are generally located in the county town. Even in counties like Cork, Limerick, Galway and Waterford which have separate councils for city and county, the county council offices are located in the city. As highlighted in Table 8.1 above, Irish citizens have the lowest number of local authorities per head of population of any European country.

In January 1995 the Government established a Local Government Reorganisation Commission under the provisions of the Local Government Act, 1994, to carry out a review of town government with a view to establishing a modern and efficient system of local government at this level. Addressing the members of the new Commission, the Minister of the Environment, Mr Howlin, said: "The town authorities of the future will need to be more relevant to the people they serve, more responsive to their needs and more ready and able to promote local initiatives and capitalise on local ideas, energies and resources" (Howlin, 1995). The absence, until very recently, of a regional tier of local government has been criticised not only in the national arena but also in international fora such as the Organisation for Economic Co-operation and Development (OECD, 1987) and the European Parliament ("Hume Report", European Parliament, 1987). A recent government-commissioned *Report on Industrial Policy* ("Culliton Report", Ireland, 1992) was very critical of Ireland's over-centralised administrative system, which, it claimed, inhibits local development. The Report recommended that decision-making functions on local development be devolved to the regional level (*ibid.*: 82). The failure of successive Irish governments to devise an adequate

regional policy has resulted in the continued growth of the East region, especially the greater Dublin area, at the expense of other parts
of the country (Walsh, 1991). The NESC Report, *Rural Areas: Change
and Development*, published in 1978, reached the conclusion that
"Regions and regional development constitute the most appropriate
framework for both national economic growth and rural development"
(NESC, 1978: 105). The recent NESC Report, *New Approaches to Rural Development*, continues to endorse a regional context for rural development: ". . . rural development requires a regional planning
framework which can set out key long-term objectives and strategies,
and achieve the co-ordination of certain policies at regional level"
(NESC, 1994: 34). It remains to be seen to what extent the newly created regional authorities will perform this function.

Absence of Civic Leadership

A combination of the limited role of local government, tight party
discipline, the dual mandate and the persistence of localism and cli-
entelism in local and national politics have all militated against the
emergence of strong local political leadership in Ireland. Of the TDs
who were elected at the 1992 General Election, 73 per cent were also
members of a local authority and 90 per cent had been a local councillor at some stage in their political careers (Gallagher and Komito,
1993: 150). Membership of a local authority is essentially sought as a
launching pad for national politics, and then as a means of keeping in
touch with issues in the constituency. The office of chairperson of the
local authority — mayor in the boroughs — is rotated on an annual
basis among members of the largest political party or coalition on the
council. The result is the absence of local "notables" on the local political scene. In their submission to the Advisory Committee on Local
Government Reform, the Community Workers Co-operative (1990: 24)
recommended that there should be an elected full-time mayor for the
life of the authority. An elected local mayor would "provide the clear
political leadership and legitimacy currently lacking in Irish local
government" (Collins 1987: 207) and "give a badly needed focus for
local leadership which would give competition to the centre and also
share the burden of leadership with the centre" (Garvin 1991: 53).

The absence of political leadership at the local level was highlighted in a recent survey of the impact of EU membership on local
government (Coyle, forthcoming). The general perception of local
politicians, which emerged from the survey, was that they were un-

interested and uninformed about the local authorities' EU activities and certainly not a catalyst for action. "Lack of enterprising politicians" was deemed to be "not a major barrier" by 61 per cent of the local authorities. This is in sharp contrast to other European countries where the local mayor has generally been the motor force behind the EU initiatives of the local councils, actively lobbying EU officials at the highest levels for funding or to secure the location of European institutions in their locality (Goldsmith and Klausen, forthcoming). It reinforces the general perception of the pre-eminence of officials over elected representatives at the local level, as discussed earlier.

A report prepared for the Combat Poverty Agency, *Urban Poverty*, similarly found that community groups preparing submissions for funding for government ministers or EU representatives were more likely to receive assistance from the local clergy than from their local councillors who ". . . are not expected to play important parts in these negotiations" (Donnison, 1991: 101–2). In his evaluation of the operation of the Third EU Poverty Programme in Ireland, Harvey noted the striking absence of elected local authority councillors from the partnerships which "marked the Irish partnerships as quite different from their continental European counterparts, most of which involved councillors or the local mayor" (1994: 112).

The absence of civic leadership at the local level is a manifestation of a wider public indifference to local government. There has been very little public outcry at unilateral government decisions to postpone local elections or to abolish a local council and replace it with an appointed Commissioner. Observers have been led to conclude that "the public is relatively unconcerned about local democracy" (Collins, 1987: 51) and that "Ireland is a country where democracy has deep roots, but the democracy is *parliamentary*, not local" (Barrington 1991b: 141).

This situation highlights the inadequacy of representative democracy at the local level. This inadequacy is compounded by the fact that citizens do not have equal opportunity to participate in the electoral process. As pointed out above, there is no uniform system of sub-county local government in Ireland. The result is that some citizens live in an area with only one tier of local government (the county council) while others may have an additional tiers in the form of urban councils or town commissioners with the corresponding additional franchise. This situation is further exacerbated because:

The illogical divisions currently in place serve to deny the possibility of any democratic principles applying to equal franchise in local government. Local urban administrative units can vary in population between 525,000 and 1,600 in population, and county population levels between 422,000 and 27,000 (Community Workers Co-operative, 1990: 6–7).

There is also an enormous variation in the number of electors per councillor, ranging from 914 in the most highly represented area, Dromahaire, Co. Leitrim, to 8,376 in the least represented, Pembroke ward of Dublin Corporation (Colgan, 1992: 372).[3] The current system of local representation is based on 1981 census figures, which are now seriously outdated. This results in a situation that favours voters in rural areas. Colgan's analysis of voter-turnout at the 1991 local elections showed that "despite other factors, the percentage of electors turning out to vote declines as the number of electors per council seat in an area increases" (*ibid.*: 371). Moreover, as Colgan points out, "Because councillors make up the vast majority of those who elect forty-three of our sixty senators, . . . [t]he effect is the election of a rurally-biased Seanad with unrepresentative, predominantly rural values and interests" (*ibid.*: 373). Thus, despite the shortcomings of the current system of local representative democracy, it would appear that voters in rural areas are actually better represented than their urban counterparts.

Lack of Experience in Local Economic Development

Irish local authorities have not generally been regarded as agents of local economic development or facilitators for local community development groups. Although local authorities were designated as developmental agencies for their areas under the Local Government Planning Act, 1963, this function has never been properly exploited. The reorganisation of local government and the strengthening of its financial base, which were envisaged as necessary concomitants to this new role, were never implemented. Local authorities have never availed of the provision in the Local Government Act, 1941, permitting them to assist local groups in community development (Commins and Keane 1994: 110). Indeed, until they were formally included in a variety of partnerships for local development from the late 1980s on-

---

[3] Figures based on the position which obtained at the 1991 local elections.

wards, local authorities have had a poor track record of engaging in dialogue with community groups and the voluntary sector. Rather, the developmental role of the local authorities has been essentially confined to providing infrastructural support for industry and the preparation of five-year development plans for their areas. Until recently local authorities were said to be acting "ultra vires" — outside their powers — if they performed functions which were not specified in law. This resulted in a cautionary reactive style of management, which focused on their core role as providers of infrastructural services. The withdrawal of their role in the provision of social services over the years has meant that they had very little involvement in the "software" of local development. The Local Government Act, 1991 abolished the ultra vires restriction and conferred on local authorities a general competence to act in the interests of the local community.

The County Development Teams (CDTs), which were established in the Western counties in 1965 and subsequently became more widespread, represented an earlier attempt at an integrated approach to rural development within the local government structure. The CDTs comprised representatives of the main public-sector agencies. However, they essentially performed an administrative role, rather than the wider function of actively promoting local development. Once again the financial and technical support available to the CDTs was inadequate to carry out the very ambitious briefs they were given (Commins and Keane, 1994: 105). In 1993 the CDTs were effectively replaced by the County Enterprise Boards (CEBs).

Since the late 1980s, local authorities have been involved in the sub-regional groups which prepared submissions for inclusion in the two National Development Plans which were forwarded to Brussels for EU Structural Funds. This was a new experience for the local authorities to work alongside representatives from non-statutory bodies such as the trade unions, the farming community and local community groups. The creation of 36 County Enterprise Boards in 1993, composed of representatives of local business, farming, trade unions, community interests, and public-sector agencies, including the local authorities, is intended to provide a new forum for the promotion of local indigenous development through a partnership approach between public and private interests.

Many of the local authorities applied to set up projects under LEADER I. However, the view of the Department of Agriculture at the time was that it was inappropriate for state agencies to head-up LEADER projects as the spirit of the initiative was to empower local groups to develop their own communities. One LEADER group was subsequently administered by a local authority, but this was caused by the lack of alternative local community structures. The local authorities also had representatives on 13 other LEADER group boards — they had no representation on three of the groups. In their evaluation of LEADER I, Kearney et al. (1994: 106) point out that in those LEADER Groups where the local authority has not been formally involved, the omission has contributed to misunderstandings and reduced the overall effectiveness of the group. They go on to say:

> The involvement of local authority and state agencies in local partnerships is important not only because they contribute much of the physical and financial resources but also to guarantee accountability and to ensure that they are fully aware and supportive of the local objectives (*ibid.*: 21).

The Department of Agriculture guidelines for LEADER II requires local groups to establish a close working relationship with public-sector agencies, including the local authorities (Department of Agriculture, 1994).

ADMINISTRATIVE STRUCTURES AND RURAL DEVELOPMENT

In assessing the role played to date by the local authorities in stimulating local economic development, it could be concluded that their potential was seriously constrained by the ultra-vires restriction and the lack of adequate financial and technical resources. This led to a cautionary, reactive style of management. Local authorities are frustrated at the fact that they have lost out to ad-hoc community groups in the allocation of EU funding for local development. Against this background, local authorities are likely to experience difficulties in adjusting to the new strategy of local development, which involves dealing with the voluntary sector and community groups in a partnership arrangement. Equally, in the absence of opportunities for consultation and co-operation with local authorities in the past, voluntary and community groups are likely to have a negative, if not indeed hostile, attitude to the involvement of the local authorities in community-development programmes.

The NESC Report, *New Approaches to Rural Development* (1994), is very negative in its evaluation of the potential for local government to play a central role in rural development. It argues that ". . . the existing structures, procedures and role of Irish local government are such that its involvement is unlikely to enhance current initiatives for rural and local development" and that ". . . even reformed local government structures are unlikely, in combination with central government, to constitute an adequate institutional arrangement for the design and conduct of rural and local development policy" (*ibid.*: 114). Indeed, the Report suggests that any increased role for local authorities in rural development might actually have a negative impact and "could damage the innovative or collaborative nature of many recent initiatives" (*ibid.*: 155). In the opinion of NESC, an increased role for the local authorities in rural and local development should only occur in the context of:

- Proven performance of CEBs in the formulation and execution of strategic development plans;

- Partnerships of statutory, voluntary and local bodies; and

- Reform of local government (NESC, 1994: 146).

There is a good deal of unease about the multiplicity of organisations and programmes which have sprung up recently and the absence of any co-ordinating mechanism. There is now a complex web of urban and rural development programmes, special employment measures, enterprise initiatives, and EU-funded community projects, which operate through a mix of institutional arrangements. The absence of an adequate mechanism for horizontal co-ordination of programmes and partnerships at the local level and vertical co-ordination between agencies at the local, regional and national levels is likely to result in a considerable degree of deadweight (activity which would have occurred anyway) and displacement of existing activity. The NESC Report on Rural Development (1994: 153) points out that the structures and organisations that have evolved in Ireland in recent years in the area of rural and local development differ from those in other European democracies in the extent to which they are in partnership with central, rather than local, government and with national, rather than regional, statutory agencies.

Both the NESC (1994) and the Commins and Keane (1994) Reports on rural development endorse an area-based rather than a sectoral/functional policy approach to rural development — that is, rural development should be undertaken by a territorial organisation. This view is supported by those with experience in LEADER Groups, PESP Partnerships and Anti-Poverty Programmes (NESC, 1994: 147).

The NESC Report, however, points out that the administrative implications of establishing a nationwide sub-county network of local development organisations requires some consideration since it would
involve a considerable increase in the number of partnerships. It also
cautions that "the approach to rural development adopted in the
short-run should be consistent with a general and long-run approach
to national and local economic and social management (*ibid.*: 131).
    The programme for government states that:

> The Local Authority must become the focus for working through
> local partnerships involving local community-based groupings, vol-
> untary bodies, the private sector, and public agencies. A particular
> focus must be to co-ordinate the efforts of existing groups such as
> County Enterprise Boards, LEADER, and ADM Partnerships
> (Government of Renewal, 1994: para. 70).

Despite the limitations of Irish local government discussed earlier,
there is a strong case for making the local authorities the core administrative organisation for co-ordinating local and rural development,
rather than setting up a new nationwide organisational structure.
Although the inadequacies of local representative democracy were
highlighted earlier, in proposing this arrangement, the principle of
public, private and voluntary partnerships would remain central.
However, the local authority would become the focus for the horizontal co-ordination of local groups and the vertical links with national
administration. There are a number of considerations which would
favour such an arrangement.
    The recent establishment of regional authorities and the govern-
ment's commitment to introducing a comprehensive system of local
government at the sub-county level will put local government in the
unique position of having an integrated system of administration at
sub-county, county and regional level. This three-tier structure will
enable the local authorities to provide horizontal co-ordination for
development groups at each level (sub-county, county and regional),
as well as providing vertical links between the three levels. It will
also allow the local authorities to adopt an integrated strategy for
local development between adjacent urban and rural areas and also
between sub-county, county and regional levels. It would be difficult to
replicate such an integrated administrative structure in any new institutional arrangement for local development.
    Even with limited finance at their disposal, the local authorities
are in a position to offer those benefits in kind which can be a drain

on the resources of voluntary and community groups such as premises, technical expertise, statistical information, etc. Local authorities also have the organisational skills, a track record of managing public finance, and experience of dealing with state agencies, national government and EU officials. These are all resources which are generally lacking in local groups and which create a serious imbalance in power when local groups have to deal with national agencies, government departments and EU representatives.

Local authorities can also provide permanence and stability to local partnerships. As Curtin points out in Chapter 7, community development programmes are characterised by their temporary nature. Therefore, they cannot engage in long-term planning or engage the services of professional staff except on a temporary basis. Also, voluntary groups may lose interest in the partnership when their own project has received approval. Research indicates that rural areas, which are already disadvantaged from limited public services, appear also to be less well served by voluntary agencies (Storey, 1994). *Forum*, the rural development project in Connemara, was hampered in its efforts to involve the community sector by the absence of representative councils or associations in many areas. This was also a problem in the first LEADER programme, where one LEADER group was administered by a local authority owing to the lack of alternative local community structures. This problem is likely to be exacerbated with the extension of LEADER II countrywide.

The expansion of what has been termed "the non-elected local state" constitutes a new form of corporatism at the local level. Jones and Stewart (1992) suggest that what has been created is "a new magistracy" — a lay non-elected élite where elected representatives are being replaced by a burgeoning army of the selected. In their recommendations for the Local Development Operational Programme under the 1994–9 round of Structural Funds, FitzGerald and Keegan state:

> There is a serious danger that the introduction of new untried structures involving ad-hoc community groups could give rise to problems in this area. We would recommend that the existing local authority structure should be used (FitzGerald and Keegan, 1993: 63).

This view is based on the fact that local government "has the advantage that it is subject ultimately to democratic controls" (*ibid.*).

The NESC Report on Rural Development disagrees with FitzGerald and Keegan's prescription for putting the emphasis on the avoid-

ance of corruption and for according primacy to officials in the conduct of rural development policy (1994: 140). NESC's approach is "to
focus on economic, administrative and political reality rather than abstract administrative or democratic principles." (*ibid.*). As Marsh and
Rhodes point out, however, the legitimacy of networks is not political,
but resides in the claim to superior expertise and/or to increased effectiveness of service provision. "(G)iven that policy networks are a
species of private government, it is imperative to devise effective
forms of political accountability" (Marsh and Rhodes, 1992: 265, 268).

The concept of accountability underlies the entire process of democratic government: power emanates from the people and in exercised
in trust for them. The exercise of power needs to be legitimate and
accountable; decisions must emanate through a rightful source of
authority.

> A legitimation deficit undermines public support and commitment
> to programmes of change and ultimately undermines the ability of
> power-holders to mobilise resources and promote co-operation and
> partnership (Stoker and Young, 1993: 14).

The elected, representative nature of local government provides a
process of decision-making that is open, understood and accountable
and better placed to promote balanced social and economic development. Ultimately, however, the case for giving local authorities a more
central role in local and rural development is based on the rationale
that no other organisational structure is as well equipped to undertake the role. Moreover, the rationale is not based simply on their
particular powers, structure and resources. Rather it rests on their
potential to offer real community government. In July 1995 the Government established a *Devolution Commission* to oversee the process
of local government renewal. According to a Government statement
on this development:

> The government believe that a renewed system of local govern-
> ment can provide a more effective focus for the delivery of a wide
> range of public services, for the better development and well-being
> of local communities, and for promoting more local development
> and enterprise. Partnership and participation can be fostered
> through local government, and local identity and local loyalties can
> be harnessed to foster social inclusiveness, equality of opportunity
> and a tangible sharing of the burdens and rewards of society
> (Government Information Service, July, 1995).

References

Advisory Expert Committee (1991): *Local Government Reorganisation and Reform*, Dublin: Stationery Office.

Barrington, T.J. (1991a): "Local Government Reform: Problems to Resolve" in Walsh, J.A. (ed.), *Local Economic Development and Administrative Reform*, Dublin: Regional Studies Association — Irish Branch.

Barrington, T.J. (1991b): "The Crisis of Irish Local Government" in Hesse, J.J. (ed.), *Local Government and Urban Affairs in International Perspective*, Baden Baden: Nomos Verlagsgesellschaft.

Blackman, T. (1993): "Tenant Participation or Community Development?" *Administration*, 41(3): 299-306.

Christiansen, T. (1992): "Regionalism and Supranationalism in Western Europe", Seminar Paper, Florence: European University Institute, March.

Colgan, J. (1992): "Local Elections: Behind the Results" *Administration* 39(4): 370-375.

Collins, N. (1987): *Local Government Managers at Work*, Dublin: Institute of Public Administration.

Commins, P. and Keane, M.J. (1994): *Developing the Rural Economy: Problems, Programmes and Prospects*, Dublin: NESC, No. 97

Community Workers Co-operative (1990): *Community Groups and Reformed Local Government*, Dublin: Community Workers Co-operative.

Community Workers Co-operative (1993): *The Same Old Story: The Irish National Development Plan, 1994–1999*, Dublin: Community Workers Co-operative.

Coyle, C. (forthcoming): "European Integration: A Life-Line for Irish Local Authorities" in M. Goldsmith and K.K. Klausen (eds), *Black Holes and Bright Stars: Local Governments in European Integration*, London: Edward Elgar.

Department of Agriculture (1994): *Information Note — LEADER II*, July Dublin: Stationery Office.

Department of the Environment (1991): *A Plan for Social Housing*, Dublin: Stationery Office.

Department of the Environment (1995): *Local Authority Estimates*, Dublin: Stationery Office.

Donnison, D. (1991): *Urban Poverty, the Economy and Public Policy*, Dublin: Combat Poverty Agency.

Dublin Corporation (1993): *Lord Mayor's Commission on Housing*.

European Commission (1993): Consultative Document *The Future of Community Initiatives under the Structural Funds*, Directorate General for Regional Policy, XVI/180/93.

European Commission (1994): *Guide to the Community Initiatives 1994–99*, Luxembourg: Office of the Official Publications of the European Communities.

European Parliament (1987): *Hume Report on the Regional Problems of Ireland,* Document B 910/85, 6 April.

FitzGerald, J. and Keegan, O. (eds.) (1993): *EC Structural Funds: The Community Support Framework — Evaluations and Recommendations,* Summary of Report to the Department of Finance Dublin: Economic and Social Research Institute.

Gallagher, M. and Komito, L. (1993): "Dáil Deputies and their Constituency Work" in Coakley, J. and Gallagher, M (eds.), *Politics in the Republic of Ireland,* Limerick: PSAI Press and Folens.

Garvin, T. (1991): "Democracy in Ireland: Collective Somnambulance and Public Policy", *Administration,* 39, 1: 42-54.

Goldsmith, M. (1993): "The Europeanisation of Local Government", *Urban Studies* 30,4/5: 683-699.

Goldsmith, M. and Klausen, K.K. (eds.) (forthcoming), *Black Holes and Bright Stars: Local Governments in European Integration,* London: Edward Elgar.

Government Information Services (1995): *Government Statement on Local Government Reform,* July, Dublin.

Government of Renewal, A: (1994): *A Policy Agreement between Fine Gael, the Labour Party and Democratic Left,* December, Dublin.

Hart, J. (1990): *Completion of the Single European Market: Training and Development Implications for Local Government,* unpublished report prepared by Laois County Council.

Harvey, B. (1994): *Combatting Exclusion — Lessons from the Third EU Poverty Programme,* Dublin: Combat Poverty Agency.

Howlin, B., T.D. Minister for the Environment (1995): *Minister Launches Town Council Review,* Government Information Services, January.

Ireland (1989): *Ireland: National Development Plan 1989–1993,* Dublin: Stationery Office.

Ireland (1992): *A Time for Change: Industrial Policy for the 1990s: Report of the Industrial Policy Review Group* ("Culliton Report"), Dublin: Stationery Office.

Ireland (1993) *Ireland: National Development Plan 1994–1999,* Dublin: Stationery Office.

Jones, B. and Stewart, J. (1992): "Selected not Elected", *Local Government Chronicle* 15, quoted in Stoker, G. and Young, S. (1993): *Cities in the 1990s,* Harlow: Longman.

Kearney, B, Boyle, G.E. and Walsh, J.A. (1994): *EU LEADER I Initiative in Ireland: Evaluation and Recommendations,* Dublin: Department of Agriculture, Food and Forestry.

Keegan, O.P. (1993): "Social Housing: The Role of Housing Authorities — The View of the Lord Mayor's Commission on Housing", *Administration* 41(3): 276-289.

Marsh, D. and Rhodes, R.A.W. (eds.) (1992): *Policy Networks in British Government* Oxford: Clarendon Press.

McDonagh, M. (1993): "The Plan for Social Housing and the 1992 Housing Act: New Thinking on Social Housing?" *Administration* 41(3): 235-248.

NESC (1978) *Rural Areas: Change and Development,* Report No. 41, Dublin.

NESC (1994): *New Approaches to Rural Development,* NESC Report No. 97, Dublin: National Economic and Social Council.

Organisation for Economic Co-operation and Development (1987): *Innovation Policy: Ireland,* Paris: OECD

Peterson, P.E. (1981): *City Limits,* Chicago: University of Chicage Press.

Report of the Task Force on the Travelling Community (1995): Dublin: Stationery Office.

Roche, D. (1982): *Local Government in Ireland,* Dublin: Institute of Public Administration.

Smith, A. (1995): "Going Beyond the Democratic Defecit: The European Union and Rural Development in Networked Societies" *Regional and Federal Studies* 5(1): 45-66.

Stohr, W.B. (ed.) (1990): *Global Challenge and Local Response: Initiatives for Economic Regeneration in Contemporary Europe,* London: Mansell.

Storey, D. (1994): "The Spacial Distribution of Education and Health and Welfare Facilities in Rural Ireland" *Administration* 42(3): 246-268.

Stoker, G. and Young, S. (1993): *Cities in the 1990s,* Harlow: Longman.

Walsh, J.A. (1991): "Regional and Local Development in Ireland in the 1990s in Walsh, J.A. (ed.), *Local Economic Development and Administrative Reform,* Dublin: Regional Studies Association — Irish Branch, 1991.

9: Poverty in Rural Ireland: Policy and Practice

Hilary Tovey, Chris Curtin and Trutz Haase

This book has been written in order to provide an understanding of the causes and consequences of rural poverty, and an analytical framework for the formation of policies aimed at the alleviation of rural poverty. It has drawn primarily on the political economy approach and has focused attention on the way that the organisation of the economy produces poverty through different forms of investment and dis-investment in rural areas, how the state plays a critical role in influencing the life chances of rural dwellers, and how rural areas comprise individuals and groups with varied and often conflicting interests. An attempt has also been made to overcome some of the limitations inherent in the political economy approach. In particular, the contributors have sought to avoid a narrow economic determinism and argued for a view of rural poverty as the outcome of economic constraints, public policy choices and the way inhabitants of rural areas respond to these economic and political processes.

One of the themes that has been central to this book is that the life chances of people in rural Ireland are strongly constrained by social and economic forces, many of which are located outside the rural setting — indeed, in some cases, outside the national society itself. Land values, for example, may play a major part in shaping access to housing in the rural locality, or to resources needed to generate a livelihood for the rural household, but the factors that establish land values are largely to be found outside the local setting — for example, its attractiveness to urban holiday-makers or second-home owners. The chances that Irish farmers have of making a living from farming are inextricably bound up with processes of change occurring at international and global levels, as transnational agribusiness and food corporations jostle for position in world markets, and as powerful states try to support their own food industries through, first, the imposition, and later, the removal of protective tariff barriers and financial supports.

It is argued here that while these powerful forces moulding life chances at the local level are particularly easy to identify in a study of rural poverty, they are equally influential on poverty in urban settings, and no approach to the problem of poverty can afford to ignore the national and international structures within which it is constructed and embedded. However, this study does not adopt a position of determinism in relation to poverty in general or to rural poverty in particular. While structural pressures can be immensely strong they are never absolute. In the view of the editors, this is one of the central messages to be derived from recent and contemporary developments in sociological theory, which emphasise the continuing possibilities available to individual actors, groups or institutions to exercise agency — to collaborate, to resist, or to negotiate new paths forward — even in the face of what may appear to be overwhelming structural constraints.

As many chapters in this book show, the issue of poverty is seldom directly addressed by policies for regional and rural development. This lack of a poverty focus probably results from a number of factors. The rural poor are not segregated from those who are not so disadvantaged but rather are widely distributed throughout the countryside; the poor are often unwilling to identify themselves as being poor and disadvantaged and the image of the integrated rural community often acts as a screen to cover over individuals and groups who are marginalised and experiencing economic and social deprivation. Even allowing for the particular difficulties that the changing global economy has posed for rural areas, one of the conclusions of this book is that the policy response to rural poverty has been both inconsistent and inadequate. Like the three-card trick at the village fair, the promise of real progress has emerged only to disappear when the time for action arrives. The odds have been stacked in favour of economic rationality and of more powerful interests. The rhetoric of concern for rural decline has not been matched by the consistent commitment of state resources to challenge that decline. The failure to focus on the causes and consequences of rural poverty has also resulted in setting policy goals that cannot be achieved. For example, as Jackson and Haase observe in Chapter 2, an implicit and undeniable assumption of a static homogeneous rural population replacing itself in a balanced way in the same areas has dominated thinking on rural demography. What is required, however, is a dynamic model of population change which does not assume "that rural decline is necessarily or inevitably the consequence of population decline".

In addressing the policy implications of the analyses of rural poverty given in the preceding chapters, then, a central question must be how people living in rural areas can take back into their own hands at least some control of the forces that are pushing rural society and the rural economy in directions which exacerbate inequality, poverty and social exclusion in rural localities. The editors would argue that, contrary perhaps to immediate appearances, this is not a marginal or uninteresting question for people living in what has been called late-modern society or "high modernity" (see, for example, Giddens, 1990, 1991). It is in fact of immense salience and is central to the emergence of a wide range of new social movements (ecological, feminist, communitarian and peace movements, for example), some of which are exercising increasing influence on society at political and cultural levels. To say this is also to maintain that it is quite inappropriate to characterise rural Ireland, as has so often been done, as an irrelevant backwater, segregated from the really important and interesting arenas in modern Irish life. Rather, rural space, and rural places, are primary locations for the global restructuring which is currently occurring and which is transforming social reality in profound ways. Moreover, any ways that can be identified in which the rural poor can be helped to take hold of the changes and use them to their own advantage may contain valuable lessons for dealing with poverty throughout Irish society as a whole.

Within this context, one major policy issue which the book addresses is poverty among farming households. The discussion in Chapter 3 makes very clear the extent of inequality that already exists within Irish farming today, the extent to which it is likely to be amplified in the future, and the high risk of poverty faced by farmers with the least assets, who can be roughly identified as farmers with land holdings of less than 50 acres, particularly those located in the West or Northwest of the country and/or dependent on specialised dry cattle production. What, if anything, can be done to improve the situation of such farm households?

Commins' analysis leads to the conclusion that future developments within farming itself, even including various forms of farm diversification, which could provide solutions to the problems of high-poverty-risk farm households are unlikely. The farming structure that has emerged in contemporary Ireland, which is as much the result of several decades of policy interventions under the CAP which have had regressive effects on farm incomes, as of international economic restructuring processes, is "not entirely appropriate for a modern farming economy". The changes that have been occurring are characterisable as trends towards "economic rationalisation". In this context, possibly the most successful "survival strategy" that smaller farmers have been able to take up has been off-farm employment, although the availability of this is spatially unequal and some of the farm households in greatest need would in any case, given their demographic and educational characteristics, probably be unable to take advantage of off-farm opportunities if they did exist locally. Small-farm households apparently can escape poverty, if at all, only by becoming less engaged in farming.

Neither should one rely too blindly on the continued willingness on the part of the EU to provide income supports for such farmers. The EU is at present more concerned about problems of economic and social exclusion in European cities and towns than in rural areas, and unless a strong case can be made that small farmers provide valuable services for European society as a whole, their leverage on Brussels funding is likely to diminish sharply. The responsibility for dealing with their problems will probably revert to Member States. However, Cummins' analysis of state policy towards farming over the past two decades, which illustrates how it has progressively withdrawn from intervention in those areas of agricultural structure — such as land distribution and the provision of development advice — of greatest significance for small farmers, inspires little confidence that the Irish state will take up the responsibility in a positive way.

What responses should those concerned about rural poverty make to this analysis? Two remain highly relevant. First, pressure must be maintained on the State to ensure that the levels of welfare available to farmers whose income from agriculture is insufficient, and who have no prospects of earnings from off-farm work, is such as at least to raise them above minimum poverty levels. This, however, should be part of any package of measures to combat poverty which include using the social welfare system. Second, it is clearly extremely important to create and maintain non-farm employment opportunities in rural areas, whether in industrial or service sectors or, for example, in self-employment in natural resource exploitation. The difficulties in maintaining a relatively egalitarian dispersion of jobs into rural areas in the conditions of the mid-1990s, and of ensuring that such jobs as become available to rural people are not particularly badly paid or do not involve very poor conditions of employment, have been addressed in a number of chapters of the book (for example, Chapters 4, 5 and 7). Possible ways of dealing with them will be discussed later in this chapter.

It may also be useful to look again at the argument that the structure of farming in Ireland is not entirely appropriate to modern agriculture, in that it is not fully "economically rational". There is some evidence to suggest that food consumers in late modern society, at least in the richer countries of the Western World, are not primarily concerned about economic rationality in food production, in the sense that when they purchase food, their choices are influenced by other factors besides price. A number of surveys of German consumers, for example, suggest that information about the conditions under which the food has been produced — particularly in the case of meat or live-stock products — is an increasingly important influence on their purchasing choices. Vegetarianism is a growing phenomenon in European countries generally, and many of those who still eat meat will do so only if assured that the animals experienced no cruelty in being farmed; others have general concerns about the levels of chemicals used to produce food in intensive, "productionist" forms of agriculture.

Irish farming tends already to be perceived in Europe as accept-able on both counts, and this is, in large part, because of its perception as a country of small farmers. Without wishing to overemphasise the possibilities for Irish smallholders which such trends among food con-sumers may open up, it may nevertheless be premature to accept that low-output producers have no future within Irish agriculture or that the persistence of fairly large numbers of such producers within the agricultural structure is somehow "not modern". One way of address-ing poverty among such smallholders may in fact be to consolidate their existence, through such measures as the construction of an ad-visory and development agency specifically geared to meet their needs, deliberate and sustained attempts to promote their produce on appropriate markets, the extension to them of the sorts of supports recently made available to long-term social welfare recipients who are trying to set up in business, and so on. It would appear that organic forms of farming are already attracting increasing numbers of small farmers in Ireland, and intensive study of, and co-operation with, the more successful of these might suggest a number of ways in which state intervention and support could be utilised.

In a situation where even large-scale and intensive farm producers are receiving a small and declining share of the price paid by the end consumer of their produce, it would be of particular importance to de-velop means by which small farmers could avoid selling through mid-dlemen corporations, or could bring onto the farm as much value-added as possible in the form of further processing of their produce (this is already proving successful for growing numbers of artisanal cheese producers, for example). It is notable that compared to other European countries which are regarded as important food producers, such as France, the artisanal food sector in Ireland is extremely small. The pressing need to create jobs throughout the past three decades or more led the Irish state to encourage and massively to support the develop-ment of an industrialised food sector. Its policies in this area should be reconsidered and re-evaluated to see how links might be built between small farmers and artisanal food producers to the benefit of both.

A focus on the development of small farming along these lines might be one way of making the sort of case for support for small-farm households which, Commins argues, is going to be needed to maintain EU funding for them. There already exists a developing vocabulary and discourse, which has currency in EU Commission circles, and which could be appropriated to add symbolic and political power to such a case. This is the discourse of "sustainable development".

As Chapter 4 suggested, this is an ambiguous concept, which can, unless used with care, turn out to be a two-edged sword. It cannot be assumed simply that small-scale farming is always more sustainable, in the sense of ecologically friendly, than large-scale food production (some sustainable agricultural techniques may be available only to those with access to considerable amounts of capital or may be profitable only if used in conjunction with high levels of farm output). Nevertheless, there is potentially a strong case to be made that when we consider not just food production on its own, but food production in conjunction with a number of other desired or desirable rural goods (maintenance of certain "traditional" scenery, facilitation of access by the public to farmland, co-existence with a variety of other forms of natural resource use which rely on an "unspoiled" natural environment, maintenance of a relatively distinctive rural society, which in turn depends on the presence of reasonably high levels of the farm population in rural areas, and so on), "sustainable rural development" must include maintenance of, and support for, small farm households which are prepared to adopt environmentally friendly farming methods.

Rural poverty, of course, is not confined to agricultural groups in Ireland. While small-farm households need access to off-farm work if they are to be able to enjoy more than a minimal standard of subsistence, this is even more true of those rural residents who own no property beyond perhaps a small boat or a house site carved out of a relative's land. Many contemporary poor people in rural Ireland are surplus agricultural labourers (particularly in the east of the country) or (in the west) the non-inheriting children of small farm families or their descendants, who would in previous times have emigrated but who remained at or returned to home during the peak period of rural industrialisation and subsequently, when factories closed down, found themselves unemployed and trapped within their locality by the stage of the life cycle they had reached. Chapter 4 discussed the potential for eliminating poverty among a wide range of rural groups, which derives from other forms of natural resource exploitation besides that of agriculture. A number of issues with important policy implications arise from that discussion, of which two in particular are discussed here. First, the way in which natural resource development is carried out — specifically, under what property forms this occurs — can lead to very different outcomes for the rural poor and, more broadly, for levels of equality or inequality within rural society. Aquaculture, afforestation and rural tourism all provide examples to illustrate this point. Certain forms of aquaculture, particularly salmon farming, have attracted large investments of capital from national, and more often, transnational corporations. Capital-intensive production of this type tends not to be very labour-intensive, and many of the claims that were initially made for fish-farming as a significant provider of jobs in rural areas appear to be aspirational rather than realistic. The jobs they have provided, moreover, tend to be fairly high-skilled, which appears to have posed problems for local applicants in the early period of development, although increased access to appropriate training courses in recent years may have reduced these. Mussel-farming, on the other hand, has generally been developed as a labour-intensive form of production with low capital requirements for entrants. It has thus been a much more accessible form of employment for poorer rural households, and has proved itself suited to collective and co-operative forms of local management and control. However, the returns from it have not generally been enough to support households above poverty levels, although this may be offset in some cases by the fact that its labour demands are such as to allow it to be combined with other forms of employment.

Similarly, rural tourism, which is controlled and developed by large concerns in the hotel or tour operator industries, may be much less valuable in the number or type of jobs that it offers to local people, and in the extent to which earnings are ploughed back into the locality concerned, than, for example, farmhouse tourism, particularly where this is developed, as seems to be the case so far in Ireland, on smaller rather than larger farm holdings. However, in both the cases described — aquaculture and tourism — while there are advantages in encouraging labour-intensive and locally embedded forms of development, there is also a danger that we may be confining access to them to those individuals and families who are already property holders, and even, to a small extent, excluding the property-less from participation. That type of intervention would therefore need to be balanced against the possible benefit in terms of employment creation to be derived from more capital-intensive and externally initiated forms. It may well be the case that no general rules can be laid down around this issue but that what type of development one chooses to encourage will differ depending on the specific features and needs of the rural locality in question — remembering, as was emphasised in Chapter 4, that national and international restructuring processes in the period of late capitalism tend to increase the differences between rural localities, rather than to homogenise them.

Secondly, certain forms of rural resource development — most notably, mining and other types of materials extraction, but forestry might also be included — while having the capacity to bring wealth into a locality can also be very disruptive of local social life and destructive of its capacity to reproduce itself over time. The disruption may be a result of an unstable demand for labour over the life time of the development — both afforestation and mining, for example, require larger amounts of labour in the initial construction or planting periods than in later periods of production. Or it may be the result of environmental damage which temporarily or permanently prohibits other productive enterprises from carrying on their activities — for example, where mining produces pollution of air or soil, which in turn makes local food production impossible, or where afforestation changes the conditions in local rivers, which in turn leads to a decline in angling or other water-based forms of tourism.

It would be extremely important, where such types of rural development are proposed, to have some means of ensuring that the balance of costs and benefits at the end stages of the project is weighted towards the rural locality, and particularly its poorer residents, rather than, as is so often the case, to the national or transnational investors in the development. Conventional Cost/Benefit Analyses or Environmental Impact Assessments, while important and now legally required in many such cases, are not really satisfactory as means of ensuring this. Cost/Benefit Analysis, as a number of authors have pointed out (see, for example, Adams 1995: 99, 100), generally makes a presumption in favour of development rather than in favour of those who might try to prevent it (it generally operates by assessing what objectors would be willing to accept as compensation for their losses if the development goes ahead, which implies that they have no rights in the status quo). Environmental Impact Assessments are usually carried out by researchers from a natural science background, who have little insight into social structures and relationships or into the inequalities and conflicts which structure local social life — thus, their capacity to assess the social impacts of given forms of development is generally extremely limited.

An alternative approach which has been generating considerable interest in some circles in recent years is that of the Social Audit (see for example, Mayo, 1994; Zadek, 1994). Social Auditing is seen by its proponents as primarily a way of bringing about change, in a massively unequal world, from below rather than above. In other words, it does not try to challenge global power structures directly, but tries to make the main global power-holders — the banks and transnational corporations — more accountable to those whose lives they affect. This is done by focusing on the concept of "the stakeholder". Stakeholders are not just, as in conventional accounting, those who own shares in or can otherwise make claims on the property of the corporation — they include "all those individuals and groups who are affected by, or can affect, the activities of the organisation", and Social Audits are a means of assessing "the social impact and ethical behaviour of an organisation in relation to its stakeholders" (Mayo, 1994: 7). Social Auditing is thus a way of giving a voice to, and taking into account the interests of, a much wider range of individuals and groups whose lives are in some way shaped by the operations of the corporation than has hitherto been the case.

Social Auditing has already been adopted by a small number of transnational corporations, and organisations (such as banks) in more than one country. However, it has been adopted voluntarily and because of special features of the reputation of the companies or the principles of those who run them. It would clearly be a long battle to get some similar procedures accepted into EU or national law. Nevertheless, precedents are already in place in terms of environmental regulations and requirements on companies in the EU and the US. The major challenge is to persuade powerful groups within Europe that the social damage which results from irresponsible forms of development is as great a problem and just as unacceptable as is environmental damage.

Such issues continually lead to the question of how change can be brought about, or whether there are indeed any grounds for believing that the rural poor possess some capacity to exercise agency in relation to their life chances. It seems clear that reversing the current trends towards increasing inequality and amplifying poverty within Ireland could only occur with the intervention of the Irish state. But is there any reason to believe that the state would be willing or would have the capacity to act in ways that effectively run counter to global economic tendencies? Or at least, to do so in ways that go beyond merely trying to alleviate the worst sufferings of those who are marginalised or impoverished by these tendencies?

The contributors to this book are broadly in agreement that the current models of rural development held by the Irish state — to the extent that they exist at all, and are not assumed to be subsumable into national development strategies — are not directed towards the elimination of poverty as a significant goal. Even to return the issue of poverty to the rural-development agenda may be an extremely difficult task, and there are clearly powerful interests both outside and inside rural and agricultural Ireland, which would strongly oppose any change in policy priorities that they might interpret as downgrading their own concerns. Commins, in concluding Chapter 3, reminds us that there are constraints on state autonomy, and that policies which the state adopts are often better understood "not so much as *solutions* to problems but as the *outcomes* of bargaining processes among diverse interests with unequal influence".

The implication of this is that while rational appeals to the state to take this or that action to resolve poverty may have some limited effect, in the end the only really effective approach for those who want to bring about social change must be to engage in these bargaining processes, and to bring to them as much power as possible. In Chapter 2, Jackson and Haase outline six reasons why the rural poor in Ireland have tended to be largely invisible — not just socially, but also politically. Rendering them — or helping them to render themselves — highly visible, politically, may be the most important way in which change can be brought about and may be the most important topic to which this book could contribute.

One important area in which political demands could be made more strongly is that of the distribution of highly subsidised manufacturing jobs. As Boylan argues in Chapter 5, the perceived tension between the requirements of national economic growth and the needs of regional development has, over the past 15 years, effectively led the state to abandon any attempt to direct new large-scale industries to more rural locations. However, addressing rural poverty requires a specific and spatially focused strategy. In the absence of a policy commitment to industrial dispersal at this level, the potential of the currently pursued local development strategies through County Enterprise Boards and Area Partnerships remains questionable, at least in relation to what may be achieved in terms of a revival of the underlying economic base of the more disadvantaged rural communities.

The problem of rural poverty is associated not only with policies for economic development, but also with policies that are concerned with social-service provision. Indeed, given the socio-economic profile of the rural poor, inadequate provision of social services has played a highly significant role in contributing to the numbers experiencing poverty and social exclusion. Because of such factors as low population density and dispersed population, provision of social services cannot be costed and evaluated on the same principles as in urban areas. Yet economies-of-scale and efficiency arguments have been used to justify the rationalisation of critical social services in rural areas. As O'Shea argues, however, the "welfare state must also guarantee the social rights of people as well as nurture feelings of civic belonging and community if citizenship is to mean the same thing to all people". What is required is a social policy based on a commitment to rural life and influenced by notions of fairness, equity and justice, as well as notions of efficiency and economies of scale. Denying poor people services because of where they live further undermines shared citizenship rights and communal solidarity. Policies should also be targeted on those in rural areas who are most at risk, and particular attention should be focused on innovative and flexible responses that help to overcome the problems associated with access and distance.

In relation to health care, what is needed is greater commitment to community-care services and additional resources for the public-health-nurse service, home help, day-care centres and day hospitals, and improved access to general practitioners. Also central to tackling rural poverty are policies that contribute to the provision of pre-schools and remedial education facilities, acknowledge the critical role of local schools in the cultural and social life of rural communities, and provide much needed adult education. Since poor housing remains a feature of many rural areas, policies that facilitate the improvement of the existing housing stock and the provision of new housing by both local authorities and voluntary organisations are of great significance. The non-availability of transport as a means of access to social services is a major factor contributing to social exclusion of poor people in rural areas. Free transport is of little value to the rural elderly when transport services are not available in their areas. At present a transport policy for remote rural areas does not exist. Yet the Forum initiative in north-west Connemara has shown what can be achieved through an integrated approach to transport provision. Evidence is available from a variety of local projects on how innovative measures can be put in place to provide social services in rural areas. What is required now, therefore, is not more studies of what could be done, but a commitment to implementing a programme of social services in rural areas as a practical manifestation of the value of social citizenship and solidarity.

In the past decade, a growing interest has developed in the role that communities can play in counteracting economic and social exclusion. Individual community initiatives and community-development projects supported by the Poverty 3 Programme, LEADER, the Area-Based Partnerships and the Department of Social Welfare provide valuable insights into how a community-development approach can contribute to tackling rural poverty. A major strength of community-based strategies is their capacity to respond flexibly to varying circumstances. Some of the limitations of community development have also emerged, including the difficulties of ensuring participation by the poor and the uneven spatial distribution of community initiatives. The pressing necessity now is to ensure that the lessons learned from these numerous projects are incorporated into mainstream public policy. What is required, therefore, is a policy environment that identifies the particular strengths and weaknesses of community groups, recognises that community development cannot replace mainstream public provision, provides consistent and ongoing support for community organisations, and, in particular, ensures that they can draw on a professional and dedicated staff.

An important policy consideration is what the appropriate institutional arrangements are for managing and implementing measures directed towards tackling rural poverty. Irish Local Authorities have not been regarded as agents of local economic development or facilitators of community development. The potential of local authorities for tackling pressing problems of rural poverty and exclusion has been seriously constrained by a number of restrictions. These include the absence of any direct link to key government departments arising from their regulation through the Department of the Environment; the withdrawal of their role in the provision of social services over the years, resulting in a reduction of their involvement in critical aspects of rural development; and the absence of financial autonomy which has curtailed local authorities' scope for independent action. The outcome has been a cautious reactive style of management, which has focused mainly on the provision of infrastructural services. Even in this function, financial restrictions have meant that local demands for good quality roads, sewerage systems etc. are often disappointed.

Local authorities have had, in the main, a poor track record of engaging in dialogue with community groups. The failure to avail of the provisions in the Local Government Act, 1941, facilitating their assistance of community groups, has left them with particular difficulties in adjusting to development strategies that involve partnership arrangements with voluntary and community groups. The result has been that, compared to other European countries, both elected councillors and officials from local authorities have had, at best, limited participation in partnership initiatives. In many other European countries, the elected leader of the local authority, the Mayor, is to the forefront in EU community support initiatives. Evidence is also provided by the Scandinavian countries of how local authorities can play a critical front-line role in rural-development programmes.

Despite the identified limitations and the inadequacy of the present system of local representative democracy, Coyle makes the case for the local authority as the core administrative organisation for co-ordinating local- and rural-development initiatives. In this context, the Local Government Act, 1991, envisages a more central role in local development for local authorities. Also, the recent establishment of Regional Authorities and the current proposals to introduce a comprehensive tier of Sub-County Local Government, should facilitate local authorities in adopting an integrated and strategic planning perspective to rural development. In addition, the elected-representative nature of local government provides a process of decision-making that is open and accountable and well placed to promote balanced social and economic development. Coyle's argument is therefore that what is required is more, rather than less, effective civic leadership from democratically accountable local authorities. Local authorities offer the possibility of providing permanent and stable environments for local partnerships. To fulfil this function, they require additional financial support and the freedom to recruit new staff with expertise in local and community development. More effective leadership by local authorities, more democratic accountability, and a more welcoming and inclusive stance on the part of the state towards local community initiatives — these are all aspects of a process of distributing power downwards to rural residents and particularly to the most impoverished and marginalised among them which, in the view of the editors, is essential if any progress is to be made towards addressing and dealing with rural poverty.

In the end, one of the things that a political economy perspective on poverty highlights most clearly is that studying poverty is also all about studying power. It is not just that, as the increasing use of the concept of "social exclusion" is intended to indicate, those who are poor are also those who are powerless in society. It is also that the production and reproduction of poverty is, in contemporary society, the result of the routine exercise of power to ensure that the structures, institutional arrangements and developmental processes which persist in an increasingly globalised economy and polity are those that best suit the interests of the power-holders themselves. The empowerment of previously disempowered groups, such as the rural poor, challenges existing power relationships and would be likely to meet with strong, if often hidden, resistance. Collective mobilisation, which can provide a means for countervailing resistance, is one source of power which disadvantaged rural groups can, and perhaps must, draw on if they are to escape from the systematic construction of disadvantage. Another power resource is knowledge. It is hoped that if this book achieves nothing else, it may provide some insights into the dynamics of poverty in contemporary Ireland, which may help in the process of empowerment and self-empowerment of people who are poor in rural Ireland.

References

Adams, J. (1955): *Risk*, London: UCL Press.

Giddens, A. (1990): *The Consequences of Modernity*, Cambridge: Polity Press

Giddens, A. (1991): *Modernity and Self-Identity*, Cambridge: Polity Press.

Mayo, E. (1994): "Strategies for Socialising the Economy — TNCs and accountability", paper presented to the Permanent People's Tribune on Industrial Hazards and Human Rights, London, 28 November.

Zadek, S. (1994): "Ethical Accountability and Strategic Planning — The Social Audit Approach". London: New Economics Foundation.